Connie Monk grew up in Reading and, following her marriage, lived in the Thames Valley area until 1974, when she moved to Ringwood in Hampshire. After her husband retired they moved to Shaldon in Devon and she began to write, her first novel, *Season of Change*, being published in 1984. She has since written twenty novels including *From This Day Forward, The Sands of Time, Different Lives, Water's Edge, Family Reunions, The Running Tide, Beyond Downing Wood, The Apple Orchard* and *Tomorrow's Memories*. Two of her books, *Jessica* and *A Field of Bright Laughter*, were nominated for the Romantic Novel of the Year Award.

Also by Connie Monk

Season Of Change
Fortune's Daughter
Jessica
Hannah's Wharf
Rachel's Way
Reach For The Dream
Tomorrow's Memories
A Field of Bright Laughter
Flame Of Courage
The Apple Orchards
Beyond Downing Wood
The Running Tide
Family Reunions
On The Wings Of The Storm
Water's Edge
Different Lives
The Sands Of Time
Something Old, Something New
Echo of Truth

From This Day Forward

Connie Monk

PIATKUS

All the characters in this book are fictitious and any resemblance to real persons, living or dead, is entirely coincidental.

Copyright © 2000 by Connie Monk

First published in Great Britain in 2000 by
Judy Piatkus (Publishers) Ltd of
5 Windmill Street, London W1T 2JA
email: info@piatkus.co.uk

This edition published 2001

The moral right of the author has been asserted

A catalogue record for this book is available from the British Library

ISBN 0 7499 3318 6

Set in Times by
Action Publishing Technology Ltd, Gloucester

Printed and bound in Great Britain by
Cox & Wyman Ltd, Reading, Berkshire

Chapter One

Autumn 1905

Jane stared straight ahead. She couldn't close her ears to her father's tirade but at least she could refuse to look at him. Never had he used that tone to her; to other people perhaps, but never to her. And even now she had no real doubt that, once his first anger subsided, she would be able to steer him into seeing things *her* way. She was as certain of that as she was certain that *her* way was right.

'I won't have it, Jane. It's not right to have you hanging around those sheds. I'll not have you laying yourself wide open to gossip amongst the men. I've told you about it before.' Amos Bradley's still good-looking face was flushed with the intensity of his feelings. All too well he knew that Jane was a force to be reckoned with. The stubborn set of her shoulders was answer enough. 'Damn it, Jane. It's got to stop!' Emphasizing his words he brought his clenched fist down to thump on his desk.

Sure that she knew the way to handle him, Jane answered in a voice as soft as his was harsh. 'Oh, Dad, you've always taken me there, you've been proud as Punch to show me off to the men as long as I can remember.' Amos could tell that just beneath the surface there lurked a smile as she recalled his pride in having her at his side, and hers in being there. Even when she'd been no more than a small child she'd been able to persuade him to take her with him

1

to the family brewery, the combination of her own delight in accompanying him adding to an inborn instinct in knowing just how to mould him to her will. Even when she'd needed to stand on an upturned box to watch the crushed malt being turned in the mashing tuns, she hadn't been too young to appreciate her father's pleasure in having her there. The rich, heady smell of the yeast, the familiar West Country drawl of the men's voices, sometimes talking to her and sometimes calling to each other, the ringing of their hobnailed boots on the stone flags of the floor, all these things were ingrained in her memory.

If Amos regretted not having a son, he showed no sign of it. And no son could have taken more interest in the business than she did. She knew each stage of the process of beer making. Some children are enthralled by the magic of fairy stories: not so, Jane. She had never tired of watching the men, asking questions, learning, always learning. By the time most girls of her age had been working on their first cross-stitch samplers, she had been able to gauge from the colour of the malt what the end result would be, whether it would be pale ale, brown ale or porter. As a child, it was what the brewery produced that had enthralled her; she'd seen it as little short of magic that from the basic ingredients at the beginning of the process the final liquid could emerge. But as she'd grown up, she'd recognized there was more than that to running a successful business, and willingly Amos had taken her under his wing, secretly pleased that she showed no sign of finding a husband and flitting the nest.

Not that she spent every hour of every day at the brewery: frequently she would take the train from Deremouth to Exeter for a visit to her dressmaker, never attempting to resist the temptation of new materials or the fun of choosing hats. Although at two years old she'd lost her mother, her life had lacked nothing. She'd believed the same could be said for her father. Even when he'd brought Dulcie Wainwright to visit the house, it hadn't entered

Jane's head that he might be considering marriage. That was when she'd been nineteen and in months life had changed. Maybury House, the Bradleys' home in Moorleigh, a few miles inland of the Devon coastal town of Deremouth, had found itself with a new mistress.

'I'm not blind, you know.' Amos got up from the swivel chair behind his desk. 'I've said I'll not have a daughter of mine hanging around the sheds. But *you* know as well as I do what I mean. I've seen you chattering to that young cooper, Harriman. Chattering? Making sheep's eyes at him, more like it. Either it stops or he goes.'

'I never make sheep's eyes – at him or anyone else! Anyway I doubt if you so much as know him. Dad, you can't judge a person just by the job he does. He isn't like the other coopers. You'd be surprised how much he knows about the trade – he's *interested* – intelligently interested.'

'I don't doubt he's interested! Interested in the main chance!'

'That's not true! And it's unjust to say things like that about him when you don't even take the time to know him. You've always been fair minded. Talk to Ian—'

'Ian!' He almost spat the name at her. 'The man's name is Harriman. Either you keep away from him – or he'll find himself looking for another job.' Before she had a chance to argue, he snapped, 'That's all I have to say about it – and we'll let that be the last we hear.' Was he honestly expecting to be obeyed? Then, as if there had been no cross words between them, he added, 'Now then, Janie, let's go over Dayton's advice notes together, I've got them here. Their monthly account came this morning. If you nip along to get the deliveries book from Hawkins, we'll call over what deliveries of malt we've had from them this month to make sure it's in order, then we can pay our debt on the dot. That's the way I like.' The only sign of his previous agitation was the way his fingers drummed on his knee as he sat back in his chair.

Jane looked at him with grudging affection that almost,

3

but not quite, allayed her own anger. Nearer to the truth, what she felt was disappointment rather than anger. It would be so much easier if he could have met Ian with an open mind, accepted him as a guest at the house without argument. She wished that was the way it could have been. But, failing that ... Today nothing could destroy her happiness. If only she could have told her father how she and Ian felt *now*. But it would need patience and diplomacy – and neither came easily.

Hawkins gave her the ledger in which, in his copperplate hand, he recorded all goods received – barley, hops, yeast – and she returned to Amos's office ready to tick off each delivery charged on the monthly account from Dayton's, the maltsters at nearby Chalcombe. On the surface they worked with the same companionship they always shared: Jane imagined her father had put Ian out of his mind; Amos tried to believe Jane had put Ian out of hers. The truth was, for both of them, the thought of him was just beneath the surface.

Well satisfied with her appearance, Dulcie Bradley turned away from the long mirror on the door of her mahogany wardrobe. Small wonder that a smile tugged at the corners of her mouth.

For more than two years she had been Amos Bradley's wife, mistress of Maybury House, but still the pleasure of choosing new materials, having gowns made to her order, gave her the same thrill as it had when first he'd married her. Employed by Sir Roland Elphick as companion to his cantankerous wife, fate had dealt her a hand of trumps when Amos Bradley had visited the house. In normal circumstances, having eaten with the domestic staff below stairs, Dulcie would have spent the evening in her room. There was precious little freedom for a paid companion, expected always to be on hand at her mistress's whim. Dulcie had only taken the post because she needed a roof over her head and what she lacked in experience she more than made up for in self-confidence. On the night that Amos had been visiting the Elphicks for dinner and an evening of bridge, the fourth player had sent her footman with a note of apology and an explanation that she was unwell. So Dulcie had been sent for. Hearing the maid being instructed to tell Mrs Wainwright that she was needed, Amos's spirit had sunk. He'd imagined some downtrodden servile widow whose skill went no further than the basic rules of the game. Then Dulcie had appeared. For Amos, an evening of bridge had lost its appeal; he'd wanted just to look at this pretty creature, and to encourage her to speak so that he could listen to her husky voice with its unfamiliar accent. When she'd told him that she'd spent many years in America it only added to her mysterious attraction.

In an age when most women had left youth behind them before they approached fifty, Dulcie had a quality that was ageless. He'd seen her as a woman who'd not always been treated kindly by life, and yet had retained the trusting expectation of youth. He had noted everything about her, he'd found himself wondering whether her legs would be as slim as her ankles hinted, or whether they would be in keeping with the plump softness of her body. His gaze had been drawn again and again to the deep cleavage just visible from the low-cut neckline of her gown, a cleavage made more evident by the way her pale breasts were forced high by her tightly laced corsets. He'd seen her as a woman whose experience of life had only added to the beauty of youth. As she'd studied her cards he had watched the way she'd pursed her voluptuous lips; his imagination had run away with him. That evening he'd played a poor hand of bridge, for concentration had seemed beyond him. If her appearance had surprised him, so too had her bridge. Playing as partners, it had been due to her that the Elphicks hadn't completely destroyed them.

The following week he'd brought her to Maybury House. Nearly a quarter of a century earlier he'd loved and married

Suzanne, Jane's mother. When he'd lost her he had poured all his affection on their young daughter. Nothing had prepared him for the consuming passion he'd felt – and still did feel after two years of marriage – for Dulcie. The thought of her had come between him and his work, the thought of her had haunted his dreams both waking and sleeping. Within two months of their first meeting she had become Mrs Amos Bradley.

Married twice before, one time divorced, one time widowed, Dulcie had entered her partnership with Amos with no doubts about her future. By nature she was an optimist – and certainly, with the exception of his unmarried daughter, there was nothing to hint at any clouds ahead. There wasn't open antagonism between Jane and her, but scratch the surface and there was mistrust. In her opinion, Amos had pampered and spoilt Jane for too long. At twenty-one it was high time the girl found herself a husband and moved out. And, seeing that she appeared to have no interest in looking for one for herself, Dulcie had gone out of her way to introduce anyone eligible. And what a waste of effort that had proved!

Studying herself in the mirror, hardly aware of the smile of pleasure at what she was, Dulcie let her mind dwell on her step-daughter, the one person who came between *her* and the whole of Amos's affection. Jane may not have been a beauty, not in a delicate, feminine way, but she wasn't unattractive. Finding her a husband should be easy enough – if only the stupid girl would show a little interest. Then Dulcie's thoughts moved to what she knew had been on Amos's mind over these last weeks. Her smile deepened; play her hand carefully, and Jane's stubbornness might even yet prove to be a Godsend.

As Dulcie turned from the looking glass she heard the noise of a motor car, a rare sound in the village of Moorleigh and one that told her Amos was home.

'I'm up here,' she called, leaning far out of the opened window.

6

She didn't need to say, 'I'll wait for you here,' she knew he would come straight up to find her.

'I'll put the motor in the coach house, Dad. Leave the engine running and I can slide across the seat when you get out.'

'Sure you can manage? There's not a lot of spare room in there.' His pride in this daughter of his was plain to hear.

'Out you hop,' she laughed. 'Of course I'm sure.'

For a woman to sit behind the wheel of an automobile was almost unheard of, but Amos had never been able to refuse her anything. Proudly he'd taught her to handle his motor car with dexterity the equal of his own. He delighted in sitting at her side, aware of how the heads turned at the sight of her. With the canvas hood folded right back, sitting tall, with her hat anchored with extra pins to hold it against the breeze, he knew he had cause to be proud of this daughter of his. Manage? He smiled as he watched her pull away towards the coach house, a cloud of smoke in her wake. On the surface their earlier battle was forgotten. From his appearance no one would guess the foreboding that filled Amos's heart when he remembered his growing suspicions, and the sight of Harriman and Jane together walking back towards the brewery that very day after the works mid-day break ... talking, laughing, their hands touching lightly. Jane was less worried. She was far too happy, too certain that what she wanted was right, not seriously doubting that her father would come to see things her way.

From upstairs, Dulcie watched them, her enigmatic expression giving no hint of what was in her mind. Then she went back to the dressing table to put a dab of perfume behind each ear, and another below her throat. A flick of her Queen Alexandra fringe with her silver-spined comb (part of the dressing-table set Amos had given her) and she was ready to greet him.

'I waited up here so that I could show you by ourselves.' Her husky voice had all the excitement of a young girl as she slowly twirled for him to admire her new gown. 'Don't you think it's about the prettiest gown I've ever had?'

'I think you look enchanting. Whatever you wear, you're lovely. You know that.'

'And the dress? It came this morning. I wanted to wear it right away. Say you like it.' Then, catching her full bottom lip between her teeth and looking at him with the sort of expression that might have sat comfortably on the face of a mischievous child, 'It's costing you a lot of money.'

'And every penny of it well spent, my precious girl.' Drawing her into his arms he let himself drown in the soft warmth of her embrace. If anything could banish his troubled thoughts, then it was Dulcie.

'What is it, honey?' She moved her fingers on the back of his neck, not attempting to draw away from his hold. 'You're worried. I could see when I watched from the window.' Had he not been worried, her words would have been enough to stir any shadows into life.

Releasing her, he dropped to sit on the edge of the bed. Immediately she was on her knees in front of him.

'Is it that young cooper? Didn't you have a chance to talk to Jane, to tell her how it worried us? Surely she can see we are only concerned for her own good?'

He shook his head.

'She won't hear a word against him, she tells me I ought to get to know him. She says if I were fair minded I would see that he's interested in the business.'

'But, Amos honey, doesn't that tell us he's no more than a gold-digger? Brought up to make barrels, what has that to do with producing ale? It's like saying I know about tailoring because I can sew a button on a coat. What do the men who work with him think of him, I wonder?'

'I've no idea. He comes and goes on his own. I've watched him for weeks – watched the pair of them. You know I have. I've tried to believe she's no different from the way she might be with any of the men – a friendly girl, she always has been. But it's worried me – bless you, my

8

darling, it's worried both of us. Twenty-one years old, yet what experience has she had of men?'

'I've done my best.' Wide-eyed, Dulcie looked at him. 'You know how often I've arranged little dinner parties just so that we can bring some suitable young man into the home. But you can't force anyone into falling in love.' Did he imagine it, or did she purse her full lips as she looked at him? 'One day the right man will come, then she'll find true happiness. My darling Amos, I hate to see that nasty furrow on your brow.'

How soft her hand was on his forehead.

'What can we do? She can only be heading for trouble unless you forbid her friendship with him.'

'I talked to her this afternoon. You may be sure I have forbidden it. I've made it plain that I'll not have him received here—'

'You mean she suggested *that*? The idea of it! She must realize it would be impossible. I've seen the man, remember, you pointed him out to me when we were in town together. Handsome, oh yes, he's handsome enough to turn any girl's head. And Jane is so naïve for her age. She just loves to be with you at the brewery.' Her affectionate laugh seemed to encompass Amos, Jane and the brewery too. 'What does she know of men? She must suppose they are all as upright and honest as you. We have to put a stop to it; in her innocence she's bound to be hurt. Handsome he may be, and she's too young and gullible to see beyond. The man is coarse, a rough workman. I'm just so thankful you've told her it must finish.'

Amos shook his head.

'Jane has a will of her own. She always has had.'

Rubbing her cheek against his, Dulcie decided on her next move. Yes, Jane would never be told how to live her life. Order her one way and, more likely, she'd go another.

'If you find they are still seeing each other, then honey, you must get rid of him. Sack him. There's no one else in Deremouth likely to employ a cooper. But it won't come to

9

that. Jane loves you too dearly, she couldn't bring herself to hurt you by going against your express wishes, not in a matter like this.' She stood up from where she'd been kneeling in front of him. 'Now that I know you like my new gown and aren't cross with me for such extravagance, I'll go down while you get changed.' Then stooping to rub her cheek once more on his, she added, 'And I'll tell Meg to bring you some hot water so that you can get rid of those nasty, scratchy bristles.' He heard the caress in her soft husky voice and for a second Jane and the cooper were pushed out of his mind just as Dulcie intended. Then pursing her lips in a mock kiss she left him.

Jane changed into a dark green silk gown for the evening. She sat down on the stool in front of her dressing table and unpinned her straight, dark hair, brushed it vigorously before she twisted it back into its customary coil. Bending forward, her chin resting on her upturned palms, she gazed at her reflection as if she were looking at a stranger, a starry-eyed stranger. She felt the whole of her life had been building towards this day – no, not *this* day, but all that lay ahead of her. If only her father had been ready to meet Ian, to stop thinking of him simply as someone from the workshop ... but it would soon happen. Her smile was full of secret confidence as she fixed the small emerald and pearl earrings to her lobe, her thoughts less than half on what she did. What was it Ian had said? Her white teeth clamped her bottom lip as her half-smile tried to turn itself into a laugh. 'Box clever – use your girlish charm.' In her imagination that's what she was doing, the scene in Amos's office overshadowed by the affection of years. Dad's never stubborn just for the sake of it, he'll see for himself that we're like two halves of the same whole. Softly she hummed the tune of 'After the Ball is Over'; two days ago she'd bought the music so that she could play it on the piano – in better tune than her vocal offering.

Still humming, she hurried downstairs. Tonight she'd let

the subject rest, she didn't want Dulcie voicing her opinion. It's nothing to do with her, Jane thought childishly.

It was as she came to the closed door of the drawing room that she halted. 'After the Ball is Over' silenced, her expression changed.

His face freshly shaved, his suit changed, Amos joined Dulcie in the drawing room where she was waiting alone.

'Jane not down yet?' An unnecessary question and one she didn't answer.

Instead, she said, 'However worried you are, worried or angry, promise me you won't talk about it at dinner. The last thing we want is for gossip to spread in the kitchen. It's bad enough that the silly girl must be making a laughing-stock of herself in front of the workmen at the brewery.' Not a hint in her concerned tone to suggest that she'd heard Jane's step crossing the hall.

'A laughing-stock? You think that? No, surely not. They know her too well.' Even so, he chewed nervously at the corner of his mouth.

'How else can the men see it? They must have held her in such esteem, seen her as your right hand. Then she chases after a rough workman at the flick of his fingers. Hush, I think I hear her.' She had done more than hear her, she'd seen the movement of the door handle. 'You've told her there's to be an end to the nonsense, so now we'll put the whole thing out of our minds. He's not the first ambitious young man to try to wheedle his way up the ladder this way.'

Just as the sound of the gong echoed across the hall, Jane flung the drawing-room door wide and jumped straight into the trap Dulcie had baited.

'You don't know what you're talking about!' She had taken criticism from her father, but Jane couldn't keep silent while Dulcie interfered.

'Hush, hush, do, Jane.' Dulcie looked at Amos, her pretty face a picture of anguish. 'Just do as your father tells you. Let's all of us put it behind us. You'll come to see that what we say is for your own good. All we want is your happiness.'

Purposely Jane turned her back on her and faced her father.

'It doesn't matter to me what *she* says. But Dad, I love Ian. I love him and he loves me. I don't care what anyone says. He's asked me to marry him and I've said yes. Yes, yes, yes.'

Amos felt as if he'd lost his grip on the situation. They'd talked this afternoon – talked? Argued, more likely – she'd said nothing then about marriage.

'I don't understand . . .'

'You're making it up,' Dulcie came to his side, slipping her hand into his. 'Your father talked to you this afternoon, you didn't tell him this then. You're making it up just to upset him.'

'Yes.' Amos collected his wits. 'That's it, isn't it, Janie? You'd have told me—'

'I didn't tell you because it wasn't the right time. This isn't the right time. When you've talked to him, got to know him, you'll be glad for me. You'll be glad for yourself too. He'll be like a son—'

'The man's a gold-digger,' Dulcie stood her ground. 'Honey, tell her what you told me. Tell her that unless she puts an end to this nonsense, you will get rid of the wretched man. Perhaps that's what you ought to do in any case. Even if you can trust Jane to keep her word, you wouldn't be able to trust him. Love! Love of himself more likely!'

'You keep out of it,' Jane turned on her angrily. 'I'm talking to Dad, not to you.'

Dulcie's huge blue eyes swam with unshed tears, tears of humiliation that Jane could talk to her with less respect than she'd use to young Bessie in the scullery. She clenched her teeth on her trembling bottom lip. Helplessly she looked at Amos.

'I'll not have it!' He rose to the bait, his arm around her. 'How dare you use that tone to Dulcie. If this is what mixing with the dregs does for you, then the sooner the bastard goes the better. You hear me? I'll not keep him another day. Now let that be an end to it.'

His words hung between them in the silence of the seconds that followed. The atmosphere was charged with an undercurrent that terrified him; his chest felt tight, his pulses throbbed with the beat of his heart. It was as if he'd reached the edge of a precipice and there was nowhere to go except forward.

'No, Dad,' Jane answered him, her quiet tone so different from the way she'd crushed Dulcie, 'no, this isn't an end. For me it's a beginning.'

'Janie, I can't stand by and see you throw your life away. You're too young to know.'

'Many women have children before they're my age—'

'I did,' Dulcie sniffed into a lace-edged handkerchief. 'I had no caring family to stop me marrying when I hadn't the experience to see my error. I was twenty when Franchot was born. Babies hold you together, that's what I thought. But it's not true. So much unhappiness . . . I know what I'm talking about . . .' She didn't attempt to stem her tears, lifting Amos's hand in hers to hold against her wet cheek.

How different these two women were, both of them so dear to him. Warm, soft, clinging Dulcie – only he knew the hungry passion beneath that gentleness; a day never passed when he didn't thank God for bringing her to him. Jane, since she'd been no more than a toddler, she'd been his shadow; she'd looked on him as her mentor in all she'd learnt, always capable, loyal, loving, his friend and companion, his helpmeet and his pride. No man is an island, the words echoed silently in his mind. Yet in those seconds that's what they were, none of them able to bridge the gulf that divided them. Dulcie – no doubt upset by memories of a past he hadn't shared; Jane, standing tall and erect, young and confident, her head high, only feet away from him yet already beyond his reach. Amos clenched the fist of his free hand and forced it against his chest. And

13

wasn't it evidence of how wrapped up they were in themselves and their own thoughts that neither of the two people who made up his world so much as noticed the movement. A heavy heart – another figure of speech pushed itself into his thoughts, a figure of speech based on truth. His own heart felt like a great weight aching in his chest and stabbing between his shoulder-blades.

He made one more attempt.

'Tomorrow he'll be gone, at any rate gone from the brewery. That'll show him clearly enough that you aren't his ticket to a free ride in the business—'

'Stop it! You make me ashamed!' Still Jane spoke quietly. 'You inherited the brewery from Grandpa, did you see that as giving you the right to have a free ride? Or me? Just because I was born a Bradley, does that give me the right? I'm not a puppet with strings for you to pull. I'll marry Ian because I love him. He's a *proper man*, you could have come to look on him as a son.' Then, as if she'd suddenly remembered Dulcie's presence, 'Not like the nincompoops you produce, hoping to get me married off.'

'Of course I wanted to see you with a husband, one who would give you a good home. You've never been kind to me, you always misjudge what I do.' And, filled with self-pity, Dulcie believed it was true. Jealousy and hate come hand in hand and she had known right from when she came to Maybury House something of Amos would never be hers, she would never come between him and Jane.

'This is too much!' Amos shouted, actually shouted, at Jane. 'Damn it, girl, how dare you speak to Dulcie like it!'

Jane turned and left the room, closing the door behind her with a clink of finality.

'Was it my fault?' Dulcie looked hopelessly at Amos. 'Did I make things worse? It's just that I can't bear to see you so upset. Promise you'll send him packing. She's young, it's the first time she's fancied herself in love. She'll get over it once he's out of the way.'

But with woman's intuition, Dulcie knew Jane better.

'Excuse me, m'um, sir,' Babs, the young maid tapped and opened the door a few inches on one action, 'Mrs West said for me to ask if you're ready to go in. I did sound the gong. Things are getting spoilt, see.'

'We'll come, Babs,' Amos answered. 'Just put everything on the table and leave us to serve ourselves. Then go up to Miss Jane and tell her the meal is waiting, if you will.'

'Yessir.' Babs was glad to escape. There was something uncomfortable about all of them this evening. She'd like to have told Mrs West she thought the missus had been crying, but best to say nothing. If something had upset her it wouldn't be right to have them all gossiping and wondering what was wrong. Anyway, Mrs West was always looking to find fault with the missus and that just wasn't fair when she was so friendly and nice. Not like some of those stuck-up friends they invited for their bridge evenings. No, she wasn't going to set them all wondering what had upset the missus.

So Babs carried no gossip back to the kitchen, not even about what she saw when she opened the door of Jane's room to deliver her message.

'I've come to say goodbye.'

Dressed in hat and coat, a strapped hamper behind her on the hall floor, Jane stood in the doorway of the dining room.

'What in God's name are you talking about? Just take off your hat and coat and behave yourself.' Amos was on his feet. Out of his depth, he blustered. His voice was loud, uncontrolled, even to his own ears it sounded unnatural. 'Stop playing games and come to the table.' But what a stupid thing to say: Jane didn't play games, not over something as serious as this. 'Janie,' desperately he tried again, 'where do you think you're going at this time of evening?'

'To Ian, of course. Where else would I go? I've packed some things.'

Something in him seemed to snap. He brought his

15

clenched fist down on the table with such force that the crockery rattled.

'Dear God! What have I done to deserve this? This is your home, this where you'll stay.'

'If this is my house, then he is welcome in it.'

Their gazes met and locked. For a second Jane thought he was weakening, then he seemed to remember Dulcie and the spell that held them was broken.

'The man is no good to you. If he were, would he be so insensitive to the feelings of your family? Would he expect you to accept the kind of life he can provide for a wife? When a man asks for your hand, I expect him to speak first to me—'

'You won't even talk to him. It isn't Ian who is insensitive. Don't talk about it any more. I'll write to you, Dad. I'll tell you where we are.'

'Can't believe what you're saying . . .' He slumped back into his chair.

'It needn't be like this. I'm marrying Ian—'

'No,' but this time it was no more than a whisper, a sound of disbelief that this could be happening.

'You only have to say the word and we shall come home.'

'Do you even know what you're doing – what marriage means?' His anger had evaporated, he almost pleaded with her.

For a second she lowered her gaze, but only for a second. There was something in her expression he couldn't understand. Defiance? Apology? Pride?

'Janie, how can you do this to your family? The bastard seems to have bewitched you.'

'It's not the way I expected it to be either, Dad. When I've gone you'll realize how narrow-minded and bigoted you've been.'

'Don't talk to your father like that. What he says is right.' Dulcie weighed in behind Amos, but neither of them so much as noticed.

16

A million memories crowded in on Jane, all of them shared with him. Yet none of them shook her resolve; what she was doing was *right*. Once she was married, once he understood that what she and Ian felt for each other was real and strong, then he would change his opinion. It had happened before – remember how he'd refused to let her have her first pony – but she'd wheedled him around; remember when she'd been no more than five or six and she'd wanted to swim, how he'd forbidden it. She knew now that he'd been fearful for her, but at the time she'd seen him as unjust. So what had she done? Alone she'd taken to walking by the river, then knowing no one could see her she'd taken off everything except her knickers and slid off the bank into the water. She hadn't told him about her escapades until she could swim on both her front and her back, then she'd taken him to the water to demonstrate. There had been many times through the years when he'd given her what she wanted without a battle of wills; but there had been many more when she had had to do things her own way, knowing that in the end she would win him round. Either way, in the end she'd always had her own way and he'd realized she'd been right all along. And that's how it would be this time . . .

She moved towards him. They couldn't part like this.

'Dad . . .?' He didn't look up.

'Just go. If you choose to come back, this is your home. But as long as you're with him, then the door is closed to you. Go . . . just go . . .'

But she couldn't, not with the shadow between them of all that had been said. Without so much as glancing at Dulcie, she went past her to Amos and stopped to kiss the back of his bent head. Then she left them.

Daylight had long faded as, leaving the village behind her, Jane walked. She carried her hamper by the strap, but it was cumbersome and knocked against her leg as she strode out along the familiar road across Picton Heath and finally over the main road and down the long hill into Deremouth. Alone under the dark sky, she felt more certain with every step.

Ian had worked at the brewery since the beginning of summer, she'd noticed him right from the start – just as she'd known he'd noticed her. For weeks they had been meeting, Sunday afternoons walking on the cliffs, late evenings by the Dere upstream of the estuary. When had she realized she was in love with him? Perhaps right from the afternoon at the end of May when she'd been shopping in town, just a week after he'd started working at the brewery. With a hatbox in one hand and her umbrella held well forward against the fine rain that was driving in from the sea, she'd not seen him coming towards her.

'You look laden, Miss Bradley. Why don't you let me carry your box?'

Harriman, the new cooper. Of course she'd been aware of him, any girl would have been aware of such a man. Tall above average, well built, even in the workshop she had seen him as the epitome of masculinity, his sleeves rolled up exposing muscles that looked as strong as steel. With dark curly hair and clipped beard his appearance was striking as he'd looked up from his work to find her watching him and had smiled at her, showing perfect white teeth. Was that the moment when she'd felt the first recognition of what was to follow? Or was it not until the following Saturday when he'd waylaid her in the rain with the same easy confidence he might have shown had they been introduced over a friend's dining table. There was nothing servile in Ian Harriman; they had met as equals.

'That's kind,' she'd smiled her pleasure at his offer. 'I have the automobile, it's only just along the street.'

As if some weather god had heard her, a tap in heaven had been turned full on. Rain that minutes ago had been fine suddenly drove at them like silver needles, dancing on the thoroughfare and making them run towards the shelter of the motor car.

18

'Get in till it eases,' she'd shouted as she ran. It was only afterwards that it occurred to her how he had made straight for the passenger's side of the vehicle, leaving her to put down her dripping umbrella and open the door for herself. Used to driving with her father, it was habit for him to have it held while she climbed in. But that day had been different: everything about that day had been different.

Cut off from the storm while the rain beat on the canvas hood and the wind rattled against the transparent weather-shields on the door, conversation had been easy and natural. He'd told her how he had come to Deremouth only a fortnight before, his object being to close down the house where his mother had lived until her recent death. Instead of following his original plan he had decided to go on renting the cottage in town and had taken work at the brewery.

'Sheer chance,' he'd held her gaze, his hint of a smile conveying as much as his words. 'That – or a kindly fate?'

'You like your work there?' She'd said the first thing that came into her head, anything to hide the strange, wild excitement that surged through her veins.

He shrugged. 'Like it? There's always satisfaction in doing something you know you do well. But making barrels is outside the real work of the brewery. The whole process is interesting, fascinating.' He watched her, weighing her reaction to his words.

'I've been going there as long as I can remember. My father explained things to me even when I was young.'

'You're an only child, I believe? He must wish he had a son to carry on.'

'Oh, Dad won't be thinking along those lines. Someone else carrying on implies that he's nearing the end of his working life – and he's most certainly not. Anyway, he has me.'

When the rain passed they'd hardly noticed. It was only when the pale sunlight had found a gap in the clouds and the empty road had, for a minute, sparkled temptingly that she'd suggested they might drive up the track that led along the cliff top.

'Will you swing the starting handle?' she said. Then, as he climbed back into his seat and the engine chugged healthily: 'From the highest point you get the best view in the district. Look right and you can see across Deremouth and the estuary; look left and you see Chalcombe, the fishing village the other way.'

Five months later, striding confidently through the night towards his terrace cottage in Chandlers Wharf, that afternoon merged with so many in her memory. Exactly when that easy friendship had turned into the emotion she felt now – they both felt now – she didn't question. This afternoon he had told her she was the most important thing in his world, he had begged her to marry him. They'd been alone in the stable, alone expect for one dray-horse who'd looked on solemnly, missing nothing.

'Yes, oh yes,' she'd whispered, her eyes telling him even more than her words. And a few minutes later, when all the promises, the embraces, were interrupted by the sound of the hooter for the start of the afternoon's labour, 'I want you to come home, get to know Dad – and for him to get to know you. Then we'll tell them. I'll tell him this afternoon that I want to bring you home . . .'

And so had begun the hours that had led to where she was now. She was taking a short cut through Union Way, no more than a narrow alley leading to Chandlers Wharf when, just as she came to The Jolly Sailor, a man the worse for drink was propelled through the door to come to a staggering halt in front of her. For a moment he stood there swaying, whichever way she stepped to go round him, so he moved to block her way. 'There's my lovely,' he slurred, lurching to grab her as she backed away, then belching with the effort of speech.

'Excuse me,' she said with all the dignity she could muster, thankful that she was almost at journey's end.

''Scuse you. 'Scuse me . . .' She'd not realized what he

20

was doing until she heard the sound of him urinating, laughing as he sprayed whichever way she tried to dodge past him.

'You're disgusting!'

'Don't come on like that to me, young madam.' Finding her not amenable to being touched, like so many the worse for drink, he was set for a fight. 'Here, here you, wait while I put m' ol' man to bed – here, come back when I'm talking to you.'

But she'd got round him and was gone, only his uncertain steps telling her that he was following. Head high she marched on, determined not to run until she'd rounded the corner and was out of his sight.

At last . . . journey's end . . . no. 5 Chandlers Wharf. The front rooms were in darkness. Please don't let him be out, please, make him be here. She banged the knocker on the door as hard as she could, already hearing the drunkard's footsteps. No reply.

'So 'at's where you are. No one home, eh? Good lookin' gal like you, what you doing alone, eh? Ah, good looking, gal . . .' He started up the short path towards her. She could smell the beer on his breath as, holding her hamper between herself and him, she forced him off her. Then, in an instant it happened.

'Get out, you drunken slob!' Ian! She'd not even heard him coming along the semi-lit road. With one hand he took the back of the man's jacket, with the other the seat of his trousers, then he carried him out of the gate and dropped him in the road. 'Now sod off!'

Watching him, Jane marvelled at his strength, she marvelled at everything about him. So why was she crying? It was as if, here in surroundings so alien to all she had known, she was brought face to face with what she had done. 'Janie . . . this is your home.' If one soul can call out to another, surely her father's was calling to hers.

Then Ian unlocked the small front door and ushered her into the dark passage.

Chapter Two

Through the weeks of summer Amos had encouraged himself to believe that he was imagining Jane's attraction to the cooper; sometimes he'd succeeded, for her interest in the brewery never lessened and there was nothing new in her natural friendship with the men employed there. She'd known some of them for years, but why should that mean she'd be less than friendly towards someone just taken to join the workforce? Perhaps the real difference wasn't so much in Jane as in Harriman's manner towards her. It was that, more than anything, which had bothered Amos.

Jane had never been in the habit of coming to town with him regularly each morning. On some days she'd not come at all or on others she'd join him later, bringing herself on her bicycle. However she spent her time, she liked to cram her days full. Sometimes tempted by a clear blue sky, she would saddle up her horse and ride out towards the open moors. Or there would be other mornings when, with the energy of youth, she would help Jim Bailey, the elderly gardener, with the winter digging. There had been plenty of days when she'd leave her bicycle at Deremouth station and take the train to Exeter, arriving back in her father's office in the afternoon, keen to parade before him in some frivolous and utterly delightful hat she'd acquired and charged to the account he would pay willingly. He'd delighted in knowing she was as free as a bird, coming to the brewery because she wanted to be there and not because it was expected of her. During that summer, though, she'd spent more time than usual at her desk – there, and where else? If Harriman were half a man, he would have realized that *her* life and *his* were poles apart.

Now she'd gone ... gone to that bastard ... Amos couldn't bear to imagine ...

With her departure, the dining room was filled with silence, except for the way Amos beat a tattoo on the table with his clenched fist.

'It's my own fault!' His voice was loud and rasping, not like his own. Yet Dulcie felt he wasn't even aware of her presence, he was simply speaking his thoughts. 'I should have stopped it weeks ago, stopped it before it got to this stage. I'm going after her—' He pushed his chair back with such force that it clattered to the ground.

'No. Amos, listen to me, my honey.' Dulcie got up from her place and went to him, retrieving the chair and gently forcing him to sit in it. There was nothing in her loving manner to hint at the raging jealousy that tore at her. Damn Jane! Spoilt from the day she was born! Thank God she'd gone. If *I* walked out, would he behave like this? He looks half out of his mind. What does she care? Nothing. And why? Because she knows that, just like she always has, she'll twist him around her finger. Well, this time she won't! This time I'll see to it that she doesn't! 'We'll sort it together,' she cooed, cradling Amos's head against her soft breast. 'If you got the motor out and chased her, yes, sure you could catch her. You might even force her back here, for nothing less than force would bring her. But would she love you for it? Not tonight, she wouldn't. Tonight she would see you as her gaoler, her enemy. Give her a day or two, let her have time to realize for herself what a mistake she is making. She's strong-minded –' wilful, pig-headed more likely! – 'she won't bend to anyone else's will. We saw that this evening. Let her be the one to make the first move.'

As he turned his face towards her a sob escaped him. It was his downfall. Amos, whose voice was always deep and strong, lost all control as he cried. Even the sound made a stranger of him, high pitched, desperate.

'. . . Can't lose her . . . can't . . . that swine touching her . . . Janie . . .' Dulcie could hardly understand his words as they disappeared into a squeak.

'Of course we shan't lose her, precious. Tonight you must give her her head.'

'Tonight – with him – can't bear to think – Janie—'

'He wouldn't touch her – not like you're thinking – she's upset by all this too, my darling.' Not touch her? Of course he'll touch her – and she'll want him to. She's not going to chase after him and then sleep alone! And by the morning she'll know there's no turning back. Her low, caressing voice didn't alter. 'In the morning she'll come to the works, she'll talk to you, you'll both be calmer.' She didn't believe a word of it, but the sight and sound of him frightened her. She'd known he was besotted with the wretched girl, but she'd never expected a man to behave like this.

Often Jane had visited the workers' houses, perhaps gone to see a new baby or a sick wife. That their homes were so unlike her own was something she'd accepted without much thought. But to be in Ian's home was quite different. He'd taken her up to the bedroom at the front of the little terrace house. By the light of a single candle she saw the iron bedstead, the chest of drawers that, with the aid of a mirror on top, doubled as a dressing table, and a chair with a hole in its wicker seat. The poverty of her surroundings added to the feeling of unreality that shrouded everything that had happened. Rather than make her see what she was doing as a mistake, it made her love Ian more. It wouldn't always be like this for him. But tonight, alone with him, it wasn't the future she thought of. There was nothing for her but the present, the longing that ached in her for them to share all that they were.

Just for one moment as she took off her earrings and laid them on the chest of drawers, then unbuttoned the bodice of her blouse, her mind was thrown back to the moment when, in her own room, she'd taken off the green gown she'd been wearing and replaced it with a simple blouse and skirt. From there it was but a short jump to be thinking of her father, of the way he'd refused to look at her as she'd bent to kiss him goodbye. But none of it had the power to dent her confidence in what she was doing, or to stem the longing that drove her. How often she'd dreamed of love, hardly knowing, only half understanding. Even now she didn't really know, still she only half understood, but she was driven by desire as they hurriedly stripped off their clothes. She wanted nothing but herself and him. Just as she was, she wanted to be part of him, to – to – she didn't know, except that she had an inextricable yearning for whatever these next moments would bring.

He was as perfect as she'd known he would he. He was tall, broad-shouldered, strong-muscled, the dark hair on his chest as tough-looking as that on his head. Her gaze was drawn down, her heart raced as she moved towards him.

By the light of the flickering candle he pushed her back on to the bed.

'It's going to hurt. You know that, don't you?' he whispered urgently, climbing above her without waiting for her answer.

'Yes, yes. Yes. I want you to hurt me, I want . . . I want.'

She knew the simple fact of the act of love-making. Artlessly she wrapped her long legs around him, her mouth opened to his as she felt his tongue probe; she heard the sound of her own voice, half sigh, half moan, a sound full of the craving that filled her.

Yes, it hurt her. But she rejoiced even in the pain. How he must love her to be moved to such passion! When his climax came she felt she had lived all her life for this moment. He recovered enough that they wriggled between the bedclothes, but in seconds he was asleep.

How different this bed was from her own. At home her sheets were changed every few days, they were starched and smooth. She burrowed her face into the pillow, it seemed to carry the stale smell of the oil he used on his wiry hair. Tonight she liked the feeling of the crumpled bedding. The candle was flickering to extinction or she might have realized the sheets weren't simply crumpled, they were also far from clean. Soon they would be in a home of their own, somewhere in Deremouth not too far from the brewery. Their house would be comfortable, their bedding well ironed. So her thoughts wandered, not believing herself to be dreaming dreams, but simply looking ahead to a future she thought was certain.

She must have dozed even though she didn't want to waste a minute of this precious night. Perhaps it was that determination to fight off sleep that woke her somewhere in the small hours. Now she knew what love was like: total, all-consuming love. Even the pain of it had been unbelievably wonderful. Life held no mysteries for her. She wished he'd wake, she wanted to tell him that even the pain had been glorious. Would it be like that for them always, every night? Even as she thought it, he stirred from this first exhausted slumber.

'Next time it'll be good for you too,' he whispered, drawing her hand to hold it around him. Excitement stirred – in her, in him. Nearby a church clock struck one. The night had scarcely begun.

It wasn't difficult to persuade Ian they should leave Deremouth. The last thing he wanted was a face-to-face encounter with Amos at this stage. Jane had given him the gist of what had happened between her father and her, adding:

'It's a storm in a teacup.' Then with an affectionate smile tugging at the corners of her mouth, 'Dad and me could never fall out – not really deep down fall out. We're much too close for that. Once he realizes we're together and we're not going to be driven apart, then he'll just want us to be happy. He'll be there to walk me up the aisle – you'll see.'

Together they breakfasted on boiled eggs (unfortunately hard and unappetizing eggs) and bread and butter, then while Ian packed his clothes, Jane washed the dishes. For her, washing dishes was a new experience, and on that morning each new experience added to her sense of excitement and wonder. She wasn't even perturbed by the greasy bowl, rather she liked to dwell on the contrast between what Ian's life had been and what it would be in the future.

'Is there anyone you have to say goodbye to? Can you just pull up your anchor and leave? What do we do about the house? Is it yours to sell? And then there's the furniture?' She was impatient for them to set out on the future they would share, but he must have ends to tie up first.

'There's nothing here that's use for anything more than firewood. And the house is rented. I'll write to the landlord, settle up anything I owe and tell him he can either dispose of this lot or leave it for the next tenants. They'd have to be pretty desperate to want this rubbish.'

'They were your mother's things. Isn't there something you can keep?'

Even the scullery maid at Maybury House was given a room better furnished, but she wasn't going to let a hint of that show in her tone. She tried to imagine what his mother must have been like; she was filled with pity for her, living alone and in such squalid discomfort.

'Pay cartage to keep any of this? What an idea! If the landlord can get a bob or two for it he can post it on to me. No, Jane, this is a new beginning for you and me. I want you to be able to write home to your father and tell him how good things are for us.'

'So they are. I wish I could tell him so this morning – after last night, I mean—'

'I have a feeling that last night wouldn't endear his future

27

son-in-law to him.' Cupping her chin in his hand he tilted her head, willingly she looked at him. 'Not like it endeared his daughter to me.'

She nodded, frightened to speak and filled with an emotion that ached in her arms and legs. Wordlessly she leant against him, conscious of the cheap, rough material of his shirt, rejoicing in the solid strength of him.

A few minutes later, without a backward glance they left Chandlers Wharf, she carrying her unwieldy hamper and he a battered case – their worldly possessions. Uninvited, a picture sprang into her mind of her father, the many times she'd brought her purchases back to the brewery and how he'd always carried the packages out to the motor car. But she stamped on the thought almost before it had a chance to take root.

They walked up Quay Hill and turned towards Waterloo Street. If she looked to the left along Queen Street, she could see the chimneys of the brewery.

'Come on, don't dawdle or we'll miss the train.'

'Suppose I were to go to his office, talk to him alone without Dulcie. Just you and me, I mean—'

Far better to give him time, let him realize she could manage without him, that was Ian's opinion.

'He'd want you to go home until the wedding. We've gone too far for that, Jane, we belong to each other. Don't leave me.'

As they'd talked they'd slowed almost to a standstill. She imagined her father alone in his office. 'Janie, draw up a chair, I want to talk to you about . . .'

She shook her head. 'Let's hurry.' She slipped her free hand into Ian's. He was right. She'd do nothing until she could write and tell her father her new address, tell him the arrangements for the wedding. By then he would have had time to see things her way. With all the confidence of youth she imagined herself walking up the aisle on his arm. Her imagination jumped ahead, she saw herself and Ian living in Deremouth, somewhere in a good residential part of town;

in her mind's eye she saw Ian becoming increasingly involved with the business of running the brewery. She could almost hear the comments as news of her marriage spread: 'How delighted her father must be to have a new son in the business with him.'

So, still held in the aura of the night's wonder, she entwined her fingers with Ian's as she strode out by his side along familiar Waterloo Street to the railway station. He had told her they would catch the London-bound train, getting off at Reading. From there they'd go on the branch line to Brackleford. Willingly she'd agreed, proud of his decisive organizing.

'What's Brackleford like?' she asked as, sitting opposite each other, alone in their otherwise unoccupied third-class compartment, they travelled eastward. 'Will it be easy to get somewhere to stay, just until we go back to Deremouth?' For she knew that he'd lived there until his mother's illness.

'It's a town like any other. Bigger than Deremouth, but Reading is the county town. Of course I could always get work there. But Brackleford's better, I know they'll be glad to see me back at Ruddicks, they'll take me on straight away.' Something in the way he smiled at her made her heart skip a beat. 'It'll only be until your father sees that I mean to take care of you. You say you're certain of your father?'

She laughed. 'Of course I'm certain. I know Dad couldn't really let us part like this. And once he knows you, he'll understand about us. He'll love you like I do.'

'Like you do?' Raising his eyebrows he looked at her teasingly, his expression drawing her to him from where she'd sat opposite. 'It oughtn't to have to be like this for you. I know how you must hate it that you and he are pulling in different directions. But, what else could we do? It couldn't be right for us to give each other up. What we have is – oh Jane, it's wonderful, glorious – you've got to make him understand.'

29

'I will. I will, darling.' She moved closer, standing between his parted knees, holding him close as he leant forward to rest his head against her breast. 'As soon as I have an address so that he can write back to me, I'll send it to him. He just wants to be sure I'm happy. And I am. I never knew there could be happiness like it.'

Pulling her down to his level, his mouth found hers. His fingers moved up and down her spine, setting her pulses racing as her lips parted and she felt the probing caress of his tongue.

'See what you do to me. I could make you happy again – this very minute. Alone,' he whispered, pulling out her hat pin and taking off her hat, 'no more stops until Reading . . . nearly an hour . . . Jane . . . Jane.' His hand was warm on her leg above her stocking top. There was no corridor; in their small compartment the world was theirs alone.

Fifty minutes later, her heart still pounding, she stood uncertainly in the rocking carriage, straightening her clothes. She looked in the mirror that was set in the wall beneath the luggage hammock and flanked on one side by a sepia photograph of the Tower of London and on the other, one of a Cornish coastal scene. Her reflection smiled at her, no wonder she smiled back. She felt she could have shouted for sheer joy. A strand of her straight, dark hair had escaped – or been pulled – from its pins; his beard had made a bright pink patch on her left cheek, his hungry mouth a red wheal on her neck. But it was her eyes that told their story, dark eyes that shone as if they'd seen a vision.

She twisted the loose strand back in place and fixed it securely, then put her hat on and stabbed it with two hat pins just as the train rattled and jolted over the points on the approach to Reading station. Flopped against the back of the seat, Ian's eyes were half closed. She looked at him and sent up a silent 'Thank you'. To him? To fate for bringing them together? Only hours before, she had lain gazing into the darkness, believing that there could be no greater wonder. She knew now, that had been but the beginning.

Last night had been like a miracle. And now? This last hour? A miracle perhaps, but one that she knew would be theirs to reach for time and again, bringing them always closer.

'Ian ... Ian I think we're almost at the station. Wake up.'

Running his fingers through his wiry hair he grinned at her.

'I wasn't asleep. Just in the recovery position. You look remarkably cool for a lady who's been raped in a railway carriage.'

'But then I wasn't raped,' she chuckled, bending to touch his mouth with hers. 'Come on, time to get up.'

The advantage of going to Brackleford was that Ian was no stranger there. From the railway station he led the way along Mechin Lane – better known to the locals as 'smelly alley' – to the town's main thoroughfare, then up a flight of steps at the side of a building and into a door on which was a sign 'Skinner and Highworth, Letting Agents'. Five minutes later, two weeks' rent in advance handed over and nothing in his manner to hint that it had left his pocket almost empty, they were on their way to No. 4 Mill Lane. This was where they would stay until the 'storm in the teacup' was over and they could go home, as she thought of Deremouth.

While she unpacked, he went to buy their supper. The wonder came from being with him; and it was that wonder that gave her this sense of adventure in her new and humble surroundings. What furniture there was in the cramped terrace house was basic, of poor quality; indeed, although cleaner, it was as cheap and tawdry as what they'd left behind in Chandlers Wharf. But after a life of comfort the very difference added colour. She had always delighted in buying clothes, delighted in it and yet taken it for granted. Now, though, she wished she'd been able to bring more with her, but there had been limits to how much she'd been able to cram into a hamper. It took no time to fold away her silk underwear in one drawer of the chest, and hang her few outer garments in the wardrobe. Next came Ian's things. There was something thrillingly intimate about undoing his case, taking out his few personal possessions. Carefully she refolded the collarless shirts he wore for work and put them in the second drawer. Then came two spare collars for the better shirt he'd worn for their journey, vests, two pairs of long underpants, two pairs of short, a few none-too-white handkerchiefs and socks in varying stages of wear. Lastly she unpacked the hobnailed boots he wore for work, in which he'd stuffed his shaving mug and cut-throat razor. His entire wardrobe ... how could she fail to compare it with the clothes that hung in her father's dressing room. She sat on the edge of the hard bed, her hand smoothing the rough wool of his underpants, her mind hardly able to accept that she was actually here, these were his most personal items, he was part of her life and she was part of his. How scratchy the material was, how harsh to wear next to his skin. Soon it wouldn't be like that. Her own undergarments were silk, their touch was a caress. Ian in silk? She chuckled at the thought. Could there ever have been a man so splendid, so masculine, so strong, so passionate, so demanding? Demanding? No, that sounded as if she weren't willing. Oh, but she was ... Hark, that was his step, that was something she'd learnt to recognize even at the brewery. He'd bought their supper.

'Come on, are you still up there? Let's eat these while they're hot.'

She pushed his pile of clothes into the second drawer and ran downstairs.

'What have we got? Smells gorgeous.'

'Faggots. Faggots and peas. A quarter of tea, half pint of milk and a loaf. I forgot the butter, but you can shop properly tomorrow. Bring the plates.'

Jane had no idea what went into the making of a faggot,

but food had never tasted better. Faggots, peas, a wedge of bread, all followed by a pot of tea. For a second she imagined the dining room at Maybury House, Babs carrying in a tray loaded with dishes of steaming food, Dulcie, plump, pretty and purposely trying to give the impression that there was a secret she shared only with Amos. Dad, dear dear Dad. Now, in her newfound joy of living, all her anger had vanished. Have I made Dad miserable? Perhaps I have, but he won't be, not when he knows how happy I am. Joyously happy – except when I think about *him*. But then it's easy for me, I've got Ian, I've got all the wonder of loving, being loved. I know Dad's missing me. But it won't be for long . . .

'Well? Good supper?'

She nodded.

'The best meal I've ever eaten.'

He laughed. 'Must be the company. I can't believe faggots can compare with the sort of meals you've been used to in the evening.'

'I'm glad we're here, living like this. I've often thought of couples who set out – to the New World perhaps, starting a completely new life together – I've often thought of the challenge, the . . . the *unity* they must have felt. Don't you see, it's much, much better than starting off secure and comfortable. I'm *glad* we shall have this time together even though it won't be for long. When we go home and look for a house in Deremouth, this will be like a secret life we've shared. I'm not saying it very well . . .'

'You're saying it splendidly, my sweetheart. When we go to Deremouth, you say. You sound so sure. Perhaps your father will decide you've made your bed so you must lie on it.'

She laughed, cutting herself another slice from the crusty loaf.

'Dad do that? Of course he won't. We were very angry with each other – me as much as him. Now all that's over. I just know I love him and not for the world would I ever want to hurt him. And he feels just the same.'

'He wouldn't be the first irate parent to wash his hands of an errant daughter.'

'Dad and me aren't like that. If Dulcie hadn't been there I believe I could have made him understand right from the beginning. Once you find work and we have the wedding arrangements made, I'll write to him. Ian, I hope he isn't too miserable. He'll have been to your house, he'll have found that we've gone and he won't know where.'

'If he has time to worry, then he'll be all the more thankful when he hears from you. Tomorrow I'll go along to Ruddick's, where I used to work, they make the barrels for the mill. They'll welcome me back, start me working straight away, you may be sure. I shan't tell them that it'll only be until your father sees I'm making an honest woman of you.' His expression when he said it set her pulses racing. 'When he knows we've gone too far for him to be able to change your mind, he'll find he's *glad* to have a son in the business. But I shan't say that to them at Ruddick's – and mind you don't tell anyone either.'

She hardly thought it was likely that she would, for who could she possibly tell?

He was a skilled cooper and, just as he expected, Ruddick's welcomed him back. So Jane went alone to the vicarage to make arrangements for the wedding.

'Vicar's in his study.' Edith had been a servant there throughout the incumbency of two priests prior to the Reverend Marcos Warburton, and she assumed the right to know what was going on. 'What name shall I tell him? Better if I can give him an idea what it is you've come about.'

Some visitors might have been annoyed by such open curiosity, but Jane told her all she wanted to know. What was there to hide in the fact that she and Ian were to be married? Willingly she would have shouted it from the rooftop. If she'd also told Edith her address, no doubt she would have been kept waiting on the doorstep, but experience had taught the retainer to recognize 'a lady' when she saw one.

'You'd better step inside and wait here in the hall while I tell the vicar you're here.'

If Jane expected to be greeted by someone of the vintage of Moorleigh's Reverend Hislop, she was mistaken. Not that she was sufficiently interested in Marcos Warburton to speculate on his age, whether he was twenty-five, thirty, thirty-five, didn't register with her. She saw him simply as a necessary player in the act of binding her life to Ian's.

The impression she made on the priest was far more positive. She wore the outfit she'd travelled in to Brackleford, indeed the only outdoor clothes she'd brought, the soft lightweight wool of her well tailored tawny-coloured autumn coat silently pronouncing that she was someone of comfortable means. She may not have been a beauty, not as his wife Alayne was, but there was something about her confident manner, something in her firm handshake and in the way her earnest eyes met his gaze, that held his attention. As he wrote down the information she gave him in answer to his questions, he became puzzled. Jane Bradley, twenty-one years old, her father a master brewer, her mother deceased, all that seemed in keeping with the slim, erect girl who sat facing him across his desk. Only when he asked for her address did she hesitate.

'Here – or where I come from?'

'Your permanent address at the time of your marriage. Either you or the bridegroom must be resident here for at least three weeks.'

'Oh, I see,' she smiled, not a bit put out as she told him, 'that's all right then, we shall both qualify for that. We're at No. 4 Mill Lane, the same address for both of us. We were in Devon – that's where I've always lived – we came here yesterday.'

'And you'll be married from the home of your in-laws?'

'No. I didn't mean that. Ian has no parents, both of them

are dead. We've taken the house for rent.' Then, for the first time, considering how the world would condemn their situation (The world? And did that include the priest?), she rushed on, her feathers ruffled, 'You can't tell me you believe I should be living in some miserable bed-sitting room because we have to wait three weeks before we can be married? We live together because we want to be together. If you don't want to marry us, then I'll go to the town hall and arrange it at the registry office. Perhaps that's what I should have done in the first place.' Already she was on her feet.

'Did I say that, Miss Bradley?' He willed her to meet his gaze.

'No. That was rude of me. And I'm sorry. I expect I'm prickly.'

'Not with me, I hope.' She heard the smile in his voice and, for the first time, looked at him with more than cursory interest. The thought sprang to mind that the women of the parish would find it no hardship to fill his pews on Sundays. There was something almost foreign in his appearance. His well cut hair was that dark brown that is almost black, thick dark lashes fringed eyes of an even deeper brown than her own, his olive complexion might have come from roots in some Mediterranean country. She found herself staring and quickly looked down, only for her gaze to fall on his well kept hands.

Dipping his pen in the silver-topped inkwell on his desk, he started to write out particulars of the bride and groom. But his mind was on what she'd said. Prickly. What made her prickly? The answer was obvious: the couple had met with opposition. This girl came from a background very different from the residents of Mill Lane. Had she not brought her birth certificate with her he would have suspected she was an under-age runaway; he felt she was poised ready to defend her actions. He wanted to set her at her ease. 'To go back to the arrangements: will you want the choir and the organ?'

'No. It'll be very quiet.' Then, as if she defied him to argue: 'My father will come up from Devon to give me away, of course.' She said it with such conviction that she persuaded herself it was the truth. It had to be.

And it was those words that set Marcos Warburton's doubts at rest.

Walking back down the drive Jane came upon a young woman filling her trug with dahlias. Responding to the smile she wished the woman a cheery 'Good morning'.

'I don't think we've met, have we? Are you new to the town?' The woman's voice was soft and gentle, in keeping with her appearance. Jane had never seen anyone so lovely.

'Yes, I arrived yesterday. I came to see the vicar about my wedding.'

'I'm his wife.' The secateurs were gently laid in the trug and a soft, white hand extended. 'Welcome to the parish. I hope you'll feel yourself to be one of us. On Tuesday afternoons I hold a knitting afternoon here at the vicarage, the ladies of St Stephen's you know. Perhaps you might enjoy coming to join us. That would give you a chance to meet people.'

'That's kind of you, but—'. In time she stopped herself saying she wouldn't be in Brackleford many weeks. 'But I've never knitted. And just at the moment I have a lot to do, with the wedding so soon.'

'Afterwards then. Perhaps you sew, or do crochetwork. We busy ourselves making little garments for the poor in the parish. Even in a town like this, you'd be surprised how little some people have to live on. We should all try and show our gratitude in whatever way we can, don't you think?'

Looking at his lovely wife, she pictured the vicar. What a handsome couple they made. Faced with such a beautiful, compassionate woman she felt gauche, her laugh loud and forced, holding defiance rather than humour.

'Even the poor wouldn't be seen wearing the sort of effort I'd produce.'

'Made with a loving heart, you might surprise yourself.'

Of its own volition, Jane's imagination took her to the brewery, to the part she'd played there. That had been a man's world but she had fitted into it effortlessly, a square peg in a square hole. Wishing gentle Mrs Warburton goodbye she hurried away.

On the way back to Mill Lane she called at the stationer's and bought a penholder, a box of nibs, some ink and notepaper – the best quality the shop could supply. For Ian's sake the heavy parchment was essential for her letter to Maybury House. Once indoors she sat at the plain wooden table and started to write. Holding the thought of Dulcie firmly to the back of her mind, her letter was simply to her father.

My dear Dad ... know you must feel like I do ... quarrels never come between us ... you'll be worried ... we are both so sure ... here because I love him just as he does me ... three weeks Saturday at two o'clock ... please, Dad, be with me to take me up the aisle ... I know you will ... we can't hurt each other, not you and me ... if it's my fault, then I'm sorry ... no other way, we are right for each other ...

On and on she wrote, sometimes repeating herself, every word written from her heart.

... wish I could be with you when you get this ... must have been deep down miserable just as I have, even though I've found joy I never knew existed ...

With the thick pages folded, it was a fat envelope she dropped into the postbox at the end of Mill Lane. Tomorrow it would be waiting on the breakfast table. Jane could almost see the expression on her father's face as he pulled out the folded bundle ... relief, joy. Would he answer it before he left for the brewery, or would he take it with him and write to her in his office? Yes, that's what she liked to imagine. Either way, by Friday morning she would have his reply, the cloud would be lifted.

The letter posted, she bought two slices of steak, some

38

potatoes, carrots and greens. Tonight would be the first meal she'd cooked for Ian – the first she'd cooked at all. In her mind she imagined the end result, the steak as succulent as Mrs West sent to the table at home, the potatoes light and fluffy, the carrots tender, the cabbage a fresh green.

She wasn't the first not to have instant success, but surely she had a right to expect at least *something* to turn out as she'd imagined. Supposing meat should always be cooked in the oven, that's what she did with the steaks; and believing that somewhere she'd heard that meat cooked for a long time was more tender, she allowed three hours. The cooker had three rings, so she filled three saucepans with cold water, and put all the vegetables to boil at the same time.

According to the agent, No. 4 Mill Lane was fully equipped and ready for occupation. She hunted in all the cupboards but could find no serving dishes any more than she'd been able to find more than one well-worn tablecloth. As for the cutlery, nothing matched and the only thing the selection of forks had in common was that they all gave the impression that someone's strong teeth had been chewing them. In an effort to give the table a festive appearance for this, their first home-cooked meal, she went into the tiny back garden and managed to find three Michaelmas daisies and two sprigs of greenery cut from the privet hedge. The nearest thing to a vase was a fish-paste pot which some previous occupier had carefully washed and stored in the cupboard probably for the very same use as she was putting it to. With only one tablecloth discovered, she knew it was useless hunting for napkins, so she took a sheet of her high quality notepaper and wrote 'Napkins, tablecloths, vase ...', the start of a shopping list. Her ignorance of house-keeping on a working man's wage was much the same as her ignorance of cooking. Into her mind came a picture of the dining room at Maybury House, the highly polished silver, the gleaming glassware, the delicate china. It was the very difference between that and her present surroundings that challenged her. It wasn't in her nature to accept defeat and she certainly wasn't going to be beaten by the lack of a few creature comforts!

When Ian came in she wanted to hear about how he'd been received on applying for his old job back.

'I told you – there was no question about whether they wanted me. It's been a long day with nothing but a crust of bread and cheese. What have you got for me?'

'I'll have to put it straight on to our plates. They said the house was equipped, but there are no dishes.'

'Won't be on my plate long, I could eat an ox.'

In a shroud of steam she dished up her first effort: potatoes that had boiled into sloppy puree, yellow cabbage, hard carrots, and steak cooked beyond recognition.

'What do I do with this? Sole my boots?'

'Wasn't tough – was lovely steak—' Disappointment made her frightened to speak.

'How the hell long have you cooked it?' He knocked it with his knife. 'Even a dog couldn't eat it.'

She pushed her plate away.

'I'm sorry,' she bit hard on her bottom lip, trying to control it. It wasn't unhappiness that brought the threat of tears, it was disappointment, it was the difference between the meal she'd dreamt and the meal she'd brought to the table. 'I'll buy a book, see how to do things—'

He managed to overcome his first spontaneous anger.

'Never mind, sweetheart. And how did you afford steak from the bit of money I left you for shopping?' They'd not talked about what money she'd brought with her, so despite the inedible meal he took some comfort from supposing she hadn't come empty-handed. 'What would you know about looking after a poor man, eh? There's always been someone to put the food in front of you. I shouldn't have opened the door of your golden cage and let you out.'

'That's not true!' In a second she was out of her chair and kneeling by his side. 'I'll learn. Honestly, I'll do better tomorrow. I'll buy a copy of *Mrs Beeton*, that'll tell me everything. It's just that I'd never done it before.'

40

'We'll have to have something else for our supper. What else is there?'

'Nothing.'

Just as she had, he pushed his plate of untouched food away from him. The action was a play for time.

'There are more important things than supper. In a minute we can get something from the pie shop but first – did you write your letter?'

'Of course I did. First I saw the vicar, then I wrote and told Dad.'

'Even now it's only two days since you had that row with him. You don't think you ought to have left him a bit longer? Let him get really anxious?'

'Of course not. He'll be worried to death – like I would be if he'd walked out on me. I can't leave him not knowing where I am. I was angry on Monday night, just as angry as he was. But you can't stay angry when you're as happy as I am. I hate to hurt him.'

'You have a right to choose your own partner.'

'And so I have chosen my own partner. I know Dad as well as I know myself. By now he'll have had time to see things from my angle. Just you wait until Friday morning, you'll find we shall hear from him that he's coming to give me away.'

Ian stood up from the table, hoisting her to her feet and pulling her into his arms. Yes, Friday they'd hear that the pig-headed old fool had realized the choice of a husband had to be her own. And from there on everything would be plain sailing for them. In fact, the more Ian thought about it, the better pleased he was that they'd had this break from Deremouth. It would act as a lesson to Amos Bradley that he couldn't dictate their lives.

Friday's post brought no letter from Deremouth, nor yet Saturday's. Monday came and went, Tuesday ... Wednesday ... a week since she'd written.

She'd bought a copy of *Mrs Beeton's Household*

Management. It was lying on the table when Ian came home.

'That's an expensive book.' Frowning, he picked up the heavy tome to look at it. 'A good thing I'm to marry a lady of means.'

'Means, by no means,' she laughed. 'But I didn't pay for it from the money you gave me for housekeeping.'

'My idea of being a lady of means may not be as exalted as yours. At least you have something behind you to draw on, you don't have to wait for a pay packet at the end of each week.'

'Ian, I have no money. Not in an account, I mean. Dad always gave me spending money, just so that I was never without. Of course I could have asked him for more if I needed it.'

'My dear, sweet innocent, the coat you put on your back probably cost what we have to think of as three months' wages – perhaps more. And you say "Dad always gave me spending money."'

'Clothes aren't money. What I mean is, I charged anything I wanted to his account. I just never needed spare cash except for my train fares and perhaps buying my lunch while I was in Exeter, that sort of thing. But I had enough in my purse for *Mrs Beeton*, so I'll make a cook of myself yet.'

He had turned away and was looking out of the window at the street. No money ... she had nothing of her own ... surely if her old man cared two hoots about her wellbeing he wouldn't leave her like that ... no, there must be a letter in the post ... or perhaps at the weekend he'd walk in and surprise them ... no money, just about enough for that bloody cookery book. Well, he just hoped it proved worth having. Thank God she had more talent between the sheets than she had in the kitchen.

But her culinary efforts remained at best unappetizing and, more often, at worst inedible.

'He's paying you back, that's his game,' Ian told her when he came home on the Thursday of the second week to find the afternoon post had still brought nothing.

'He wouldn't do it for that,' she defended. 'Perhaps the post got held up. Perhaps he never had my letter.'

So she wrote again. But still no answer came.

When their wedding day arrived both of them donned their best clothes just as they had for their journey from Deremouth.

'He'll be waiting at the church,' she said as she anchored her hat with its long pin. 'Yes, that's what he'll do. He'll want to see my face when he surprises me.' She turned to Ian, her eyes bright with hope at this new thought. 'He has all the arrangements, he'll be there, I know he will.'

As the Saturday shoppers pushed to be served at the stalls, the bride and groom made their way to St Stephen's church at the end of the Market Square.

Make him be here, make him glad about Ian and me . . . But the only person waiting in the church porch was the vicar. In an instant Marcos Warburton felt he understood the situation. He remembered the way Jane had told him her father would come; he couldn't fail to notice that she wore the same hat and coat as she had when she'd first come to see him. Had she been thrown out of her home because this man had made her pregnant, could that be the cause of the trouble with her family? For that there had been trouble he had no doubt.

He held out his hand to her as he waited at the top of the steps leading into the church, making no reference to her having said her father would be there.

'You told me there were to be no guests,' a slight variation of what she'd actually told him, but it was accepted without correction. 'My churchwarden is in the vestry and my wife has been doing tomorrow's flowers, she hasn't left yet. Perhaps we ought to ask them to be on hand to witness the signing of the register?'

He'd spoken to Jane, but it was Ian who answered. By contrast with the vicar's, his voice was brash, lacking in courtesy.

'Up to you, Vicar. You know what's necessary, we're new to this game.'

It was impossible to read Marcos's thoughts – or Jane's either.

'Thank you. If they wouldn't mind waiting, we'd be grateful,' she said. In her expression he saw the disappointment she couldn't hide.

Turning into the church, he led the way to the chancel step. Experience had taught him not to judge a person by appearance – and in any case Ian Harriman was a handsome man so appearance didn't go against him. There was something in his manner that made Marcos uneasy. Yet was that fair? Jane, with a quiet dignity and assurance, was patently in love with him.

The short service was spoken, vows were made, a plain gold ring slipped on Jane's finger. Then Marcos took their right hands and brought them together.

'Those whom God hath joined together, let no man put asunder.' He spoke quietly. Except for the three of them the lofty building was empty, the churchwarden and Mrs Warburton were waiting in the vestry. 'Forasmuch as Ian Bernard and Jane Elizabeth have consented together in holy wedlock ...' He'd conducted many weddings, but he'd never been more aware of the solemnity. It was the lack of guests, the stillness in the atmosphere that added meaning to those simple words. And, too, was it something about the couple he'd united, a couple who on the surface seemed ill-assorted? The groom, a man who had clearly meant every word he'd said as he'd made his responses, a man who had experienced life and who had no doubts for the future; and the bride, serious, trusting – and yet there was an underlying sadness about her. Marcos remembered the confidence in her voice as she'd told him her father would be there to give her away. '... I pronounce that they be man and wife together. In the name of Father, and of Son, and of Holy Ghost.'

As far as Jane and Ian were concerned, he was no more

than part of the necessary formality of marriage. They signed the register, stood back while the churchwarden and Mrs Warburton added their signatures, then in the absence of a best man Ian handed over the fee to the same churchwarden while Marcos wrote the certificate of marriage. Then it was done, man and wife they walked out of the church, down the steps and into the Saturday afternoon bustle of Brackleford market. Neither of them turned back, so they weren't aware that the vicar watched them. And, even if they had been, they could have had no idea of the memories that crowded in on him.

Chapter Three

Each day Jane made a conscious effort to hang on to the magic. Perhaps it was in trying that she held it always out of reach; perhaps she tried too hard to rekindle the easy companionship, the ready laughter they'd shared all the summer; perhaps it was the conscious effort she made not to let herself be offended by Ian's behaviour. But as winter closed in on them she could no more rekindle the spirit of those first days than she could bring back the warmth and hope of the season that was gone. So was she to blame for the change? If only, just once, he'd look at her as he had in the beginning, the smile in his eyes an unspoken confirmation of his pleasure in their being together. It was easier to let her thoughts follow that line than admit to herself the times she averted her gaze rather than watch him. She was ashamed of her own irritation; reason told her it wasn't his fault that he'd always lived where the way he behaved was normal. The change wasn't in him, it was in her. She recoiled from the daily sight of him, his working shirt unbuttoned at the neck as he 'washed' at the kitchen sink each morning. (He didn't so much as notice that she had bought a second bowl, happily he would have used the same as dealt with vegetables and dishes.) Only a few months before, the sight of him peering into a mirror making sure his beard was evenly trimmed would have made her gaze at him in adoration. Yet by the time their

46

first winter held them in its grip she tried not to see, tried not to hear as he started the smokers' ritual of coughing, clearing his throat and finally spitting in the sink. She told herself that these things were superficial, the fault was as much hers as his; she ought to be able to tease him good-humouredly, gradually smooth out the rough edges. But she couldn't. The one thing she had learnt to cook well was soup and the large cast-iron pot was usually on the range, its warm and nourishing contents helping to disguise her other disasters. Thankful that he would eat it without criticism, yet she'd come to dread the moment she brought their steaming plates to the table. Into the first bowl he would stir great lumps of bread until it was almost solid, then he would push his plate down the table to her for a refill which he would scoop into his mouth in noisy spoonfuls.

But over the last few weeks, there had been something else at the front of her mind. They'd been married for three months, how could he not have noticed that it was nearly two since her one and only period? Each day her hope grew stronger, more certain. He'd not seemed to notice as night after night, wordlessly he mounted her, wordlessly rushed to a climax then wordlessly fell asleep, not caring that she felt unloved and frustrated. How could she tell him her hopes when he never looked at her as he used to, never touched her with tenderness? Would he feel as she did, that a baby would draw them close? Or would telling him lead to that all too familiar uncontrolled anger she dreaded? It was easier to dwell on superficial irritations than to let herself face the desolation of where her life had brought her.

She remembered the miracle of those first weeks. Had she failed him so badly that he had turned against her already? No, of course he loved her, just as she loved him. Time and again that's what she told herself, all her hope and trust on the thought of a child. But supposing tomorrow, when her next period would have been due, nature mocked her.

She folded a pile of semi-dry washing, the sight of a triangular scorch mark on the tail of his shirt a reminder of her daily failures. Could she blame him if he was disappointed in her? He worked hard for his meagre wage, and what did she do? Nothing that was useful, nothing, nothing, nothing. A picture of the brewery flashed into her mind. If she closed her eyes she seemed to see the familiar scene, hear the sound of hobnailed boots on flagged floor, breathing in she imagined the heady smell of the fermenting brew in the mash tuns. Always there had been life, action – and she'd been part of it, what she'd contributed had been important. She looked around the tiny kitchen, ashamed of her own uselessness, ashamed that she was failing Ian, frightened to face the wedge that was already forcing its way between them.

Consciously holding her straying thoughts in check she spread an old blanket on the table (a very old and torn blanket, with scorch marks that gave her the comfort of knowing some previous tenant had had failings too). Two flat-irons were heating on the range, the clothes she'd washed the previous day had been hung to dry on the string line attached to either end of the mantelpiece. Hours of her day were spent in this room, the windows wet with condensation while, outside, day after day was either cold, wet or both. I wouldn't care if only he'd still be like he was, I'd never let any of these sorts of things beat me. Other women manage, they don't moon around feeling sorry for themselves. No, and neither will I. If he sees me as different, then it's because I am different. Just look at my hands! They're red and chapped, they're rough. And my face ... as if to bring home to herself how plain she looked, she moved to the freckled mirror that was attached to a string fixed to the window bolt in front of the sink. She bit hard first her bottom lip, then her top, trying to bring colour to them; she pinched her cheeks.

Pull yourself together, Jane Bradley – Jane Harriman. That's what wrong with you, you fancy yourself still as

Jane Bradley. Well, you're *not*. Dad doesn't think of you as Jane Bradley, he's washed his hands of you. Christmas, even at Christmas, he didn't answer your letter. Jane Bradley ... you were always cock-a-hoop enough about knowing how to run the business – in those days you would have looked down your nose on the sort of jobs you do so badly now. But when it comes to it, there probably isn't another woman in the street makes such a poor fist of running a house. No wonder they never stop when you say hello to them. The walls are thin, probably the woman next door hears Ian shouting ... Self-pity threatened to destroy her, she felt her eyes burn with tears she wouldn't shed. It's my own fault. He must dread what he'll find when he comes home each evening. Her glance fell on the cookery book that was to have been her guide to efficiency. Yet still her cooking was at best mediocre. Yesterday she'd made a fruit cake, it had taken her hours and cost more than she could afford for the ingredients. Despite the way she'd kept poking at the coals in the range, the fire had done no more than smoke sulkily. Her masterpiece had started to smell quite appetising, yet each time she'd opened the oven door to see whether it had started to look as good as it smelt the well in the middle of the cake had sunk lower. In the end, angry and humiliated, she had scraped it out of the baking tin and carried it to the park to feed the birds.

Anyway, cooking, ironing, cleaning, all the things I know I do badly, I wouldn't mind any of them if only sometimes he'd look at me as though he loved me. If, just sometimes he'd say, 'That was nice', about something I cook. Even if it hadn't been splendid, I always make sure there's *something*, and failures wouldn't seem nearly as bad if we could laugh about them together. Other wives don't grizzle, I bet they make their tiny houses comfortable, welcoming. As if to prove her point the woman from next door called across the garden fence to her other neighbour, both of them happy with their lot. She'd always despised self-pity – she was frightened even to think the word, lest it took hold of her. She spread Ian's thick vest on the table and took up her iron.

The trouble is, I'm cold. At home no one seemed to have any problem in making a fire burn, think of the welcoming red glow in every room. Taking the poker she stabbed at the coal, breaking a lump in two. For about two seconds a yellow flame flickered with promise before it gave way to a pall of sooty smoke. It had been the beginning of October when she'd left Maybury House. What few clothes she had brought with her had been warm enough for those days of autumn and she'd been confident of being home to collect the rest of her things long before winter set in. No wonder she was cold. She imagined the wardrobes in her old room, she remembered how at the turn of the season her summer things would be stored away and replaced by heavyweight materials for the winter. Involuntarily she shivered. It wasn't Ian's fault that she had nothing warm to wear. Most brides, even those without the advantages she'd always taken for granted, collected a trousseau before their wedding; they didn't come with nothing.

Taking the previously scorched shirt from the top of the waiting pile, she went back to her ironing. But her thoughts weren't on what she did; instead she was mentally composing a letter. To write it would be to show she accepted that her father didn't mean to acknowledge her marriage. After the ceremony – and this time unbeknown to Ian – she had written to him again; then as Christmas drew close she had sunk all her pride, believing he must surely do the same. She had begged that he would accept. If he didn't want them back in Deremouth, at least wouldn't he write to her? When, even then, he hadn't replied she had known the position was final, he would never accept Ian as his son-in-law, nor would he forgive her for marrying him.

The letter she would send today would hold out no olive branch, this time she would be brief and to the point.

It was mid-afternoon some four days later that Jane opened

the door to the station carrier's knock, for one moment her smile lit with relief. This was the answer to her letter to her father. At last the silence was broken.

Her first doubt came when she recognized Dulcie's writing on the labels but, even then, hope lived on. Dad must have put a note in with my things, she told herself, then left Dulcie to see to having them sent on. She unstrapped the trunk and lifted its lid . . . nothing. Item by item she took out the garments, shaking each one in the ever-diminishing hope that a sheet of paper would flutter to the ground . . . nothing. She surveyed the pile of garments, pleasure and excitement swamped by disappointment. If anything were designed to force her to face the truth that he would never accept what she had done, then surely this was it.

Surrounded by clothes that had been shaken and dropped to the floor around her, she closed the lid of the empty trunk. What if he and Dulcie could see her now. Not that she cared a rap what Dulcie thought – but Dad, what if he could see me here unpacking my things? Remember how when I bought something new and pretty he always wanted me to show him, the way he used to smile when I paraded up and down his room waiting for the praise I knew would come. How proud he was of what I did at the brewery. 'It's the way I've trained you,' he always said, remember the twinkle in his eye as he said it, knowing that he could take days off and leave me to see to things. What if he could look at me now, see just how useless I am. Why, I can't even make a good job of running a little house like this, Babs could do better; I can't make Ian's wages go round to feed us properly and pay the rent. What if he could have seen me in the pawnbroker's with my earrings? What if he could see my hands, if he could know how hard I try but what a rotten mess I make of things? Would he feel triumph? Or pity?

She wanted neither. As if she were escaping what she wouldn't let herself see she bent to pick up the garments then, not for the first time, was assailed by a feeling of nausea. Yesterday and again this morning she had been horribly sick. With no knowledge of what to expect in pregnancy, she looked for other reasons as she steadied herself against the table. Perhaps the kippers she'd cooked for breakfast hadn't been fresh; even now, half way through the afternoon, the smell of them was everywhere. Involuntarily she retched as she blundered out of the back door and into the shed. The sight of the wooden seat holding the unsavoury bucket was her undoing. Clinging to the wooden wall she bent over the bucket. In those seconds she thought neither of her father nor Ian, not even of the cheap, fatty bacon joint that was boiling on the range.

Five minutes later, back in the house, she was feeling better. In fact she began to feel quite hungry. By the time Ian came home she was dressed in a winter-weight wool dress of russet brown, her feet were shod in comfortable leather slippers that seemed to caress her feet.

'My, my!' He greeted her, with a light in his eyes she hadn't seen for weeks. 'I do believe this is the girl I fell in love with. You've heard from him at last?' His voice was bright with hope.

The doubts and misgivings she'd been frightened to acknowledge vanished.

'I feel like *me* again.' She twirled in front of him. 'Do you like it?'

'What did he say? Let's see his letter.' He held his hand out expectantly, his mood seeming to match her own.

Jane's excitement died like a lamp turned out. She shook her head, hating to put into words what she knew she had to accept.

'Damn it, why shouldn't I see it?' Ian's expression changed. 'Still sulking, is he?'

'There wasn't a letter. Just clothes – I'd written and asked for them. It's no use Ian, I can't go on hoping. If he wouldn't come to see me – if he wouldn't have me home – none of that would matter if only he'd say he forgave—'

'Forgave?' He spat the word at her. 'It's that what you've been thinking all these weeks? Daddy's little girl, wanting to be forgiven! Is that what you are? Seems he's got other ideas. Perhaps you were no more use as a daughter than you are as a wife. Christ, if I could get my hands on the arrogant old bugger—'

She covered her ears with her hands, her eyes tightly closed. She couldn't look at him.

'Stop it! Ian, please don't!'

When he didn't answer, she opened her eyes and let her hands fall to hold the back of the wooden chair. She could not read his expression. Disappointment? Hurt? Something more than those, something she couldn't fathom. His anger had died as quickly as it had flared. Coming towards her he opened his arms. The bad moment had passed, everything was forgotten except that they were together again.

'Forgive me, Jane. I shout at you, I hurt you. Don't know what happens to me. Didn't want it to be like that for us.'

'You were disappointed, just like I was. But Ian, we've got each other. I'll do better, honestly I will. I am getting better – aren't I?'

He didn't answer, just held her close to him.

Five minutes later he carved the salty, fatty, unappetizing bacon joint she'd been boiling, while she brought potatoes and carrots to the table. These days there were serving dishes, just as these days there were table napkins. When she'd bought them Ian had seen them as a forerunner of their better way of life. Now he knew differently. They represented a waste of his hard-earned money. Only hunger drove him to eat his unpalatable meal with gusto, seeming unaware of the way Jane toyed with hers.

'With a wife so smart it's a shame to go out and leave her,' he said as he wiped his plate with his remaining piece of crust. 'But I told old George he could depend on me. Just him and his daughter running the pub, neither of them fit to see to the barrels.'

She watched him go, then took the greasy plates to the sink. A handful of soda in water from the kettle and she was just starting to wash away the evidence of their meal when there was a loud knocking on the front door. She knew no one in Brackleford, for any opening gambit she'd made to neighbours had met with suspicious withdrawal. So, not surprisingly, the hope that never quite left her sprang to the front of her mind. It was short-lived.

On opening the door she was faced with a stranger, a woman in middle age. Jane was taller than fashion considered beautiful, but her visitor was even taller. Upright, her shoulders erect and straight, her bearing was out of keeping with her shabby but well-cut attire.

'Time we met,' she greeted Jane without preamble. 'I ought to have called before this, forgive me.' She might almost have said, 'I ought to have presented my card before this . . .'

Jane's smile was broad and spontaneous.

'Come in.' She opened the door wide. 'You're the first caller I've had.'

'Shouldn't worry on that score, my dear. Funny lot, some of them around here. Don't come calling on me either, but that's not to say they aren't interested enough to watch and gossip. You don't come from this area unless I'm much mistaken. If I'm your first caller, it seems neither you nor that handsome husband of yours has family hereabouts.'

'I come from Devon. That's where I met Ian. And you? Are you one of those ladies the vicar's wife talked about? Has she sent you?'

'No one sent me. Often I've noticed you in town, always on your own.' Holding up her hand before Jane could protest, 'I've not come visiting out of sympathy, I don't mean that. No, more out of hope. Every time I've seen you I've felt this pull, the pull of a kindred spirit. If you'd been about the streets gossiping like some of them are, then I'd have stayed away.'

'Hope?' Jane prompted.

'You didn't get my drift. Yes, hope. Old enough to be your mother, I dare say, but hope that we might have something between us to build on. I'd thought it often enough. Then, yesterday, hope turned to something more positive. I was waiting in the butcher's shop while he was palming off a lump of bacon on you, sure that you knew no better than to buy it. It was as if a voice spoke to me, told me you and I could be friends. Told me too that you need someone to give you a guiding hand. No, I'm not prying. My ardent prayer: "Dear Lord teach me not to pry into what doesn't concern me."'

'I didn't even notice you there. I expect I was too concerned wondering how I could turn the bacon into something vaguely appetizing.'

'And did you manage it?'

Jane shook her head. Then, taking herself by surprise, she laughed. 'It was a good thing Ian came home ravenous.'

'Are you going to invite me to sit down? Or, better still, aren't you going to give me a towel and let me wipe up those dishes you were washing?'

'How did you know?' Jane had an uncomfortable feeling that there was a good deal about her that her visitor knew without being told.

'I didn't need magical powers.' The stranger's laugh was low, in keeping with the voice that was evidence that she, like Jane, hadn't always lived as she did now. 'When you answered the door your hands were wet.'

'I'd nearly done.'

'Come on then, we'll soon turn "nearly" into "quite". Then, if that husband of yours isn't home you can offer me that chair I mentioned.'

How strange it was, ten minutes before they'd never spoken yet already Jane felt relaxed, at ease with herself and with the stranger.

'I wish I could offer you something, a glass of sherry or something. All I have is tea.'

'One accustoms one's palate. I've had nearly three years to accustom mine.'

Jane didn't ask questions. Here she was, with a woman who could have passed as a duchess – albeit a shabby one if she were judged by the clothes on her back – yet she felt no embarrassment about the squalor of her surroundings. The greasy meal cleared away, they settled themselves close to the few coals burning in the sitting-room grate. Talking, listening, it was so easy with Alice Gregson.

Alice wore a wedding ring, but when Jane called her 'Mrs Gregson' she said, 'I'd like it if you could call me Alice. One of the hard things is that there is no one, absolutely no one, to call me by my Christian name.'

'You've lost your husband?' Jane felt real sympathy for her new friend.

'I wouldn't say "lost", more like "temporarily mislaid". But temporary can seem endlessly long.'

Could she be launching into a sermon about bearing the hardships of this life in the certainty of the joys of eternity? For a second Jane felt a stab of disappointment. 'He's serving ten years. Nearly three of them gone. If you'd been on better gossiping terms with the neighbours they would have pointed me out and told you.'

'In prison! Ten years! I'm sorry. That must be so hard for you.'

'Aren't you going to ask me what it was all about?'

'No. One day, when you want to, perhaps you'll tell me.'

Alice sat a little straighter, nodding her head and sizing Jane up. Yes, one of these days she'd entrust her with the whole story, but young and smitten with that handsome rogue she'd married, there was no point in burdening her with things she didn't want mulled over in the Queen Charlotte. So, instead, she said, 'Yes, no doubt I will. And one of these days you'll come to tell me how a gently reared girl like clearly you were comes to be living in Mill Lane and having no family to care about you.'

'I didn't think we'd be here long,' Jane heard herself confide. And, once started, the words poured out. Alice heard the whole story and as it came up to date with the delivery of the trunk and hatboxes, she reached out and took both Jane's hands in hers, giving her no chance to wipe the tears that had started to spill.

'My dear, if you are married to a good man, then all will be well. And me, I think I'll go home now, before that same good man gets back from the alehouse. Funny thing this love business, gives us all a different slant on life. One woman's good man is another's bounder, I dare say. And I should know! For me, Gerald will always be that good man, keep him behind bars ten years or life. Yet there are those hereabouts in Brackleford who would tell you otherwise. Never a violent man – and no one knows him better than I do. What he did was wrong, no civilized society could let it go unpunished. "Vengeance is mine saith the Lord," isn't that what we're supposed to believe? But it's hard to leave it to someone else to give a villain his come-uppance. One of these days I'll tell you about it, but not now. We've laid our foundations, plenty of time to build on them later.'

She withdrew her hat pin, pulled her hat on more firmly, re-stabbed it, then she was ready to go home. Jane closed the door on her, her mood more cheerful than it had been for weeks. '. . . felt the pull,' wasn't that how Alice had explained her visit?

Going up the narrow, creaking stairs to the bedroom, Jane unpinned her hair, brushed it vigorously, recoiled it, then powdered her cheeks with a hint of rogue. Back down-stairs again she plumped the shabby cushions, then put more coal on the fire. Perhaps it was having a visitor that had given her this feeling of optimism, perhaps it was wearing a good gown. More likely it was her suspicion of the reason behind two mornings' sickness.

But when Ian came home he was quiet and sullen, a mood she had come to dread, his handsome face wearing an expression she couldn't fathom. It was as if some inner misery held him out of her reach. Tonight she couldn't even talk to him about Alice – and certainly this wasn't the time to break the news of her hopes for a baby. Although he sat leaning back in the fireside chair with his eyes half closed, his hands on his knees, there was nothing peaceful or contented about him. His fingers moved constantly, they drummed his knees, they twisted and untwisted as he massaged them with his thumbs.

Pride told her that if he hadn't even noticed the effort she had made with her appearance, then she should leave him alone. A silent voice reminded her of all those doubts that had been gathering strength, waiting for their moment to defeat her. But she was driven by some inner excitement.

'Ian?' She was rewarded by his opening his eyes. Certainly he looked at her, not with the smiling affection she used to see, but with the desire she longed for. Tonight surely he would love her with the passion and tenderness she yearned for, tonight they would move together to the moment of union she craved.

'Bedroom's cold as charity,' his voice was low and urgent. 'Here, we'll put this under your back.' He threw the cushion on to the floor, her own excitement rising by the second. He wanted her, he wanted her *now*. No undressing and folding of clothes, no hoisting of her nightgown, no cold sheets. Even the sulky smoking fire co-operated, the coals slipped making it burst into a sudden bright flame. 'Take this off.' Already his fingers were snatching at the buttons of her dress. Breathing hard they rushed. It was as if their moment of bliss would get away without them if they didn't hurry. Garment after garment was unceremoniously pulled off. She tore at his long, rough underpants; he snatched at the hooks on her corset until all she wore was her silken drawers that served no useful purpose for, because they were worn under the corset decreed by fashion, for the sake of convenience were no more than two separate legs joined at the elasticated waist. He lifted his hand to pull them off, but the feeling of the smooth silk on her warm body was almost his undoing. Pushing her to the worn hearthrug and forcing the cushion under the base of her spine he lay above her. It's got to be wonderful, she said silently, for both of us, together, it's got to be ... Even as she thought it her own body responded. Rather than hold her back, the hard floor excited her. Ian wanted her, like an impassioned caveman he had thrown her to the ground and taken her. Her pulses throbbed, her body arched and thrashed. So soon it was over. Like a vivid and perfect vision it was over. Just as their own flame died so did that in the grate, the coal smouldered black and cheerless. Still lying heavy on top of her, Ian shivered.

'Shouldn't have done that,' he mumbled. 'Put something on. It's cold.'

'I'm not cold. I think I have an inner fire.' She held him close, rubbing her hand on his back, wrapping her long, slender legs around him. 'Ian, I think – no, I'm sure – I'm expecting a child.' The only sound was the ticking of the clock. 'Ian ... say something.'

'God!' Blasphemy it may have been, but it was whispered with something like reverence. 'A son. How long have you known? Why the hell didn't you say something? You'd no business not to tell me.' Clambering to his feet he stood naked. 'I'm going to have a son! Christ, but that's wonderful.'

Her heart raced with excitement. He was pleased. Everything would be good again.

'You're pleased?' She wanted to hear him say so.

'That's a bloody silly question. You tell me I'm to have a son and ask if I'm "pleased".' He looked as though he'd found a fortune.

'It may be a girl,' she laughed, 'our daughter—'

'Oh no. It'll be a boy. My son.' Then, as if he was suddenly aware of her still lying on the hearthrug, 'Here, put this on.' He threw her woollen dress to her, then turned away to pull on his long underpants and shirt. The night was cold, it was wise and sensible to put something on; she tried to tell herself he was taking special care of her because of what she'd told him. And yet, even while over and over he repeated what sounded like 'Boy . . . my boy . . .' it was as if she had no part in it. He was as removed from her now as he had been when he'd come home from the Queen Charlotte. She told herself it was her imagination, she was behaving like a silly romantic young girl.

Her hair had fallen loose from its pins, the wool of her dress felt alien to the smooth skin of her naked breasts. She scooped up her chemise, corsets, stockings, garters and petticoat and rolled them in a ball. Tearing them off had been erotic; picking them up, anything but.

'You'd better take off that last lump of coal,' Ian was saying. 'It's hardly caught at all, leave it on the hearth or it will burn to waste.'

What a moment to think of Maybury House, the fires still piled high and bright when they put up the guards and went to bed. She looked at Ian clad in shirt and long pants, his bare feet thrust into his heavy boots. None of those things need matter; he wanted the baby. Everything would be good again. She wouldn't let any niggling doubt take root. Picking up the tongs she removed the dull, low-grade lump of coal to lay it on the hearth where it immediately gave up all pretence of so much as smoking.

Jane and Alice saw each other often and bit by bit, Alice's tale was told. She and Gerald Gregson had had just one child, Terry, born after they'd been married eleven years and given up hope. He'd been late in developing, walking, talking, even understanding.

'Poor wee man,' Alice said softly, 'We knew he would always be ours to care for, the world was too harsh a place for him. Because there was no guile in him, he supposed everyone was the same. Easily led, always trusting.'

'Where is he now?' But Jane knew the answer even before she was told.

'He was a grown man. He liked to go out by himself, he and his kite used to go off to Beacon Hill. A friendly, loving boy. But putty in the wrong hands. That's what happened, you see. Other young chaps, a deal brighter than Terry but a wicked lot, made a friend of him. Blithe as can be, in the summer evenings off he used to go with his kite. Then came a night when he didn't come home. Constable Timms came to our door to tell us. Terry had been caught at Blundell's, the wholesale grocer the other end of town, you know. All alone in the upstairs office he was, the lock on the side door forced. Terry would never have stolen, and as for breaking into a locked building – no, it wasn't possible. It seems a passer-by had seen a torch light shining from the window and thought something must be amiss. Chance had it that Constable Timms was nearby and he'd gone straight there.'

'Were these other lads there with him?'

'Not by the time the law arrived. The constable found the window behind Terry open, but not a sign of anyone else. Terry was carefully taking the money – not scooping it up like a man wanting to get away in a rush. Coin by coin he was putting it in a cloth bag. When Constable Timms loomed up in the doorway, the poor lad must have realized. He was alone, the window was open, his friends had left him. He would never do any wrong, not Terry; but he knew that policemen were there to catch those who did. Still shaken by what had happened, Constable Timms had to tell us. Terry had rushed to the open window, looked back just the once he said, looked back like a frightened hare, then he was over the ledge and gone.'

'You mean, the fall killed him?'

Alice nodded.

'The others must have let themselves down on the drainpipe, it was pulled from the wall.' She stopped talking. Jane wanted to reach out and touch her, but she knew better. After a minute, in a different voice, Alice said, 'You have shopping to do. I'll walk with you and see that rogue of a butcher doesn't palm off any rubbish on you.'

It wasn't until a few weeks later – weeks in which Jane's first hopefulness had turned to certainty – that she heard the rest of Alice's story. Mr Blundell had known Terry all his life, he'd been as certain as Alice and Gerald that the childishly simple young man had been obeying someone else's instruction. The Gregsons knew who the lads were Terry used to meet when he was flying his kite, Mr Blundell had his own opinion of them and was as certain as the Gregsons that they'd been behind the attempted robbery. The police were of the same opinion, but there had been no witnesses. The lads denied all knowledge; and Terry wasn't alive to say how he'd been so busy doing as his friends had told him and carefully putting the money in the bag that he hadn't noticed them open the window and slip away down the drainpipe when they'd heard a tread on the stairs. So Eric Blundell had said he didn't intend to make a case – indeed with no proof, how could he make a case? Gerald couldn't let it rest so easily. He had taken the law into his own hands.

'There's no emotion as strong as love,' Alice said. 'He was obsessed with revenge. One of the young rogues took a job as a night watchman at the timber yard, the other used to go and keep him company. And it was there that Gerald cornered them and took a horsewhip to them. Not just one or two lashings. He lost control, his thirst for blood was up. He's such a gentle man, wouldn't swat a fly if he could open a window and let it go free. But it was for Terry he did it. They were bleeding and unconscious when he'd done with them. He went straight to the Police Station and told them what he'd done. And, you know, I think he was glad when he stood in court and heard the sentence. Poor Gerald, mercy would have been hard to live with.'

Jane's sympathy for her friend was very real, but she had no true conception of how love could make a person do something so out of character. But time was to teach her understanding.

*

Alice Gregson was looking out of her window as the motor car drew up at the kerb. Her first reaction was fear: something must be wrong with Gerald! It was Dr Bingley who regularly attended the prison, and why would he come to see her if it weren't to bring bad news? She reached the front door and opened it as Matthew Bingley took hold of the knocker.

'Mrs Gregson,' he smiled. 'You must have seen me coming.'

'Trouble? Is that why you've come?' Her mouth was so dry she wondered she could speak at all.

'On the contrary. I was able to talk to your husband yesterday. May I come in?'

'Forgive me. Seeing you so unexpectedly put everything else out of my head.' She opened the door wide and stood back for the doctor to get past her in the narrow passage. 'There's only the one fire – that's in the kitchen. You don't mind?'

'That's down the passage, isn't it?' From his tone she knew he was smiling. 'A fire gives the same warmth whatever grate it's in. I promised your husband I would come. He asked so much about you, I felt I failed him that I could tell him so little.'

'Why did you have to see him? He's not ill? There's nothing wrong with Gerry is there?' She looked helplessly at the doctor. The reality of her situation hit her. Here she was in the kitchen of a tiny terrace house, sitting with a doctor she hardly knew, one pretty well young enough to be her son, talking about Gerry who had been part of her life since she'd been a girl.

If Matthew Bingley realized how her thoughts had taken wing, he gave no sign of it as he answered.

'He is keeping remarkably fit. Physically, at any rate, he isn't suffering, I promise you. Mentally . . . well, you don't need me to tell you. It's something you know about at first hand.'

'Ten years . . . ten endless years . . .' It was as if a spring in her sagged, she looked older, defeated.

'He'll be released earlier than that, he'll get early remission. The kettle's singing, do you think we might share a cup of tea while we talk.'

She nodded, fighting to get a grasp of the control that threatened to be lost.

'It's good of you to spare the time to call, Doctor.' Once again standing tall she held the teapot to the steaming kettle to warm it before she spooned in the tea. Being occupied helped, just as he'd meant it to. She had been on his mind for some time, such a solitary figure. His surgery was in the middle of town, but the Gregsons had been his patients although they'd lived in a good residential area on the outskirts. When he read about the case he'd felt sympathy for them, especially for the quietly spoken, kindly man who would be so out of place amongst the felons who were to be his companions.

Matthew had a list of calls to make, a living to earn. It was quixotic of him to sit drinking tea with the wife of a so-called criminal but he believed he was as necessary to her as to any of the patients who would be sent a bill for his services. There was something about him that melted Alice's natural reserve. Many a tear she'd shed in the solitude of her miserable little home, but never before had she found the relief of unburdening herself to another person as she did to him. He encouraged her, he listened to her talk of the past, encouraged her to voice her hopes for a future when her husband was home. At last, two cups of tea drunk, more than half an hour already gone and her composure regained, he rose to leave just as there came another knock at the door.

'Oh dear, I'm not fit to be seen. My face . . .'

'Rinse your face, I'll go to the door. Are you expecting anyone?'

'Who would call here? Not that I want them to.' Some of her spirit was returning. 'Oh, it might be Jane, Mrs Harriman. Good-looking young woman, tall – you can't mistake Jane for any of the others around here. If it's her, you could bring her through. Anyone else, just say I'm not here.'

She listened as he opened the door. What was she coming to, letting herself behave as she had in front of a young man she hardly knew? Self-pity! She'd never been able to tolerate self-pity. She pulled her iron-grey hair more firmly into its bun and stood waiting as Jane was ushered in. Instead of feeling sorry for herself she ought to be grateful that here were two young people who cared enough to spend their time with her.

'Jane my dear, have you introduced yourself to Dr Bingley?' Then, before Jane had time to reply, 'What in the world have you done to your face?' Not the most tactful opening gambit and as soon as she'd spoken she regretted it, especially when she saw the way Jane tightened her jaw. She too hated self-pity.

'I fell – caught my head on the corner of the table.'

Chapter Four

Spring 1906

Jane had come to her friend, not looking for sympathy but needing the calming reassurance of her presence. They'd known each other for no more than a few weeks, Alice was old enough to be her mother, but time and age had little to do with the natural empathy they'd both felt right from that first day. So, when the door was opened by a stranger, Jane was disappointed.

Following him into the room she kept a large handkerchief to her forehead, but already the blood was seeping through. For a second she took it away so that she could turn it about and press an unsoiled part to the wound on her temple.

'That's a nasty gash,' Matthew Bingley said, his tone professional. 'A little lower and you could have damaged your sight.'

'Yes. I was lucky.' Jane defied sympathy, she even forced a laugh she was far from feeling, 'It will teach me not to leave the hearthrug rucked up. That's what tripped me.' If only it were true! She shied away from remembering Ian's mood when he'd come home from the Queen Charlotte even later than usual last night; she tried to push his sneering sarcasm from her mind. He'd had too much to drink. He hadn't been responsible for the things he'd said; he hadn't been responsible for the way he'd almost thrown her out of his way in his rush to the back door; even if he'd heard the crash as she'd fallen it would have seemed no more than part of the horror of the moment as he'd got outside just in time to vomit into the drain; and this morning as he'd silently eaten the breakfast she'd put in front of him and collected his sandwiches and can of tea, he'd probably had no recollection of the mess he'd left for her to clean away, any more than he had of the way he'd grovelled in front of her, wailing at the miserable state of his life.

Was that what she'd done to him? She wanted to force it out of her mind in the way a nightmare can be overcome on waking. But Dr Bingley's concerned expression wasn't making it any easier.

'When did you do it?' Alice asked, giving no hint that she didn't believe the story of the rug.

'Not long ago. It'll soon stop bleeding.' Last night, not long ago! Last night, lying still and straight by Ian's side, hearing the heavy breathing of his drunken sleep, feeling the warm blood on the cloth she'd used to try to protect her pillow.

'You ought to have it attended to,' Matthew still eyed the gash and the area of swelling. 'If you've not seen anyone yet, let me look at it for you.'

'I don't need a doctor. If I thought I did, I would have sent for one.' She heard her answer as ungracious, sharper than she intended in her effort to hide the truth that doctors were a luxury she couldn't afford. To soften her words she added, 'I'm very healthy, I heal quickly.'

'Even so, you're going to be reminded of your tumble for a while. If that cut is to heal it ought to be stitched.' Then with a sudden brief smile that relaxed her despite herself, 'Why don't you sit down and let me see to it?'

'*You're* not my doctor.' She snatched an excuse out of the air. She believed that a visit from a doctor cost as much as half a crown, and even if they lived on bread and cheese until pay day she hadn't enough in her purse to pay for the sort of treatment he was suggesting.

'Then, let's not tell your own doctor, humph?'

'Let him see to it, Jane,' Alice weighed in. Then, behind Matthew's back she mouthed the words, 'I'll help you pay.'

Not knowing the silent charade, Matthew misinterpreted the way Jane bit on her trembling lip.

'I'll put something on to deaden the pain first,' he told her gently. 'Don't be frightened.'

'. . . not that. Just I haven't much money . . .' Honesty prevailed.

He hadn't believed her story that the fall had only just happened – this gash had been open for some time. The swelling, and the yellowy blue bruise, told its own tale. He saw the way she squared her jaw and made herself meet his gaze, and he was moved by an unfamiliar emotion. Respect? Pity? Perhaps both, but something else besides. When he answered, he was surprised by his own words. What sort of a living would he make if he carried on like this?

'As you just said, I'm not your doctor, and I'm not trying to poach his patients,' he laughed. 'I'm visiting here simply as a a a friend of Mrs Gregson's, just as you are. Now then, sit here Jane – Mrs . . .? – so that I get the light from the window on what I'm doing.'

'Jane Harriman. But just Jane will do.' Her smile was sudden and unexpected, she was surprised by the unfamiliar feeling of relief that gripped her. Her head throbbed, deep in her mind was a hurt beyond words, but for the moment she could put herself into someone else's hands; all responsibility was lifted from her.

Of course it hurt; she clenched her fists so that her nails dug against her palms, she held her jaw stiff and gripped her teeth together, she closed her eyes. But she made not a sound as he worked.

'Good girl,' he told her gently as, minutes later, he stood straight. 'You can open your eyes, we're finished. All that remains is to put this bandage around your head.'

'Right round my head? But it's only a cut!'

'There's no other way, The stitches must be protected. Even in bed, a sudden movement could jar them and be extremely uncomfortable, especially after a day or two as they tighten. Here we go.' And, with that, he began deftly to wrap the long bandage around her head. Giving herself over to someone else's care had been a temporary luxury; the sight of herself in the mirror brought her face to face with reality.

The episode merited another cup of tea and Jane's spirits rose as she sipped it. These people were her friends, Alice, yes and Dr Bingley too. On first meeting him, her reaction had been resentment that he should be there when she wanted the easy comfort of Alice's presence. Beyond that he hadn't interested her. But now she looked at him afresh – and liked what she saw. He must have been somewhere in his thirties, clean shaven, hair that had faded into a nondescript shade of light brown as so often follows the pale fairness of childhood. His light blue eyes gave her the impression that a smile was never far away; his slender hands were well kept – and recently scrubbed at Alice's kitchen sink before and after he had ministered to the cut. It was months since she'd been with a man so well groomed; seeing his neatly knotted necktie, the stiffly starched collar, the tailored herringbone suit and highly polished boots, memories crowded in on her. Then, in contrast another picture sprang into her mind: Ian working in the yard at the brewery. The epitome of manliness, that's how she'd seen him. And so he was, she defended loyally. No white collar, no carefully tended nails, no highly polished boots. But those things didn't make a man. Manliness came from strength, from rippling muscles, from self-confidence – no, don't think of last night, don't remember the sound of his uncontrolled drunken self-pity. That's what it had been. Ian, *her* Ian, the man she loved, he was a pillar of strength. She would put last night's scene behind her and, if his own recollections of it were as hazy as she expected, then he would believe the story she'd told him at breakfast time, the same story that she'd told Alice. What was she trying to do? To repeat it so often that it would become the truth in her own mind? That way the wound on her head wouldn't drive a wedge between them – he wouldn't have to face the guilt and shame of knowing what he'd done. Supposing the fall had made her lose their baby ... and, as early in pregnancy as this, surely it might have happened. Just be thankful that all she'd hurt was her head – yes, and take it as a sign that their baby was a growing proof of the rightness of their love for each other.

She only half listened to the conversation between Alice and Matthew, her mind a kaleidoscope of memories, some distant, some recent. Ian, on the evening she'd gone to him in Deremouth ... herself and Ian isolated in a world of their own as the rhythm of the train sped them towards their brave new life together ... and now, all that the new life entailed. Perhaps it was her own bravery that had been lost. She felt a wild longing to be with Ian, to know she was *his woman*, to know that together there was nothing they couldn't overcome. So engrossed was she with the embryo of an idea that was taking shape in her mind, that she didn't notice Matthew getting up to leave.

By the time she pulled her thoughts into line, he was putting on his herringbone overcoat, Alice standing up ready to see him to the front door.

'I'd like to keep an eye on that cut, Jane. The stitches must stay in about nine days.'

'You want me to come to your surgery?'

He smiled. 'Surgeries are for patients. Didn't we agree that I don't poach from your own doctor. Mrs Gregson has written down your address for me.'

Only then did Jane realize how deep in her daydreams she had been.

'You're very kind,' she told him. She wanted to say something more, but wasn't sure what. Then, just as it had before, honesty got the better of her. 'The truth is I've not seen a doctor since I've lived in Brackleford, I'd hoped I wouldn't need to. I'm sure there's a local midwife for when I need her – and, like I told you, I'm very healthy.'

It hadn't occurred to him that she was pregnant, but then he'd not known the tall, thin girl who'd been heir to Bradley's brewery. Now he looked at her afresh, aware of the too-tight fit of the bodice of her dress, a fit not in keeping with the good quality material or fine workmanship of the making. What was her story? He wondered about her, but his mind moved straight on; he had a list of patients waiting. So he put out his hand to meet hers in farewell, did the same to Alice, picked up his brown bowler hat in one hand and his Gladstone bag in the other, then followed Alice along the passage to the door.

When Ian arrived home at the end of a day in the cold workshop of Ruddick's, his nostrils were assailed by the tempting smell of macaroni cheese. The table was set for the meal even to the extent of some greenery from the hedge in the fish-paste pot cum vase, and the fire had been coaxed to a blaze. Jane greeted him with a smile of welcome – and her head wrapped in a white bandage.

'What the devil have you been doing?'

'I told you at breakfast. I fell against the corner of the table. Don't worry, it'll soon heal. Honestly, it's not as bad as this makes it look.'

But was it anxiety on her account that furrowed his brow?

'You sent for the doctor? Just for that? This is Mill Lane, not Maybury House in case you hadn't noticed.'

Oh, I've noticed, she screamed silently. At Maybury House Dad would have cared that I'd been hurt. Don't say it! Don't let this turn into another scene! He's miserable, that's why he talks as he does; he sees himself as failing me because I have to get used to living as we do.

'I wouldn't have sent for a doctor for a little thing like that. Whatever do you take me for?' She kept the smile in her voice. 'I was visiting Alice Gregson—'

'Who?' She heard the suspicion in his question at finding she had made a friend without his approval.

'Alice Gregson, she lives in Merchant Street. She's been very good to me.' Then with a laugh, 'You owe any improvement in your meals more to the tips she's given me than to my copy of *Mrs Beeton*. Anyway I was out shopping and I called to see her. She had a friend there, Dr Bingley; it was he who dressed my forehead. It needed to be stitched, I couldn't stop it bleeding.'

'This woman you're friendly with, what's she doing with a doctor for a friend? Merchant Street is hardly where you'd expect him to be on visiting terms – unless she's entertaining him and his sort to make a living.'

'Ian, why are you so bitter?' The words were out before she could stop them. 'She's a fine person, just she's fallen on hard times—'

'Like you have! Is that what you're telling me?'

She'd planned an evening very different from this. Her head ached, hopelessness threatened to overwhelm all her good intentions. But she wouldn't give in. Instead she moved close to him, leaning to rest the unhurt side of her face against his chest. For work he wore no collar on his shirt so, opening the top button, she moved her mouth on his skin. He stood quite still, but she knew he wasn't unmoved, she could tell by the change in his breathing. Against her chin she could feel the dark hair that covered his chest; the smell of his body was familiar, masculine. With all her power of thought she willed him to come back to her. The Ian she had fallen in love with had been brimming with self-confidence, he had felt no shame in being a working man. Was it *her* fault that his mind had become warped with jealousy of those who had more than he was able to provide?

'I'm not thinking about money, if that's what you mean. Alice Gregson has lost a son, her husband has been taken away from her—'

'Gregson!' he cut into what she was saying, 'Gregson,

you say? I remember the case. What sort of a yarn has she been telling you? Her husband is a convicted criminal, he's serving a prison sentence for almost killing a night watchman. It was all the local gossip a year or two back. Brackleford doesn't often have anything so bloodthirsty to get its teeth into, so the *Standard* made the most of it for weeks.'

'I know all about it, Alice told me.' She stood a little away from him, her eyes pleading with him to listen with his heart. 'The two young men her husband attacked had been responsible for the death of their son – a simple lad, but what difference would that make to the way they felt about him unless it was to make them love him more. Think, Ian, what if it were to happen to us, to our son—'

She was shocked by his sudden change of expression, his eyes narrowing as he gripped her shoulders. 'Simple! Our son, simple! Don't say it – don't even think it!' Did he realize how he was shaking her as he spoke? 'To imagine it might – might – damn it, Jane, it's our son you're talking about, our son who will be perfect in body and brain. Until he's born he is *your* responsibility. We don't know what sort of influence the way you think can have on him. He'll be *strong*, he'll be *healthy*. You hear me?' He stared at her unblinkingly, emphasizing his words 'strong' and 'healthy' by intensifying his grasp.

'Of course he will – or she—' Again she leant against him, almost rejoicing in his rough treatment that stemmed from his care for the child she carried. 'Ian, I've been thinking. About us, I mean. How much money would it take for you to set up on your own? The profit from every barrel you make goes to Ruddick's, even though it's your craftmanship the firm depends on. You're a fine cooper – I know that, I've seen your work. You were only at Bradley's a little while, but I could see you were the best cooper on the workshop floor.'

'Ruddick's has all the trade for this area. No one would leave a firm like that to give their business to a one-man show. Anyway, there's more to running a business than filling the orders.'

'Yes, but *I* know about that. Who do you think ordered the materials at Bradley's? Who do you think dealt with the customers? Who paid the bills?'

'Your old man, of course. I'm not fool enough to think he gave a girl her head.'

Jane laughed, rubbing her cheek against him, using every wile she knew to persuade him to consider her scheme.

'He taught me well, honestly. And he trusted me.'

'Anyway you're not at Bradley's now. No one round these parts would take their trade away from Ruddick's to give it to a man setting up on his own.'

'Nothing keeps us in Brackleford. We could move out of town. Think how good it would be for the baby to grow up in pure, fresh air. We could have a new start, a really new start, away from the noise and smells of town.'

'And what would we use for money? You can't start a business on fresh air.'

'I'll find the money. Instead of paying rent on this place we'd pay it on somewhere else. I could write and ask Dulcie to send my fur cape and one or two things that would fetch us enough to get started. My grandfather started in a very small way. Think Ian, think how exciting it could be as our own business grew—'

'If you've got things worth selling, then we've plenty of need of anything you can get for them. But not to waste on some crazy scheme.' He laughed, a sound that held mockery but not mirth. 'A cottage in the country with a shed to work in, and you think that would give us a living. You concentrate on giving me a son, leave the rest to me.' But he softened his words by raising her face and covering her mouth with his. 'A son ... my son ...'

'Our son,' she whispered, 'or our daughter.' Her dreams of the business they would build were pushed to the back of her mind. This moment was special, it had brought him close to her. Suddenly she was happier than she had been for weeks.

The macaroni cheese was brought from the oven, a dish of bubbling golden-brown perfection. The baked potatoes were white and soft inside with crisp skins just as she knew he liked them. All in all, the evening was promising to be everything she'd hoped.

'Why don't you stay in this evening?' she suggested. 'It's turning into a beastly night, cold and wet.'

'I won't be out long. But I must give George a hand if he needs to put a new barrel on. I promised – I can't break my word.'

'If he can't manage the place, then he ought to get a cellar man. It's a ridiculous way to go on, relying on a friend like he does on you.'

'We're not all made of money. One thing about us working folk, we know the meaning of friendship. I suppose that's why you've thought up this hare-brained scheme of working from some hovel outside town, to stop me giving George a hand. What have you and your gossiping friend heard about the work I do at the Queen Charlotte?'

'The last thing Alice is a gossip – and we never discuss you.'

For a second they glared at each other across the table, but he was the first to look away.

'Damn it all, I've worked like a dog every hour of the day, are you grudging me a glass of ale and perhaps a game of cribbage? What did your darling daddy do with his evenings? Did he sit by the fireside and read aloud to the ladies?' How she hated it when he took that sneering tone.

'I'll tell you what he didn't do,' she said as she stood up to collect the dirty plates. 'He didn't stagger home at night reeking of beer. You know why I have such respect for him? Because he behaves like the gentleman he is, not like some drunken so—'

He was on his feet; with one hand he pulled her towards

him as he brought the other across her face. Fortunately the bandage took some of the force of the blow.

She stood very straight, willing him to meet her gaze and this time not look away.

'It isn't working, is it, this marriage of ours?' It was as if she stood outside herself, hearing her own calm voice. 'We can't go on like this. We were both happier a year ago when we hadn't even met.'

'So that's it! You want to go back to your precious father, such a gentleman. Never done a bloody day's work in his life – not man's work.'

She tried not to hear the way his voice croaked. To hide from the storm that was brewing she picked up the stack of plates – and dishes, too, these days – and turned to carry them to the sink. 'You'll bloody listen to me when I'm talking to you!' He yelled, yanking her arm so suddenly that the crockery dropped with a crash to the floor. 'Break them,' he croaked. 'That's it, break them like you'd like to break me.'

She knelt to collect the pieces of broken china, anything rather than watch him. It was as if he were possessed by some inner devil.

'If you're going to help George you'd better go. We can't talk rationally when you're behaving like this.' She hated herself, she hated her cold voice. Cold, that was how she felt, as if all emotion had died.

'Jane!' Just as she had, he dropped to his knees. 'Think of the baby.'

'Perhaps that's why I know we can't go on like this. A child has the right to take a happy home for granted. I can't stay here to bring a baby into a home like this.'

'Don't leave me, Jane.' He didn't hide the way his face contorted, didn't try to control it any more than he did the unnaturally high pitch of his voice, didn't try to fight down his tears. 'You're not being fair,' he croaked. 'It's not just you who've had a bad time. How do you think it's been for me? You never gave me a meal worth eating. If they hadn't fed me at the Charlotte I'd have starved. You wasted the money I gave you—'

It was like listening to a stranger. She felt nothing. It was an effort to force warmth into her voice as she told him, 'I'm sorry, Ian. I honestly tried.' But he appeared not to hear her.

'How do you think it is for me, knowing you look down your nose on the home I give you?'

'Forget it. Forget everything we've said. I'm probably just tired, I didn't sleep much last night after my fall and my head aches.' She put the pile of china on the table, some broken, some chipped, one plate unharmed.

'That dish is a clean break,' he said as he stood up, his voice already returning to its normal deep pitch. 'Put it to one side and I'll glue it.'

She knew it was his peace offering for, to his way of thinking, the vegetable dishes had been an example of the way she'd wasted his money.

Five minutes later, an attempt made to control his wiry dark hair with perfumed macassar, he slammed the front door behind him as he went off to the Queen Charlotte. It seemed he had already put the scene behind him. But for Jane it wasn't so easy.

When, next morning, Jane heard the sound of a motor car drawing up outside, instinct sent her thoughts rushing in just one direction. After all this time, he must have come to find her! Her hands flew to the none too tidy coil she wore in the nape of her neck, for it hadn't been easy to brush her long straight hair and pin it securely with a bandage tied around the crown of her head.

She heard the motor car door slam shut, her heart racing with anticipation. Reason would have told her that had her father travelled all the way from Devon he would have come by train and then taken the hansom from the railway station. Perhaps it was a symptom of her own repressed unhappiness that she was deaf to reason as she ran to open the door.

For one brief moment Matthew saw her expression of pure joy – and then it was gone.

'You said nine days.' She said the first thing that came into her head. 'I thought you were someone else.' It wasn't his fault that she was disappointed, but there again reason stood no chance against the rise and fall of her tide of emotion.

'I won't keep you if you're expecting visitors. I simply wanted to reassure myself that your bandage was comfortable.'

A few months ago she would have accepted such a remark without question, but now what he said – and the courteous way he spoke to her – was in sharp contrast to her present lifestyle.

'I'm not expecting anyone. Forgive me, I was rude. It was kind of you to bother to call. Won't you come inside?'

He had calls to make in Millsham, the eastern residential outskirts of the town, but they could wait. He found himself being ushered through the door straight into the small living room where the grate still bore the signs of yesterday's fire. It was very little warmer in here than outside on this late February morning.

'It's warmer in the kitchen,' she read his thoughts. 'I don't light the fire in here until teatime.'

'Then let's go to the kitchen, shall we? I'd like just to see that your head is going along as it should, then re-do your bandage.'

'You don't have to, you know. I'm grateful, but . . .' Her voice trailed into silence as he drew the kitchen chair for her to sit on.

'Don't be, there's no need. I'm glad you and Mrs Gregson are friends. She is a very special lady – but then I don't need to tell you that.'

'I've only known her for a few weeks, but she has made such a difference to my life here. She's a sort of pattern to live by. I hope he knows – her Gerald, I mean – I hope he knows that what happened hasn't destroyed her pride and her dignity.'

78

'Pride and dignity can't be destroyed by events, even tragedy like theirs. Puffed up self-esteem, that can be knocked down, but not her sort of pride. That stems from faith in the people she loves, certainty of right and wrong. He's the same, you know. People like that make one feel very humble.' While he talked he'd unwound the bandage and inspected the healing wound. 'Before I give you a clean dressing and wrap you up again, do you want to go and brush your hair properly.'

This time when she smiled it was natural.

'You don't know just how much I want to brush my hair! I won't be a minute.' Already she was on her feet. He listened as she ran up the narrow wooden staircase, then heard her moving in the room above. What was a girl like that doing living in surroundings like this? He knew enough about Alice Gregson to be sure he'd never hear Jane's story from *her*. Hearing her quick tread coming back down the stairs, he cut a fresh piece of lint to protect the stitches from the holding bandage.

'I'll look in again in a day or so, if I may, Jane,' he told her a minute later as he collected his bag ready to leave.

It took all her courage to look him in the eye and answer. 'You ought not to. I hadn't expected you to come until the stitches had to come out. You can see, I haven't the sort of money to meet a doctor's bill, I thought you understood—'

'And I thought you understood,' his face was serious, only his eyes seemed to believe he was smiling, 'we met socially, we were introduced as friends. Of course I send bills to my patients, I have to earn a living. But I hope you can look on us as friends.'

Before she could blink them back, she felt the sting of the hot tears that welled into her dark eyes.

'Today's Wednesday, suppose I come about the same time on Friday? Would that suit you?' His manner was businesslike, careful not to let her suspect he'd noticed.

She nodded as she overcame her momentary weakness. Then, moving in front of him to open the front door, she was ready with a smile, her composure restored.

'I'll be here.' Then, making a conscious effort to speak to him as a friend, not a visiting doctor, 'And, thank you, Matthew.'

Her saying his name brought them forward a large step. It was as if the moment was imprinted on their memories. Then the charade of departure went on: he put on his hat, raised it as he turned to her in a final farewell then left her. She closed the front door and leant against it, listening to the familiar sound as he cranked the engine into life, then the roar of the motor as he drove away. What had happened to her in just a few months, that a man treating her with no more than normal courtesy could make her so aware? There had been nothing extraordinary in his raising his hat to her, it had been no more than force of habit while his mind had probably already moved ahead to his next call. No, to him it had meant nothing; yet, with cruel clarity, it had shown her what she had become. When did a man last lift his hat to her? Ian wore a cap, on one occasion she'd seen how, like every other man, he'd taken it off out of respect as the undertaker's horse had pulled a funeral cortège past them on the way to the cemetery. Hadn't she cared in Deremouth that he'd kept it firmly on his head when he'd met her? No, she hadn't. That was the truth. So who was it who'd changed, was it Ian or was it her? She knew the answer and she wasn't proud.

'You know what has happened?' Yvette Bingley greeted Matthew when he arrived home at mid-day. For nearly ten years she had lived in England, but nothing could turn Yvette into an Englishwoman; her French origin was in the way she used her hands to express herself, in her silent aitches, and in her mode of dress which was flamboyant by Brackleford's standards.

Matthew looked at her tolerantly. Whatever it was the morning had brought to his vivacious wife had clearly pleased her.

'Not yet, I don't know. But I think I'm about to hear,' he smiled.

'But of course you are to hear it. How long is it' (which sounded like 'ow long ees eet') 'since I have sung to an audience? I tell you just how long. Nine years and two months. And all those years and months I have been the wife of the good doctor.'

He laughed. 'What are you telling me? That you are no longer going to be the wife of the good doctor?'

'You make joke of it, but I will tell you. This morning a lady came to see me. She is the most beautiful lady I have even seen, she is the wife of the Reverend Warburton. It is the Reverend Warburton who sent her. There is money needed, the tower of the church needs some mending. So in the hall, St Stephen's church hall she called it, they are going to make some concerts.'

'But we've never been inside St Stephen's church, how did this vicar know you'd been a singer?'

'This is what is so exciting, Matthew. He was told that someone had seen me – me and you too – at the Christmas party at the orphanage. He heard that I had made the party happy for the poor children – she said it was someone she called a sidesman who told them about me.'

And Matthew had no doubt of the description that would have been given to the organizers of this fund-raising concert. What Yvette had was more valuable than beauty. Petite, quick in her movements, huge dark eyes ready to smile at every woman and tantalize every man, even if she knew nothing about entertaining an audience she would have been an asset.

'And you're going to sing?'

'Sing – dance – all the things I used to do. You do not know how much I have missed being a performing person. Being the good doctor's wife can be a very dull thing. I said that to the beautiful lady who came to see me. I said to her, was it not the same being the good vicar's wife? But I think she did not understand. She told me she had parties two or

81

three times every week, she said I ought to join in. Oh but Matthew, how can she call them parties? A lot of women doing their sewing and knitting together, making clothes for children of the poor; or cleaning the brass in her husband's church; or making what she said were fancy goods to sell at the church bazaar. I did not even ask her what a fancy good was, I felt so confused that she call these things parties. I told her I liked jolly things, I like to sing or to dance. Naughty of me, but I wanted to shock her. But it did not. She just nodded her pretty head very kindly and said if I could sing and dance then that would be very good for these concerts to make the money to mend the church.'

'Is it really so dull for you?' He'd heard it often, but never seriously believed her talk of boredom. Most people would look on her life as very comfortable: she had enough money to indulge her love of clothes, she always seemed to be cheerful.

She considered his question with unusual seriousness.

'I do not sit down and wait for happiness. I amuse myself – and for you, that is lucky. For how dull it must be for the poor vicar to come home to a beautiful wife who has taken her pleasure sewing with her party of ladies, or making goods of fancy. Life is a very jolly affair, even if we do have to dig deep to find the fun. And what about you, Matthew? If either you or me has a dull life, then it must be you. Always with people who have pains or spots or broken bones. Bah! I would not care for the work you do.'

'We're all of us different. I see there was a letter from Anton this morning. Is there any news?'

'What news can a schoolboy have? When you were at that school, what did you find to write home about? I think his letters are a Saturday afternoon penance.' Then, her mind jumping back to Alayne's visit, 'Perhaps for those vicarage ladies it is like that – do you think these parties are their way of doing penance for their wicked living the rest of the week?' She chortled at the thought.

'Sometimes you are a wicked woman, Yvette Bingley.'

'Only sometimes? Never let me turn into one of those so good and serious ladies.'

'Not a chance of it,' he laughed. 'Have you got anything to feed me on?' An unnecessary question for one of Yvette's delights was to make exciting meals, guided by intuition, a love of good food and owing much to her French ancestry.

'I called on the doctor's wife,' Alayne told Marcos when he arrived home from choir practice that evening, 'and she has agreed to take part in the concert. She was a singer before she was married, so I'm sure she'll be useful.'

'Good. Perhaps she and Herbert Franklin might do a duet. What is she, soprano or contralto?'

Alayne rested her knitting on her knee and raised a worried face.

'I know I ought to have asked her – but Marcos, she was so pleased to help – so excited I was going to say – I didn't like to probe. But she said she wouldn't need an accompanist so I suppose she plays the piano herself. I invited her to come to one of the women's groups, but she didn't seem interested. Perhaps, being foreign, she's a little shy of putting herself forward. Anyway, I told her I would call again and tell her when the rehearsals were to begin. I'll try and find out more then.'

'Good idea,' Marcos's thoughts had already moved on from the proposed concert. 'I know I can leave all the arrangements in your hands.'

Alayne smiled contentedly. Surely there was no role better than that of a vicar's wife – and no one who carried it out better than she did.

A few days later she again set out from the vicarage which stood in a large garden behind the Market Square, to visit the doctor's house in Millsham. The journey entailed crossing the busiest, noisiest part of town and, although she would happily have taken the trap on her own if she'd been going in the other direction where the roads were quieter, on this occasion she asked Jimmy, the garden boy, to drive her. Brackleford was proud of its trams, they rattled and clanked along their rails from Wemberton at the western edge to Millsham at the eastern, but Alayne found it unnerving the way Shandy, the pony, flicked her tail and twitched her ears as they clattered past. She enjoyed being driven through the town, for this was the heart of Marcos's parish, so she invariably saw some of her 'ladies' to wave to; it gave her a happy sense of belonging, being part of the pulse of life that beat so strongly here amongst the shops and workshops.

As they came into residential Millsham her thoughts turned to the doctor's wife. Perhaps it was because she spoke with that accent that she seemed so different from the other women ... could it set her apart so that she hadn't found it easy to make friends? ... and if that were the case, perhaps it was the very reason Mr Ashford, the sidesman, had been guided to suggest she might be approached to take part in the concert. Alayne saw it as a sign that their paths had been made to cross so that she could be the one to offer friendship. The Lord moved in mysterious ways, and she liked to feel He could rely on her to keep up with Him.

'Wait here while I ring the bell, Jimmy. But, if you see I am invited in, then you can take the trap home. I may be a little while, so I'll come on the tram when I'm ready.'

Yvette was clearly pleased to have a visitor, especially one who brought details of when and where she was to join in the fun of preparing for a concert. Somehow she couldn't imagine that those good ladies who sewed for the poor or spent afternoons making goods that were fancy would be in the cast of performers. Alayne was delighted with her reception: wasn't it evidence that the doctor's wife was in need of a friend to talk to? So many of the lady parishioners were pleased to spend their time in her good works, but seldom was she given the opportunity to feel that her mission was to help one who needed her friendship.

'You have come about the concert – yes?' Yvette smiled her pleasure.

'Partly I have. But not just that. I thought it would be nice to see you again.' There, now, that should set her visit off on the right foot.

'We will have some tea together and you shall tell me what is being arranged. What has happened to me, that I can be so pleased to entertain in the hall of your St Stephen's church?' Then, memory taking a leap back across those nine years and two months she'd talked about to Matthew, 'Different from the Café Hélène, but I will transport your good citizens so that they believe themselves to be in my beautiful Paris.'

Alayne felt vaguely uncomfortable. She knew very little about Paris, but from the way Yvette laughed as she spoke, the implication seemed to be that it was some sort of a den of iniquity – not at all the sort of thing an audience in the church hall would be looking for. Then she reminded herself of her mission and gave Yvette the benefit of the doubt: after all, she might be talking wildly simply to impress because she was unsure of herself. So Alayne made sure her smile held no hint of a suggestion that she had a twinge of doubt.

'The Café Alayne, you say?' she repeated, not recognizing the silent aitch, 'Alayne, that's *my* name.'

'What a gay place it was. There must be such places in your London – but no, 'ow could there be? Paris is the 'eartbeat of France, London of solemn, sober England.'

'How long have you lived here?'

'Since I married Matthew, nine years and two months ago. He brought Anton and me to his own country. He is a good man, kind, generous. We are 'appy.'

'But of course you are.' Again Alayne's smile didn't take the message of her thoughts: if they've lived in England all that time, surely it's an affectation to speak with such a silly accent! 'You are man and wife. It would be a sad thing if you weren't happy together. Who is Anton? Is that your brother?'

85

'Anton is my son. He is living at one of your so fine boarding schools. He speaks like an English boy – but he has the soul of a French boy. His father was an artist. Matthew went to this same school, he too played that silly rough game they call rugby. It makes a man of a boy, that is what people say. I do not know how fighting over a silly ball can make one a man. Did your vicar learn to chase after a ball?'

'Marcos played cricket. He still does. Each summer we have a match, the Vicar's Eleven versus the Town Hall Eleven. We wives do the teas. Just a friendly match, you know. I don't understand the rules of the game, but I've come to know the sort of things they like to eat.' Visibly, she snuggled further into the fireside chair; her contentment with life was plain to see. 'How sad for you. You must have been so young when you lost your husband.'

'André was married, but he was not *my* husband. But yes, I was very young. Then I met Matthew.'

Alayne was nonplussed by the matter-of-fact acceptance that the father of her son was another woman's husband. Added to that, she was irritated by the fact that 'husband' sounded more like 'osbond'. If Mrs Bingley had been in England for nine years and two months, surely she ought to be able to speak much more like everyone else. But she reminded herself that she'd been sent for a purpose, it wasn't for her to levy criticism or to judge. So, to cover her natural reaction, she rushed to say the first thing that came into her head.

'And you and the doctor? Do you have children?'

'No. In the hospital when Anton was brought from me, the surgeon made me no more able to conceive. He was a friend I had known for many years.'

'Even if he was a dear friend, how sad it must have been for you. But you have Anton.'

'I am not sad for it,' Yvette laughed. 'And have you and the vicar a houseful of children at home in your vicarage?'

'None. In the beginning I expected to have babies, I wanted babies more than anything. But it's in the Lord's hands. We had been married for nearly a year when some inner voice told me that the Lord had other work for me.' Alayne smiled gently, well satisfied with her lot.

'Other work?'

'In the parish, helping Marcos of course. We are very happy together, and I told you about the working parties I run. Once I realized that children – and living together – you know what I mean – once I realized it wasn't for us, we seemed to move forward in our relationship. We made our vows when we wed, but there must be different ways of interpreting them. We really are devoted – we are a splendid team. We shall never have children, but there are other kinds of love. Don't you think so?'

'I believe that what is important is that a loving relationship holds nothing back.'

'You mean sleeping together? No! When it's not in the hope of having children – no, I *couldn't*.' Hearing her own words, Alayne's face flushed with confusion and embarrassment. She'd never spoken about anything so intimate to anyone, not even to Marcos in those early months when they'd shared a room.

'I expect we're all different.'

'Yes,' Alayne agreed, glad to let the topic drop.

Yvette wondered what sort of a man her husband could be. In her mind she formed a picture of the unseen vicar, a picture that took away some of her pleasure in anticipating the forthcoming concert. A man who accepted rejection from his wife without a murmur, an audience made of ladies from the vicarage 'parties'. An imp of mischief prodded her: she'd add a bit of zest to their evening.

'I'll try not to hurt you,' Matthew said as he took scissors and tweezers and prepared to take out Jane's stitches. Then, to take her mind off what he was doing, he told her about the concert that was being arranged in St Stephen's church hall. 'Yvette – that's my wife, you remember – is planning to do some song and dance act.'

'Is she good?'

'She is talented, yes, a breath of life straight from Gay Paree. But good?' He shrugged, something in his expression Jane couldn't understand. 'What is good to one is dull to another; what some see as bad, others accept as a normal appreciation of all life offers. Yvette is the same now as when I first knew her – she has an insatiable appetite for romance, shall I say? She tells me her life in Brackleford is dull; by her standards I dare say it is, or would be if she let it. Perhaps there was a time when I expected things might be different. I don't know. Whatever I thought or felt is long since forgotten. There, that's the stitches gone. The scar will fade. Not entirely perhaps, but more or less. This concert – I was wondering whether you and Alice would let me take you. I suspect she seldom goes out, and it's not good for her having nothing but memories for company every evening, especially memories that can't all be happy. If you say you'll come, Jane, I may be able to persuade her.'

Willingly Jane agreed. The vicar had been important in her life only because it was he who had performed her marriage ceremony, but now she thought of him again. She remembered his handsome face, his olive complexion, his hair so dark that it was almost black. And she remembered her brief encounter with his sweet, lovely wife, surely the most beautiful person she'd ever seen. Yes, she'd like to go to the concert. Most of all, she wanted to meet Yvette, Matthew's French wife.

Chapter Five

The women of Mill Lane were a close-knit community, held together by understanding of each other's worries and experiences. They all knew the feeling of wellbeing on Friday evening when their menfolk brought their wages home, but it wasn't the 'Friday feeling' that held them together so much as the struggle to eke out their meagre housekeeping money to make it stretch for a whole week. On Thursdays the rent man called and when one or other had to stay out of sight and not answer the knock at the door, the rest of them were prepared all to tell the same lies. 'Mrs Hopkins has got called away to see her sick mother' or 'You'll likely meet Mrs Brown as you go back, she had to run to the shops but she said she'd be back. You're round early today.' Neither Mrs Hopkins, Mrs Brown nor any of them would think of keeping it a secret from each other that this week she couldn't find the money; instead she'd rely on them all to tell the same story. And somehow by the following week she would struggle to get the rent together in time.

The spirit of community went beyond the women. It bonded the children in much the same way, as they played hopscotch, football, five stones, skipping in the narrow street. As soon as they were old enough to stagger unaided they would be out there, watching, jumping with excitement, waiting to grow big enough to join in. And in the struggle for existence it was the accepted thing that as one child grew out of a garment, there would be another somewhere in the street ready to grow into it. So, poor though they were, they weren't unhappy.

The only one who remained outside the circle was Jane. Had she arrived looking down-at-heel, had they ever seen her in the street in an overall, or had she hung her washing with theirs on one of the communal lines that stretched across the narrow thoroughfare, then she would have been accepted. As it was she was looked on with suspicion. When, on her way to the shops, she passed a group of neighbours talking she invariably smiled and wished them 'Good morning' to be answered, at best, with a curt nod. It didn't worry her, she gave it no more than a passing thought and would have been surprised how often she was the subject of their gossip.

She was certainly the subject of it on a blowy morning towards the end of April, Jane and the doctor too.

'I see *he's* there again,' one of them nodded her head in the direction of the parked motor car.

'Hardly a day goes by when he doesn't come. She finished with that bandage on her head weeks ago, I saw her in the baker's yesterday and the bruising has cleared up. Never was that bad if you ask me. If it had happened to you or me we would have let nature take its course. These hoity-toities, they're all the same, make a mountain out of a molehill.'

'What she's got won't be a molehill much longer! Putting it on fast, she is. But then, that sort make a meal even out of having their kids. I feel sorry for that poor husband of hers. Running to the doctor at every turn, she'll keep him a poor man all his days. No wonder he spends his evenings in the Queen Charlotte. Goes up there hungry, so I've heard. Glad to be given a bite of something.'

'A bite, is that what you call it? More likely a nibble, from what we hear.' At which there was general laughter. Life held plenty of humour for the women of Mill Lane.

90

'Been in there pretty well half an hour already.' Interest went back to No. 4's visitor. 'Makes you wonder who's doing the treating, him or her.'

'Don't look round, the door's opening. He must have remembered he's got other folk to see to. Do you lot pay into the scheme?' The others appeared to give what she was saying their full attention, careful not to be seen watching the doctor's departure. 'George says he reckons we ought to try to manage to find the threepence a week for it. Peace of mind, that's what he called it, knowing if anyone is bad they can get seen in the surgery. Not like "madam" over there, waiting in the comfort of her own home. But it's worth thinking about, like George says, it's not just him and me, but the kids too. Peace of mind,' she repeated, proud of George's phrase, 'to know you needn't put off seeing a doctor for fear of the bills.'

Had they not been so interested in the goings on at No. 4, the sound of the door closing on the doctor and of him cranking up his engine would have attracted their attention. As it was, they studiously keep looking in the other direction.

Inside Jane leant against the closed door, listening as the engine started, listening as the motor car drove away and the sound grew distant and faded into silence. I ought to tell him not to come . . . There's nothing wrong with me now, he doesn't even pretend that there is. I ought to tell him not to come . . . Every morning I listen for the motor. He's like a lifeline of sanity . . . No, that's a dreadful thing to say, it's disloyal, it's not even true. Ian is my sanity, he is my life and my love, why else would I be here? Just as they did so often, images of Deremouth chased each other across her mind: the easy comfort of the home she'd grown up in, the sound and smell in the brewery, the affection she'd always been so sure of between herself and her father. Outside the wind was buffeting, she could feel the draught under the front door as she stood leaning against it, in sharp contrast to her thoughts. She ought to tell him not to come . . . No, don't think about him, think about the future you want Ian to agree to. Somewhere away from Brackleford – anywhere – far away – somewhere where their baby would grow up in God's fresh air, not like the children round here with nowhere to play except the street. Far away, where her ears wouldn't be tuned for the sound of that motor car. Tomorrow she'd tell him he must stop coming ... Moving away from the door she went back into the kitchen and sat with her elbows on the table.

What's the matter with me that I can let his visits be so important? Think of Matthew – then think of Ian. 'A male animal' the words sprang into her mind. So he was, perfect in all his maleness. Think of his hands, strong, calloused with hard work; think of Matthew's, well kept, gentle. Think of Ian, my darling, my love. Was that spontaneous, or did she consciously call the words to mind? She wouldn't ask herself. Instead, as if for reassurance, she moved the flat palms of her hands on the new roundness of her belly. Her baby, hers and his. Ian, the strong almost black hair growing with such vigour, on his head, on his face, on his body ... this time she guided her thoughts consciously, imagining him standing naked, aroused even before he touched her, a male animal with a male animal's natural appetite. And wasn't that what she wanted? Wasn't that what had made her fall in love with him? Don't think about Matthew ... tomorrow you must tell him to stop coming.

But her mind had a will of its own and as the morning went on and she stood at the sink trying to scrub the stains from Ian's shirt, it was Matthew's voice that echoed. Resolved to put an end to the visits she believed they both found easy and undemanding, she was frightened to imagine day following day without him.

'This evening we are all to meet in St Stephen's church hall, all of us who are performing.' When Yvette was excited her accent was even more pronounced. 'Mrs Warburton, she has called this morning. She says this

92

evening will not be to rehearse, for everyone will do that at home. She is such a *good* person, Matthew, even when she spoke to me of this evening, she said it was not a time for practising for all the performers will be doing their very best already. It is to be what she calls a "run through". Again she offered to play on the piano while I sing my song.' She chuckled as her imagination ran ahead of her words. 'I say "No, I will bring my phonograph – I thought you could carry it in your motor – but she says there is one already for me in the hall, so I need only carry the cylinder.'

Matthew looked at her indulgently. Under her façade of continental sophistication she was as excited as a child going to a party.

'What are you singing?'

'"The Glory of Love", that is how you call it in English. You have heard me sing it – I remember the night you came to the Café Hélène on your first visit, I sang it then.' And again that laugh. 'I could see you were English.' At which, teasingly, he raised his eyebrows. 'Oh yes I could. You may well laugh, but you have not my experience, you cannot sort out the English, the French, the German, the Dutch, not like I can. I did not know whether you would understand my French words—'.

'Are you singing it in French tonight?'

'But of course not. How many of St Stephen's good people do you think speak my beautiful language?' Seeing the way his brows puckered with a frown of uncertainty, she ruffled his hair. 'Do not be what you would say is a stick-in-the-mud!' she teased. 'Men in the hall of St Stephen's church are the same as men in the Café Hélène. They will like what I do.'

'You have other songs, you have other accompaniment you could put on the phonograph. Brackleford isn't Paris—'

'Do you think I do not know that? Why are the people here so *dull*, so frightened to – to—' Lost for words she raised her shoulders helplessly, she held out her hands with

93

the palms toward the ceiling, 'to take off their corsets and be free.'

This time Matthew laughed.

'You wouldn't want to embarrass anyone. Find something else to sing, humph?'

'You are as buttoned up as all the rest. I wish I had not told Mrs Warburton that I would help raise money to mend their tower.' Dropping gracefully to sit in an armchair she beat a tattoo on her knees. She was a picture of pent-up emotional energy and Matthew felt mean that he had destroyed her pleasure.

'Whatever you sing, you know no one else will hold a candle to you. You'll have them all under your spell.'

Mollified she let her hands fall still, she even gave him an impish smile. Then, the subject closed, she reached for the bell by the side of the fireplace, letting them know in the kitchen that they were ready for lunch.

That evening she took the tram from the terminus at Millsham into the centre of Brackleford town, then walked the short distance to the Market Square and St Stephen's church. The hall was next door to it and she heard the hum of chatter as she went in. Immediately it stopped, all eyes turned towards her. Attention was food and drink to her; she had thrived on it through the years she'd earned her living in Paris and, perhaps until that moment, hadn't realized just how much she had missed being the centre of interest.

'I have come,' she announced into the silence, smiling at the room at large.

'And you are extremely welcome,' Alayne said as she hurried across the hall to greet her and ushered her forward, an arm around her shoulder. 'I want you all to meet Mrs Bingley. You may know her husband, the doctor. He has spared her to us to help with our entertainment. Mrs Bingley has been a professional singer.'

There were murmurs of appreciation and admiration. Yvette was enjoying herself more by the second.

The 'run through' commenced. Her pleasure faded as one by one the volunteers stepped on to the small platform. There was a powerfully built woman who recited a poem, her rosy and rotund husband who gave a rendition of 'Because' in a weak tenor voice while his wife smiled demurely, believing he sang it just for her. The next to mount the platform was a man who clearly had an inflated opinion of himself, a daffodil in his buttonhole and a moustache trained to turn up like a child's drawing of a smiling face; with his eyes never leaving Yvette, he sang 'Tell Me, Pretty Maiden'. Some of the women looked uncomfortable at such blatant admiration, but Yvette took it in her stride. And so the evening progressed.

'I thought we'd save you until last,' Alayne told her. 'Everyone agreed with me. The others are all amateurs, bless them. They all agreed that as you have been a professional singer it only right to save you until the end – the icing on the cake, you know.'

Time dragged as the monotony of their warbling was relieved only by a plump child in a Grecian tunic and with bare feet, holding a large balloon, counting her way through a dance, her relief visible as she came to the end and the pianist pounded out the final chord. Then on to the churchwarden's 'I'll Sing Thee Songs of Araby' before Alayne smiled encouragingly at Yvette and whispered that if she was ready (if she was ready!) everyone was looking forward to hearing her.

For the performance Yvette planned to wear the costume that she'd worn when she'd sung the same song at the Café Hélène, but as she walked on to the platform this evening she was dressed simply. Unlike the other ladies, she had taken off her hat and coat, and in her black skirt and cream blouse with its high lace neck she appeared to be the epitome of modesty. There was no one there who knew her well enough to recognize that it was an imp of mischief who gave an extra sparkle to her eyes.

'The glory of love is the glory of life.' Now who could

95

take offence at that? Surely it was their duty to love their neighbour. But . . .

Her voice was husky and beguiling, the movement of her body was more than graceful. The women felt uncomfortable, as if, in what seemed to them her blatant seduction of the men's senses, she was exposing sentiments that were intimate and personal. There were those who felt offended that a respectably married woman could make such a disgraceful exhibition of herself; there were others who were embarrassed, seeing in her a reflection of their own desires and longings they didn't put into words even to their husbands. Such behaviour should be reserved for behind closed bedroom doors.

As for the men, they understood the hidden innuendoes of the words, they understood the seductive movements of her slim, supple body. At her first words they'd exchanged a glance or two of open appreciation, but by the time her sultry tones had brought them through the second verse each man was an island.

'Oh dear,' Alayne muttered to herself. Then, almost silently to those around her, 'What can I do? How can I tell her, it's really not suitable.'

'Look at that lot over there,' mouthed Ada Watson, with a grin. She worked full time in the office at Perkins Pickle Factory and was only one of the St Stephen's Ladies by dint of the fact that she voluntarily washed and ironed all the choir surpluses. 'Bert Huggins's eyes'll drop right out in a minute.'

'Disgraceful. The poor doctor will be mortified,' from the wife of the churchwarden.

'Oh dear,' Alayne bit her lip in consternation, 'it was me who invited her. I'm sure she doesn't mean to upset anyone.' She wasn't following the words of the song, enough that somehow Yvette conveyed to her audience that the glory of love was throbbing in her veins – in hers and in theirs too. If only Marcos would get back from the deanery meeting, he would know what to do.

In truth, Marcos had arrived at the side door of the building just as Yvette had mounted the platform. Coming along the passage towards the door at the back of the hall he had heard her opening bars and had meant to join the groups standing listening. He got as far as the open doorway – then something pulled him up short. Without even glancing at her, he stepped back out of sight.

'The glory of love is the glory of life,' her deep husky tones spoke to him. As she'd started to sing, most of the men listening had glanced at each other with hope and amusement – at least until she worked her own individual magic on them. But to Marcos her message was direct and instantaneous; it caught him unprepared. He'd been expecting to hear the usual ballads, perhaps a pianoforte solo … instead he felt hypnotized by the sensual tones, by the song's message of seduction.

All thought of joining the party in the hall evaporated. As her last notes died on a sigh, he went back out into the night. Why was he running away from a face to face encounter with the doctor's wife? Was it because he wanted to cling to the image her voice had created? His retreat was the church. In the darkness he let himself in through the west door, breathing deeply the familiar smell of the ancient building and the old wooden pews. As if it were a loved friend, he put his hand on the cold stone of the wall then, needing no light, moved to sit in the back row.

What was the matter with him that a few words, a voice that seemed to throb with suppressed passion, could destroy the control he'd fought so hard to build. If he'd known in advance, if he'd been prepared, if he'd been in the hall all the evening like everyone else … But he hadn't. He'd walked in out of the crisp evening air, glimpsed Alayne's look of anticipation at the phonograph's first notes – dear Alayne, so faithful, faithful to him, faithful to their work, faithful to all they knew to be right – then had come the voice that still echoed in his mind.

He dropped to his knees, a natural action in his search

for help. He didn't pray; instead he let his thoughts go where they would. And yet was that not praying? His heart was open, he hid nothing as he silently poured out his anguish and frustration.

I do love her. I've loved her for so long she is like part of myself, part of my faith, part of my work. And it's the same for her, I know that too. Look back to the beginning – that first year. She was mine then, her heart and her body too. Is that true? Her heart was mine, it still is. But her body? No, that was never mine. She wanted a baby so much. Poor sweet Alayne, imagine her with a child, our child. That's what she told me right from the start. That's why, except those nights she couldn't, she let me make love to her. 'Each time I pray,' that's what she used to say. How could I tell her it wasn't to give her a child that I wanted her. She wouldn't have understood. I can still feel my sense of shame that my needs were so different from hers. Gentle Alayne, nothing drove her except kindness. Kindness to me, kindness to everyone who needed her, but passion isn't rooted in kindness. If it hadn't been for that dream . . . Dream? She thinks of it as a vision. Perhaps it was. How she cried when she told me. The sound of her crying woke me. 'There's other work for me to do,' I can hear her saying it. 'I had a vision, a voice was telling me I was never to have a child, there was other work for me.' Nothing I said could comfort her. 'Just a dream, darling, just a bad dream.' She'd been so sure, nothing could shake her belief. We'd been married about nine or ten months. She wept with shame that she hadn't been able to accept. 'I begged to be given longer. Not in words, I don't mean in words,' think how she sobbed. 'I tried to say that bringing up a child was God's work too. And it is. It's all I wanted. But it's not going to happen. I begged for longer: "Give me a full year" – as if it's up to me, or you either, the way we're chosen to serve. But I know it won't work, no matter how we try, I know I'm not going to be able to have our baby. If He wants me for other uses, it's selfish of me even to ask.'

Kneeling in the darkness Marcos remembered how he

had held her in his arms, comforting her, even then believing that by morning the dream would have faded. Certainly neither of them referred to it. How pale she'd been at breakfast; she'd looked as though she were recovering from an illness. The day had followed the usual pattern and when it ended his spirit had soared. Passion had been heightened by relief. Alayne, usually gentle and passive, had responded as never before, arching and straining towards him. Only afterwards as they'd drifted towards sleep had she murmured, 'I prayed this would be the time, but what's the use of prayer without faith? In my heart I know it will be just the same as always.'

Marcos moved from his knees and sat on the wooden pew, the years passing through his mind like a pageant. Why had he accepted so willingly when she'd suggested they should have separate bedrooms? There was no escaping the answer. Sex wasn't a part of Alayne's life, but was he different from any other man? No man could lie by her side, feel her warm body against his, and not be aroused. In Alayne's mind a couple made love because it was part of procreation. She fought her battle to accept that other work was ordained for her so she expected that, as partners and friends, they could sleep in each other's arms and sex would play no part. For him it hadn't been possible. When he'd moved into another room it had been with something like relief. Unlike Alayne, whether lying by her side or in his own room, for him sexuality couldn't be denied.

'The glory of love is the glory of life,' that throaty voice echoed, the beat of it throbbing in his veins.

He'd given no thought to time. He still gave no thought to it as his candid memories held nothing back. He'd come to the sanctuary of the church as an escape, he'd stayed there for the comfort that came from unburdening his troubled thoughts. When at last he went out the way he'd come in and crossed the churchyard to the garden gate of the vicarage he saw there was only one light on in the house and that was in Alayne's bedroom. He would let himself in quietly so that he wouldn't disturb her.

He was at the top of the stairs when she heard a movement and opened her bedroom door.

'I've been so worried. There's nothing wrong?' Standing in her nightgown, her long pale hair tumbling in curls around her shoulders, she was like a beautiful picture. 'You poor darling, such a dreadfully long meeting. I'll put on my dressing gown and come down. You must be starved.' There was nothing of the seductress in the way she took his hand and held it to her cheek; she loved Marcos more than anyone in the world; she'd been worried that he was so late and now he was safely home.

When he drew her into his arms she didn't resist – neither did she show any excitement.

'I'm not hungry.' But he was, he was starved. Starved of love? No, never that, Alayne gave him her heart with the simple trust of a child.

'Marcos, my darling, has something happened?' She held her hand to his cheek and was taken by surprise when his mouth sought hers. But why should she be, she asked herself, a day never passed when they didn't kiss – hello, goodbye, good morning, goodnight; she saw the exchange of kisses as a silent expression of an affection too deeply rooted to need words. But, his mouth moving on hers like this ...?

'What happened?' she asked again when she could speak. 'Where have you been so late?'

'In the church.'

'I've been so worried, I was watching out of my window. I didn't see even a candle flickering.'

'I didn't need a light.'

Alayne was satisfied. To her there was nothing strange about seeking peace that way. Sometimes she did it herself, not because she was troubled but because sitting in silence, absorbing the atmosphere as a sponge absorbs water, she found that 'peace that passes all understanding'.

'Dear Marcos, we are so lucky, you and I.'

'Alayne, tonight I'm staying with you. You can't send me away ...' He seemed to stand outside himself, hearing himself saying the words that so often clamoured in his head. For a second he saw her expression cloud, the open devotion give way to – shock? Fear?

Then she nodded.

'You'd better undress in your own room. I'll be waiting, ready.'

He'd held her in his arms, he'd wanted to tear her night-gown from her back, to pull his own clothes off. Like a caveman with his woman he'd wanted to possess her. Her quietly spoken acceptance brought him sharply back to reality.

'I'm sorry, darling,' this time he kissed her forehead gently, 'I've kept you up a long time already. I'll stay in my own room.'

Alayne's immediate reaction was relief, but quickly she overcame it. She couldn't understand why he still wanted to make love but she would hate him to feel she didn't care about him. What was it Yvette Bingley had said? Something about if you love a person you should love them completely. Well, if that's what he wanted she ought to let him, she'd hate to think of him feeling lonely and rejected.

So she left her door open, got into bed and waited. When he came in she managed a smile of welcome and moved over to make room for him in the bed.

'Bless you.' Gently he kissed her cheek. 'You go to sleep. I'll stay in my own room.'

Remembering the way he'd held her, the hungry move-ment of his mouth on hers, she supposed he must have recovered. Dear Marcos.

'Never mind,' she didn't elaborate about what it was he shouldn't mind. 'You can stay anyway and tell me about the meeting.'

'It was quite short.' He got in by her side, relieved that his passion had been sufficiently deflated that it showed no

101

sign of reasserting itself. For a while they talked of the parish. It had been her afternoon to visit the workhouse, so on the way she had bought a basket of vegetables, then some bones from the butcher, and had helped the women make soup. 'It took longer than I expected, that's why I wasn't home by the time you had to leave for the meeting. Now, let me tell you about the concert, we had a complete run through—'

'Tell me in the morning. You've had a busy day, let's get to sleep.'

She gave him a light and sisterly kiss, then turned her back and snuggled into a comfortable position.

For a long time sleep eluded Marcos, and then he was disturbed by a dream of Alayne, naked except for a heavy cross around her neck, swaying in front of him as she sang, 'The glory of love is the glory of life'. But the voice wasn't hers, it was deep and husky, it hit his brain in rhythmic pulsing until it half woke him.

'What—' Alayne was pulled out of sleep in the pale moonlight to see him looming above her.

'Yes – darling – must.' That rhythm in his brain was in every thrust, 'You – you too – now – now—' Hollow words, even as he heard himself speak them he knew that to Alayne he might be talking a foreign language. But by then she had woken sufficiently to know what it was that had frightened her. And being Alayne, she rejected her instinctive semi-conscious reaction to push him away. Instead she lay still and waited until it was over, accepting it as a duty that thankfully she was seldom called on to undertake . . .

At breakfast neither of them mentioned their disturbed sleep, nor the fact that when she'd woken it was to find herself alone. The morning stillness had been broken by the sound of the church bell; the seven o'clock Eucharist was nearly over.

Marcos was in no hurry to reach the Bingleys' home. The morning was bright and clear; he told himself that was why he decided to walk the distance from the town centre to Millsham, the solid middle-class residential area about two miles from the vicarage. That that was the entire reason for him rejecting both trap and tram he didn't let himself question, but certainly he was in no hurry to meet the owner of that provocative voice.

No one seeing him striding through the town would have guessed that he was less than anxious to reach his destination. Such a handsome figure in his long cassock, the sombre black relieved only by a plain brown leather belt, his biretta seeming to set him above and apart from the shoppers. His answering smile as he replied to those who wished him a 'Good morning, Vicar', gave no hint of the conflict of dread and excitement that filled his thoughts. Last night at the hall he'd been hypnotized into listening to her voice – but he hadn't wanted the spell to be broken by seeing her as a woman. Now duty was making a meeting inevitable. He was ashamed that *he*, the early flush of youth far behind him, could feel a tremor of half understood anticipation like some lad throwing himself into his first infatuation. Yes, he was ashamed, just as he was of the wild fantasies that he'd so willingly let possess him last night as he'd forced himself on docile Alayne. Dear Alayne ... she had no conception of the intoxicating eroticism that had consumed him. Birds in the air, animals in fields and forests, they lived by urges of sex, surely it was their God-given instinct. And man's? No, man was on a higher plane than the animals, sex was but a part of love. And he loved Alayne, he told himself, 'with my body I thee worship', wasn't that what he'd vowed? But last night he hadn't been worshipping *her* body, her sweetly sleeping body, he'd been indulging the fantasy-driven urges of his own. As he bowed his head in acknowledgement to a passing parishioner there was nothing in his smiling greeting to hint at the self-abasement he felt. Alayne ... she gave all her thought, all her effort to serving other people ... she was a better person that ever he could be.

Easy to say that, and all too easy to accept it. But his must never be the easy path. That's why at breakfast, when Alayne had looked at him with her lovely eyes so troubled as she told him about Yvette Bingley's contribution to the concert, clearly he had seen where his duty lay.

'I couldn't speak to her last night, not in front of all the others. After all, she has been a professional, it seemed so uncharitable to have to ask her to select something different. But, it really was upsetting. Something about love – but – oh dear, I'm not good at finding the right word – it was – it was – impure. Does that sound silly? If you'd been there you would understand for yourself. I'm sure songs like that are popular in some of the music halls – well, they may be, I don't know – but I felt really uncomfortable. And this is for the church, for the tower.' Marcos had listened to her, letting her talk, not interrupting. 'This morning I must call and see her. I've been there twice before and she is so easy to talk to. Perhaps that will help.'

'Leave it to me.' He'd reached out to take her hand and felt her fingers clinging to his, a look of such gratitude on her face that he was ashamed. 'I wasn't there, so it will be easier for her to accept, coming from me. I can say that some of the ladies were upset—'

'Not Ada Watson. I do believe she thought the whole thing one big joke. She was watching the men, laughing at the way they – they – oh Marcos, they *drooled*. There was an uncomfortable atmosphere. I truly wish I'd never asked her. And yet she is lovely, not the usual pretty type. I expect it's because she's French. Well, you'll see for yourself, and Marcos, I'm so grateful that you've offered. I was dreading it. Be kind to her, won't you.'

He was shown into the drawing room and a minute later he heard Yvette's quick, light step as she ran down the stairs. Facing the door he waited.

'It is the Reverend Warburton,' she said, coming towards him with both hands outstretched. Then she laughed, the sort of chuckle that might be expected from a mischievous child.

'I'm so grateful to you for agreeing to take part in our fund-raising event for the tower. The maintenance of these ancient buildings is a responsibility that demands an endless flow of money, I'm afraid. But I always feel we are privileged to have them in our care; we have a responsibility to all those who have worshipped over the centuries.'

'You are right. The future has to be built on the past.' There was nothing of the mischievous child nor yet of the seductress in her solemn reply. 'I was happy' (she pronounced it 'arpy') 'to be invited'.

'I expect my wife, Alayne, told you I was unable to be there. I'm afraid I missed hearing you.'

This time her gingery brown eyes sparkled with laughter.

'If you are in need of funds, then you should drop some pennies into your box to ask for absolution for telling fibs,' she teased.

'I beg your pardon? Did she not explain that I had to be at a meeting.'

'But yes.' The laugh got the upper hand. 'Tell your tale to anyone else, your wife, *anyone*, for the truth is known only to you and to me. Reverend Warburton, while they all looked towards me, you forget it was I who saw the doorway at the back of the hall. Why did you not go away like you intended? Why did you wait just out of sight? And why did you forget that, man of God though you are, you still cast the shadow of a human? You listened to every note, every word, did you not? I know you did.' Then lowering her head slightly she looked at him very directly. 'It was for you that I sang it.'

'How can you say such a thing?' he blustered, thrown completely out of his depth.

'A question to which I have no answer.' Then, in a supreme effort to put him at his ease. 'I wondered who would call on me, you or your beautiful wife. Of course I know just why you have come.'

'No, no. How can you?' This wasn't going at all as he'd imagined – and neither had he expected to be so fascinated by the way she spoke and the way she used her hands to give emphasis to her words.

'You have come to tell me, as kindly as is possible, that my song is not in keeping with that of the fat tenor or the big-bosomed contralto.'

'Mrs Bingley, they are not professionals, they are people prepared to do the best they can to help a worthy cause. They are good people—' He meant every word he said in their defence, but he could read the laughter in her eyes. Mockery and yet, he suspected, mockery that held no unkindness.

'Oh, but yes they are good, that I could see. But even a *good* man can enjoy the – how you would say it? – the titillation of "The Glory of Love". Oh, you do not have to defend your so good friends. But are they not human too? And you? Hiding in the passage, were you not enjoying it just as they did?'

He thought of his stalwart congregation, sober and honest Jim Baker with his feeble tenor voice, burly Michael Biggs who invariably treated his listeners to "Asleep in the Deep" in a baritone. Then in his imagination he was once again listening in the passage, his senses alive with loneliness and longing. Is that what she had done to them too? The answer came to him before he could hold it off: they had wives and families, wives who didn't believe themselves to be on a God-sent mission to serve humanity. Even as he thought it, he was ashamed. Did Alayne ever complain? She who had wanted children more than anything in life, yet she had accepted what she believed to be asked of her.

'. . . in French,' Yvette was saying. 'But even in English I promise it could not offend the so pure sensibilities of your good people of Brackleford.'

'I'm sorry, I didn't catch what you were saying?' What was there about her that gave him the uncomfortable feeling that no matter what it was she'd said, she had been able to follow his thinking? 'A song in French?'

'Reverend Warburton, last night was a joke. Perhaps it was not a funny joke from where you stood, but for me it was. The ladies whispering, watching their husbands' ('osbunds') 'as if they dared their thoughts to stray where I was taking them. Oh, for me it was what in your strange language you call a lark. Tomorrow for the concert I promise you I will give you no cause to concern yourself for them,' then her eyebrows raised as their eyes met, 'I will be your so innocent rose.'

Was she laughing at him too, seeing him as one with all those others?

'Mrs Bingley, I wanted just to come here to tell you how grateful I am that you are helping our cause. We are all adults – no one ought to be offended.' He was blustering, over-emphasizing. 'For my own part, I found your singing . . . um . . . moving. Yes, moving.'

Her accent went wild. Purposely? Or did it happen when she spoke spontaneously?

'So being the so dull wife of the doctor has not made Yvette lose her skill? She still knows how to wake up the libido? Is that not so?'

'I told you. I was too far away to hear well, of course.' (Coward! You hung on every word. Wake up the libido, did she say?) 'But even from that distance I knew I was hearing a professional.' Then, feeling he'd got himself on to safe ground, he added, 'I'm grateful to you for giving your time to helping us and, too, for your understanding about changing your song. They are honest, genuine people, you know. I don't want any of them to be embarrassed. We're all of us different.' He felt rather pleased with that last sentence, it seemed to be telling her that, for himself, he had no narrow-minded misgivings.

His mission accomplished, he went home on the tram from Millsham terminus. Sitting on the hard wooden-slatted seat, as they jolted and rocked along the track, he let his mind go back over his visit. It was impossible to keep at bay the thought that Dr Bingley's married life must be very different from his own.

Next day, Jane dressed with care for her evening at the church hall. Matthew was calling for her at seven o'clock, then driving on to collect Alice. Over the last week or two she felt she had said goodbye to any semblance of her previous slim build. Slim? She was too honest to call it that – in fact it would be nearer the truth to say she had been angular in her thinness. But no more. With Alice's help and guidance she had let out seams and pleats so that buttons could still be done up. She could feel the baby moving now: each day the movements were a little stronger.

Ian hadn't been interested in where she was going. What difference would it make to him? He'd taken his departure for the Queen Charlotte before she went upstairs to change her dress and she knew she would arrive home to an empty house. But on that evening she didn't care. She was going out with Matthew and she made no attempt to suppress her excitement.

She unpinned her long hair, brushed it vigorously and re-pinned it, then thankfully lowered herself to sit on the edge of the bed. Was it normal to feel like this? Superstitiously frightened that to admit even to herself how unwell she felt for fear she would be suggesting something was wrong with her baby, even to Alice she made an effort to be cheerful and energetic. But it wasn't the truth. Over the weeks she'd watched a woman along the street, twins staggering unsteadily at her side and, from the look of her, another set due any time. Yet the woman was out there every day, laughing, chattering, straining to reach the line to hang her washing. Jane was ashamed of her own frailties. Only when Matthew came did she feel relaxed. He asked no questions, he seemed to understand how she felt without her telling him, yet he never inferred there was anything to be concerned about in not finding pregnancy easy. Perhaps it was the woman with such unflagging energy along the street who was unusual; perhaps most felt as she did – heavy, aching, like a cumbersome toy whose spring had broken.

But on the evening of the concert she was resolved to enjoy every moment; it was her first outing since she'd come to Brackleford. She forced herself to find the energy to get up from the bed and take her three-quarter-length winter cloak from the cupboard. That's when she heard the sound of the approaching motor car – as, doubtless, did the rest of the street! She had told Matthew she looked forward to meeting his wife. And that was true, but her feeling of anticipation was strangely complex. They must have been married for nearly ten years, but Jane had never been able to understand why it was that when he spoke of Yvette his tone was always overshadowed by what sounded like tolerant affection or even amusement. So why did she have this need to see them together? Was it to turn the knife in her own hurt, a hurt that came from the ever-increasing distance from each other into which she and Ian were drifting? Or was it to turn the knife in that other hurt she was frightened to acknowledge?

Arriving at the church hall they found that three seats in the middle of the second row had been reserved for them. Yvette must have arranged it. There were no curtains to the platform, so as one performer came down the steps and went off to a room behind the stage, the next mounted the stage. It was so long since Jane had had an evening out, no wonder she enjoyed each artiste's contribution, good and bad alike. She watched the plump and none too graceful barefooted Grecian dancer, but her reaction was very different from Yvette's: Yvette had seen her simply as untalented, but to Jane she was the embodiment of so many little girls (she'd been one herself not so many years ago), all her secret dreams held in the dance. Alayne's reaction was different again: as Florrie Bryant plodded her way through her hard-learnt routine, the boards of the stage creaking as she landed from each leap, Alayne's gentle smile of encouragement never faltered. Dear little Florrie, she had worked so hard to get her steps right; they must all clap extra loudly to show her how well she'd done.

Yvette was enchanting. Of those in the audience probably only Matthew and possibly Marcos understood all the words of her French love song. Miss Searl, who kept a 'School for Gentlefolk', Jane, probably Alice and a dozen or so more, could translate the occasional word. There was none of the sensuousness of 'The Glory of Love' in tonight's song, but even so Yvette had every man in the audience watching her graceful movements as if they were hypnotized. How proud Matthew must be. Jane forced herself to look furtively at him, needing the pain of seeing his pride and adoration as he listened to that husky French voice. She dreaded facing it and yet knew there was no running away. Perhaps it would bring some sort of sanity and reason back to her.

But it wasn't Yvette he was watching. For a moment they looked directly at each other. In a crowded hall amongst the excited applause and calls for an encore, in a silent room by themselves, time and place would have made no difference. Their defences were down. Such a tide of joy swept over her that everything else was forgotten.

Then, the child stirred, this time not a flutter but a hard kick. Confused, she closed her eyes. Under the shelter of her cloak she pressed the palms of her hands so that she could feel the movement.

Chapter Six

'Time' had long since been called at the Queen Charlotte, the door closed on its nightly customers, drunk and sober alike. Ian wasn't the only man from Mill Lane who liked his pint of ale and game of cribbage. As she lay in bed, Jane heard their noisy laughter as they passed her door, the father of the twins telling some yarn to someone who, from his unmistakable Northern voice, she knew to be the man from No. 10. It was Saturday night, the liveliest of the week, extra pence in their pockets and the thought of the Sabbath ahead.

But Jane's thoughts weren't on the familiar sound of the returning drinkers, they weren't even on the concert or on Yvette's magic magnetism, as she lay covered only with a sheet on this sultry July night. No matter how hard she tried to hold her mind on other things there was no escape from the memory that haunted her. For both of them, caught unprepared, it had been a moment of truth. As they'd looked at each other, they'd seen the reflection of their own emotions blotting out everything else. All these weeks she had tried to pretend she believed Matthew had been coming to see her out of kindness, knowing she wasn't riding easily through pregnancy and knowing too that she couldn't afford doctors' bills. She had been frightened to admit how important those hours with him had been to her, yet now, lying alone in the darkness she faced the truth; deep in her heart she had known

111

what was happening to them both. His many visits seemed to combine into one as she thought of the easy companionship, the relief of talking freely, sometimes of her own past, sometimes of his. How natural it had been to tell him about the final quarrel with her father and her deep hurt when she'd had no reply to her letters. Sometimes he'd talked of Yvette, always with that same tolerant affection.

She'd told him of her hopes that she could persuade Ian to move out of town. Only now did she face another truth: in leaving Brackleford she would not only be changing the noisy, dirty town for the sweet air of the country, but she would be escaping something too strong for her to fight. Yet fight it she must. Whether she would ever make Ian agree to her persuasions she didn't know. But one thing was certain, as certain to Matthew as it was to her: *now* must be the time to end something that could bring nothing but unhappiness to all of them. Wasn't that why he had delivered her home first tonight, seeing her out of the motor car while Alice still sat there? Wasn't that why when, in the darkness, she had found the courage to say, 'Don't come tomorrow. I'm not going to be home,' he had answered, 'No. I shan't come'? Who, hearing them, could have known the finality in those few words or guessed the misery behind their parting? Alice had called a cheery 'Goodnight' to her, but life had taught Alice all about grief and courage.

Listening to the raucous laughter of the Saturday night revellers, waiting for the familiar sound of Ian's tread, Jane lay on her back, her hands on her fast-changing body. When she felt a flutter of life she pressed harder as if she could will the unborn child to respond. All her suppressed love and aching loneliness were in the action.

But even now she wouldn't let herself admit that her father had been right. In her wilfulness she had refused to listen. Ian had been a God above all men. Was it his fault she couldn't talk to him? What had they in common? She had learnt never to mention the past to him; she knew it only provoked sneering and bitterness. Better she didn't let him guess how she missed the affectionate companionship she had had with her father, or how often she was overcome with longing for the sound and smell of the brewery; he would be hurt and see it as a criticism of how she lived now. So the door was closed on everything that had made up her life before he came into it. And the future? If only he would agree to her plan, let them start afresh together, start to build a business of their own. Her experience would help him, they would learn to grow close. They must. How could she believe they had nothing in common when the baby was part of each of them?

She became aware of the silence, Mill Lane's returning drinkers had gone home to wives who had probably been listening and waiting in anticipation of the ritual of Saturday night. Ian was late. Soon she'd hear his tread, on the cobbled street, on the stairs ... she turned on her side and buried her face in the pillow.

George Hamley put away the last of the washed glasses, wiped a cloth over the tables, put the chairs straight, and replaced the washed spittoon (only ever used on Saturday evening when old Jo Dibbins from the scrapyard came on his weekly visit). Finally he swept up the scattered sawdust from the floor. Then, satisfied he'd 'put the bar to bed', he turned out the gas lamp and went through to the living quarters.

'I thought Ian might have still been here to give me a hand. Went off early, did he?'

His plump and jolly-looking daughter shook her head. As natural now at twenty-three as she had been all her life, she seemed unaware whether or not nature had been kind to her. She battled with the pins to keep her frizzily curly ginger hair anchored on top of her head; her cheerfulness never failed, but her green eyes often gave away emotions she preferred to keep secret. Her snub nose was home to a thick peppering of freckles, her front teeth were set too close and tried to cross, her energy was boundless.

'Not that early, Pa. I gave him a bit of supper. And he

seemed ready for it too. That's why he wasn't in the bar with you. His wife's gone to some concert or other this evening.'

'That's what he gets for marrying a wench never been used to grafting. Reckon the lass does the best she know – but from the way he tucks in when he's here, she's got a lot to learn. You all right, gal? You look a bit umpty?' The skinny little man looked at his daughter with concern.

'Me? When am I ever umpty?' Her face was quick to react to the conscious effort she made to smile. To be cheerful was part of her nature; her mouth wanted to turn up at the corners of its own accord. 'Umpty,' and this time her giggle was genuine. 'Bet you his posh wife wouldn't know what you were talking about. Come to that, neither would most folk.' She raised her face to kiss her father's cheek. 'Can't say I shall be sorry to get to bed, all the same. Ian banked the fire and got the coal in for the morning.'

'Good lad.' Then, sitting down to unlace his boots, 'Good lad, be buggered, more likely a damn fool if you ask me. Plenty of truth in the saying "Marry in haste, repent at leisure" – he'll soon find out. That's if he ain't found out already. Does he talk much to you about Mrs High and Mighty?'

'He said she was off this evening to this concert at the church. Gone with the doctor, if you please, and that Mrs Gregson – remember, the woman whose husband got put inside for half killing those lads.'

'I wouldn't have it, if I were him. There's talk about her – not the old gal whose husband's cooling his heels. No, it's Ian's woman there's gossip about. I hear a good deal in that bar. The chaps from Mill Lane talk about her, encouraging the doctor to the house when Ian's earning his living. She's making a laughing-stock of him if you ask me.'

'You shouldn't listen to gossip. She's been pretty poorly with the baby, he told me. I bit my tongue, I didn't say that her sort's all the same. Where she comes from, having a kid may be a full-time job. I dare say they've got nothing better to do than make invalids of themselves. But folk around here have to get on with things, not have the doctor dancing attendance.'

'He wants to watch himself, that Dr Bingley. From what I hear he's too mighty thick with her if she's his patient. Perhaps I ought to say, "serves Ian right" getting tied up to a bird from a gilded cage like she is. But, despite everything, I have to give him credit for what he does to give me a lift. Life was hard-going here through those months he was down Devon way. You cut along to bed, gal,' he gave her a friendly tap on the bottom, 'another five minutes and it'll be tomorrow.'

The clock in the tower of St Stephen's chimed the hour, then struck midnight. Between the Queen Charlotte and the turning into Mill Lane was the national school, divided from the path by a low stone wall. It was here that Ian sat, bent forward, his elbows on his knees. An approaching policeman out on his nightly beat cast a long shadow on the pavement, but Ian was too lost in thought to notice.

'Come on now, time you were home in your bed.' The gruff voice brought him out of his reverie. 'The Sabbath already. Come along, on your feet now.' Adding, almost inaudibly, 'Damned Saturday nights.' More drunks on the street on a Saturday than the rest of the nights put together.

'I'll move when I'm ready.' Ian wanted him gone, he wanted the stillness of the deserted street.

'You'll move when I tell you. Frightened to stand up, is that it?'

'Certainly not. Not frightened of you and your lot either. I'll go home when I'm ready – and that's not yet.'

For all his burly manner, Constable Jenkins was a kindly man. This great giant of a fellow sitting hunched on the wall was sober as a judge, no doubt about that. And Alf Jenkins had seen enough villains to know that it wasn't crime that was his problem. More likely it was a lovers' quarrel.

'Nothing looks as bad by daylight. You'll see things clearer then – and so will your sweetheart, I wouldn't mind betting. Get some sleep, my old son. Haven't you got a home to go to?'

'Oh yes, I've got a home. And a wife in my bed. So you needn't concern yourself. I'll go when I'm ready.'

There had been warmth in the constable's tone, he had even looked forward to being given the chance to use his experience of life in giving advice. Even Ian's unfriendly manner didn't throw him completely off course.

'If you've had words, don't be ashamed to be the one to say sorry. Listen, fellow, I don't know anything about you and your missus, but I do know one thing. Never put off making up a bit of a quarrel. I had a wife too. Lost her back last winter. Happy together we were, not often did we have cross words. Rubbed along comfortably you might say, no ups and downs. But now it's too late I'd give a lot to be able to tell her what she meant to me. Truth to tell, I probably never gave it a thought till she was taken so suddenly. Understand what I'm trying to say to you?'

'Why don't you bugger off and leave me alone.' He heard himself say it and he was ashamed. 'Sorry, Constable. You mean kindly and I'm sorry you lost your wife, honest I am.' As if to make amends for his rudeness he got up from the wall. 'I'm going home now. Only just down the road to Mill Lane.'

'That's the way, man. Things'll look brighter by morning – and likely she's waiting for you, just as miserable as you are out here in the night.' Constable Jenkins had the last word, and took comfort from the fact that once Ian moved on towards the turning into Mill Lane, the street looked empty and trouble free. And so it should at gone twelve o'clock, Saturday evening over and finished. Time all good God-fearing men were in their beds. He watched as Ian walked away, congratulating himself that at least he'd been right on one thing – miserable the man may have been, but he certainly hadn't had a drop too many. He hoped his words had struck home to him and he'd go home and make it up with his wife, whatever the trouble had been. You don't get two chances in this life and there's nothing sadder than two people who care about each other getting out of step.

Jane was already asleep when Ian undressed and climbed into bed. It wasn't out of consideration for her that he was careful not to wake her for although, for him, sleep was nowhere within reach yet he didn't seek it in the physical exhaustion of lovemaking as he so often did. Tonight he didn't want to touch her, didn't want to think about her, didn't want to think at all. His only solace came from imagining the child she carried ... *his son* ... a replica of himself ... his hope for the future.

On the Monday morning Marcos went with the pony and trap to Millsham. Yvette's performance had been the main topic of conversation as his congregation had gathered in the churchyard after morning service the previous day, and again after Evensong. Underlying the appreciation and praise he detected disappointment on some of the men's part that she had changed her programme. But, since he hadn't been in the hall for the 'run through' no one enlarged on the subject to him.

'I enjoyed myself very much,' she told him. 'It is so long since I have sung, except when I take a bath!' The way she emphasized her words with the movement of her hand brought alive an image of her singing in her bath. His clerical collar seemed uncomfortably tight as he looked at her. She kept her eyes lowered demurely, so how was it that she was so conscious of the way his mind was going? And how was it that he felt sure her words had been intentionally provocative?

'I hope you won't take it as an imposition if, next time my wife arranges something on the same lines, she asks you to take part?'

'If you tell me the truth when you say you liked my singing, then I should be offended if you arrange all your singers and do not ask for me to come.' All said very solemnly, before her expression changed and those imps of mischief that lurked behind her eyes took over. 'And which of my songs did you prefer? The oh-so-good love song or the naughty one?'

Marcos eased his collar, knowing that she was laughing at him.

'You sang them both beautifully.'

'Which one?' Holding his gaze with hers, her voice teased him.

'For the church hall, the second one.'

She nodded, her eyes bright, her mouth smiling demurely.

'So next time you have a concert, I will sing you another oh-so-good French love song. See –' she opened the lid of the piano stool – 'I have many to choose from. You may come, if you like, and we will select one together.' He doubted if she meant it seriously, in fact he doubted if she took anything very seriously. Then she surprised him by speaking with what he was sure was complete honesty. 'It was a church hall – so different from the Café Hélène in my dear Paris – but to stand on a platform, to see people sitting there waiting. There is nothing more magic. Perhaps you understand what I mean, for does it not happen to you when you stand in your pulpit?'

'Hardly the same,' he made himself answer. But was it so different? He knew he was looked on as a good preacher, but that was surely different from being a good performer. In his mind he was climbing the steps to the pulpit, looking at the rows of people in the congregation, knowing they were waiting on his words ... were his feelings so different from hers as she stood on the platform feeling the audience's anticipation? For *her* there was no sin in enjoying the adulation of an audience ... he held his thoughts back from probing deeper.

'I came only to thank you, Mrs Bingley—'

'Yvette. Please, Yvette. And you have done more than thank me, you have said I may come again. May I give you a glass of madeira before you leave?'

'I've stayed too long already. We'll arrange another concert before autumn – Yvette.'

She watched him go, a smile playing with the corners of her mouth. She'd never been short of male admirers – before marriage and after too – but never had she seen a man as handsome as Marcos, his priest's garb somehow adding a quality of mystery to his perfect looks.

That afternoon, setting out from the vicarage with two or three calls in line, Alayne saw the Millsham tram pulling up just ahead of her. Signalling to the conductor to wait for her, she hurried and clambered up the two steep steps. The thought of a visit to Yvette was appealing.

'Mrs Bingley, I'm so glad I didn't miss you,' she called as, just after she alighted at the Millsham terminus, she saw Yvette hurrying in her direction. 'I was on my way to see you. See, I just got off the tram that's still at the terminus. Are you hurrying to catch it before it leaves?'

'I was only going into the town because the house is so quiet, so dull. I tell Matthew, to live in Millsham is like living in a – what is it he calls the place where they take the dead?'

'The cemetery?'

Yvette shook her head. 'I am so stupid, why cannot I remember the words I try to learn? Mork? Is that it?'

Alayne laughed. 'You mean the morgue. But Mrs Bingley—'

'Did I not ask you please to call me by my name, Yvette? You remember? Yvette.'

'Yvette, how can you liken Millsham to anything so cold as a morgue? It is the best area in the region.'

'It 'as no soul –' (surely she must know there was an 'h' on 'has', did she purposely say ''as', and did she purposely stress any word that was mispronounced?) – 'even when the errand boy comes by on his bicycle he is never whistling. Oh no, his jolly tune stops once he gets further than the tram terminus. He, like me, must feel there is cold here. How I do hate these hedges of laurels, and the houses all with dark and miserable paint on their wood. Yes, it is like living in a – mor – mor – no, you see I am so stupid, already I have forgot!'

A long speech, her hands moving in all directions and not an 'h' to be heard.

'The vicarage is in the middle of the noisy town. Even when I work in the garden I am aware of it. Indeed, I think to live here where it is peaceful must be lovely. But, don't misunderstand me. I am not complaining. There is only one place to find true happiness and that is within yourself. If you are lonely – and I dare say you are with your husband out all day long – then why don't you consider joining one of my working parties. You saw some of the ladies on the evening we had the "run through" of the concert.' As soon as she'd said it, Alayne wanted to recall her words. She would hate to hurt poor Yvette's feelings by reminding her of the embarrassing atmosphere in the hall that evening.

'Alayne, I am not like your so good ladies. I do not sew neat stitches, or make jam, or arrange flowers in vases. I would not fit into my place amongst them. So, why is it, I wonder, that I can talk without trouble to you?'

Ignoring the question, Alayne went on, 'Well, if you don't think you'd like the parties at the vicarage, why don't you consider helping at the infirmary, I'm sure there must be something the doctor could arrange. Or, there's the orphanage. I was told how the children loved you, wasn't it at the Christmas Party? I go in there as often as I can, usually on a Saturday afternoon. The staff there are pleased to have help. They really leave you to decide what you want to do with the children – for myself, I try to make sure they all learn to knit. So useful as they grow bigger. Of course, these are the older children, the ones who are at school each day – that's why it has to be Saturday. I take a basket of wool and plenty of needles and see they are all able to do something.' From Yvette's expression she didn't think the idea held much appeal. 'Once they get settled and their needles are clicking, I read aloud to them. You might like to read to them. My husband goes in once a week to lead the tiny ones in prayer, to try and teach them the things you'd expect them to learn from their parents, poor little darlings. He is so good with children. Dear Marcos. When I am able, I go with him to play the piano as he teaches them their hymns. I always wonder how it was that someone with a voice as good as his never wanted to learn to play an instrument. But I was saying, I go with him when I can, only it's awkward because he goes on Tuesdays and, if I'm honest, that really is the most difficult day in the week for me to manage. Or, if the orphanage doesn't appeal to you, what about visiting the women in the work-house, poor dears, all of them in such hardship—'

'If you like to suggest it to your husband' ('oosbond') '*I* could play the piano for his hymns. I should enjoy that. I am not from your Church of England, of course I am not, I am French, I was brought up in the Mother Church.'

'But you would agree to take part in his classes for the little ones? Oh, he will be so pleased when I go home and tell him. And that reminds me of my mission this afternoon: I have come especially to thank you for taking part in the concert last night. Everyone is talking about it, you really were splendid. I know Marcos will be glad when I tell him I've called to thank you. Look, the tram is still there. Why don't we ride into town together? He is going to be at home this afternoon, he has a Confirmation class as soon as the children come out of school. Come home with me and we'll tell him about your offer. He'll be delighted.'

Yvette's gingery eyes lit with pleasure at the thought of visiting the handsome priest. Or did that look of suppressed excitement come from the fact he clearly hadn't told Alayne of his visit to Millsham that morning? Her so-dull afternoon was suddenly filled with promise.

One day followed another, a week went by, then another, weeks became a month. Jane moved through the days, shopping, cleaning, cutting up some of her petticoats to make nightgowns for the baby, cutting away the turned-up hems of her skirts to use the material in expanding the waists. She filled every moment, anything rather than give the ghost of Matthew a chance to tap on her shoulder.

It was a month since she'd seen him. But where had that month got her? Nowhere. Despite all her persuasions, Ian showed no interest in her plan to set up his own cooperage and, now that they'd reached the beginning of August, she knew she must wait until after the baby arrived. Mrs Clampitt, the local midwife, had promised to come in when she went into labour.

Alice worried about her. She said as much to Matthew on one of his frequent visits. She asked no questions of either of them, but she didn't need telling that there had been more between them than the friendship that had so pleased her when first they'd met. Ever since Gerald had started his sentence, Matthew had called on her after each visit to the prison, but until that February day when Jane had arrived while he was with her, they had always been 'Dr Bingley' and 'Mrs Gregson'. That visit had been the start of the change in their relationship. Just as she had asked Jane to call her by her Christian name, so she did Matthew. She had isolation enough to bear in Brackleford, it meant a good deal to her to be accepted as their friend. Over the weeks of spring and early summer the three of them had often been together in Alice's humble villa, and she hadn't been blind to the affection that was growing between Jane and the doctor. In her opinion that handsome giant Ian Harriman was an insensitive hulk, but she wouldn't dream of saying so. She knew nothing of Matthew's marital affairs, only that he'd married a French girl ten years or so before. She'd always supposed him to be happy; sometimes he mentioned his wife, usually with a sort of tolerant amusement. So, in the early weeks of their knowing each other, her alarm bells hadn't rung as she'd seen what she supposed to be Matthew's kindness in looking after Jane's injured head, she had been glad to see they were friends.

Then she had begun to worry: it was nothing they said, yet there was no doubt in her mind that friendship became affection and, soon she realized, affection became the sort of love that could lead only to trouble. Then had come the evening of the concert. Neither that night, nor afterwards, did she say anything, but her heart had been torn with pity for them as they'd said their few words of farewell.

To Alice, Jane had become the daughter she'd never had.

It was a sultry, airless morning early in August, three or four weeks before the date the baby was due. At the time when Matthew had been treating her head wound, he had given her Mrs Clampitt's name and address and, over the last week or so, Alice had called each day to see whether there was any sign of it being time to alert the midwife.

Pushing back his chair and getting up from the breakfast table, Ian rammed his parcel of sandwiches and flask of tea into the canvas bag, then slung it on his shoulder.

'Going to be hot as hell today in that shed. All right for you, taking it easy here at home. Not for long though. You'll soon have the boy to keep you occupied.'

'Or girl,' she answered out of habit, just as she always did when he spoke with such certainty about his coming son. 'Did you hear that? I thought it was thunder. You'd better go, or you'll get soaked before you get there.' Trying to disguise the effort it took her, she stood up from the table and went with him to the front door. She forced a smile to her face as she raised it to kiss him goodbye. They touched cheeks, then he was gone, the door closed on him.

Relief flooded through her. She was alone. There was no longer any need to pretend to an energy she didn't have. The narrow flight of stairs met the passage at a right angle so now, instead of going on into the living room then through to the kitchen, she let herself sink thankfully to sit on the second stair. What a moment for a ghost from the past to catch her unprepared: could it be less than a year ago that she'd been that tall, slender girl, bursting with energy and good health? In retrospect the days had all been sunny, nights full of moonlight.

What's happened to me? I've been fit all my life. Is that why I believe I feel ill now? Less than a month and it will be over. My baby ... my own to love ... she bit hard on her trembling lip. 'So lonely,' she said aloud, not attempting to fight the break in her voice or the burning tears that stung her eyes, 'legs ache, back aches, so tired. Ashamed,' and so she was as she tasted the salt of those tears, ashamed and yet at the same time relieved to give way to her misery. 'Other women have babies, think of that jolly one at number eight, little twins to look after and she's as huge as I am. She must be tired, but I bet she doesn't cry like some stupid ninny. Can't help it. Never asks me if I'm tired ... even when I'm too sick to eat, doesn't notice ... Can't tell anyone, not even Alice. How can I? I want to love Ian like I used to – I *do* love him, of course I do. Be different when the baby comes, we'll be a proper family.' So why was she crying so uncontrollably. 'Miss him so much. He was like part of me, he understood everything without my telling him. Is he missing me? Does he wake in the night and remember. Just talked, that's all we did. Didn't even kiss me. Was he just sorry for me because of all I told him about Dad, about home? I'm just a fool. He's been married for years, he's happy with Yvette, any man would be happy with her. What's the matter with me? Can't stop crying ...'

Depressed and physically exhausted, it took all her effort to pull herself to her feet and go through to the kitchen. The sight of her reflection in the mirror hanging from the window latch did nothing to lift her spirit, but letting the tap run, she cupped the cold water in her hands and, over and over again, rinsed her face then rubbed it hard in the roller towel that hung on the larder door. That done, she didn't look at her reflection again; instead she carried the dirty plates to the sink. A handful of soda in the bowl, water from the kettle that 'sung' on the range and she attacked the washing up. Her sudden bout of crying was over, but rather than being replaced by determination and hope, she felt nothing. This was just another day, a day like yesterday, like tomorrow. She'd walk to the shops, being careful that whatever she bought to cook for when Ian came home wouldn't overstretch her budget. She'd scrub some washing, she'd prepare a meal knowing that Ian would bolt it, hardly tasting what he ate before he went, as he did every evening, to help his friend George Hamley. Was that what hurt most? That he found her such poor company he would rather be earning his ale by heaving barrels or serving in the bar at the Queen Charlotte? Today, tomorrow, next week, next year ... with her eyes closed she caressed the wriggling bulk she carried, gently rocking backwards and forwards, something akin to a smile touching her mouth.

Despite her secret outpouring of misery, or perhaps because of it, Jane dressed with even more care than usual before she sallied forth to the shops. The storm was still rumbling, occasionally seeming nearer, but still the rain didn't come and the sultry atmosphere reminded her of the greenhouse at Maybury House. Hot though it was, she had no alternative but to wear her all-enveloping cape, but she cheered herself up by taking her favourite hat from its box. Tipped forward on her head, it was made of pale fawn Italian straw, its wide brim curled and trimmed with handmade fruit and berries. This morning her mind had a will of its own, again it carried her back: she was in her father's office, returning from a shopping trip to Exeter and parading her latest creation, sure of his never-failing admiration. She remembered his teasing comment that he thought she'd emptied the fruit bowl on her head. She knew such frivolous headgear was out of place for a visit to the greengrocer (where the boxes of vegetables were put out on display on the pavement to be sniffed at and used as a 'comfort stop' for every wandering mongrel dog) and the butcher (where the floor of the shop was strewn with sawdust and everything smelled of raw meat). She took perverse pleasure in knowing it was utterly unsuitable for workaday Brackleford.

As she came to the corner of Mill Lane she heard his motor car. There were very few automobiles in Brackleford, but Matthew's certainly wasn't the only one. Even so, she knew it was his. She had listened for the sound of it too often to be mistaken. But he wasn't turning into Mill Lane; instead when he saw her coming he slowed down and stopped by the corner. An hour ago she had ached with weariness, but in that moment it was forgotten. She wanted to run towards him, she wanted to shout for joy as she saw him waiting with the door open for her to get into the car. Forgotten was her resolve that he must have no part in her life, she wasn't even conscious of how ungainly she must look blundering towards him. Then she saw that he wasn't alone. Yvette was with him.

'Jane, get in. I can take you into the town. You remember Yvette?'

Jane clutched at a dignity she didn't feel.

'Yes, of course I remember you, Mrs Bingley. Everyone who heard you sing at the church concert must remember you.'

'We are going to give you a ride, Mrs – Mrs – but I do not know. Matthew, he suddenly shout "There is Jane." So for me it will be Jane. We are going to give you a ride, Jane. Do not look so worried, three can get on this seat, is that not so, Matthew?'

'In you hop,' he told Jane.

'No, really, I can walk. Three might get in easily enough, but not when the third is *me*.'

'Wait.' Already Yvette was getting out. 'I go only as far as the orphanage. You get in first, next to Matthew, and I will be by the door.'

It was like a dream – a dream to be sitting between the two of them like a casual acquaintance or, as Yvette must see her, a stranger being offered kindness? All this time the engine had been chugging. Now Matthew pushed the gear stick forward and they started on their noisy way.

'You thought you were late, Yvette. But, see, there's the

vicar walking ahead.' He pointed to the tall, black-clad figure striding along the path, books under his arm.

'Marcos! See, I am here! I will walk with you,' she shouted as they came abreast the vicar. 'Stop the motor, Matthew. The vicar and I, we will arrive together.' To see her excitement as she climbed out of the car, she might have been going to a party instead of being part of the religious instruction Marcos had prepared for the orphans too young for school.

'Wonderful!' Was his voice just that bit too bright? 'I like us to have a chance to discuss the order before we face the children. Good morning, Doctor. And Mrs—?' He might not remember her name, but he'd not forgotten her marriage ceremony, the empty church, no one to give her away, only Alayne and the verger to sign the register. It seemed that his misgivings had been out of place. Here she was, well dressed – and what a delightful hat – soon to be a mother apparently. He sent up a silent prayer of gratitude that life had been kind to the dark-eyed girl who had looked so trustingly at the huge, hairy man Marcos had secretly considered a ruffian – then chastised himself for having harboured such an un-Christian thought. A silent prayer of gratitude was as brief as the second it took to form in his mind, then he gave all his attention to Yvette just as she'd intended.

Raising his hand in casual farewell, Matthew once again started the automobile forward. During the weeks since the concert Jane had so often found herself imagining being with him yet, now it was actually happening, the reality was mocking the dream.

'Are you going to Alice? Is that where you'd like me to take you?'

'No,' she heard her voice, 'I'm only going to the shops. You can put me down anywhere along here.' Her voice was prim, she was nothing but a pregnant housewife being given a ride out of kindness.

Without a word he drove straight through the busy little

town, past the shops, model laundry, past the manse, past Perkins Pickle Factory.

'Where are you going? Do you want to see a patient first?' How hard it was to sound casual, no more than pleasantly interested, when her heart was hammering so hard that the beat of it seemed to echo in her throat.

'I was on my way to the hospital—'

'But you passed it—'

'Jane.' His hand reached out and gripped hers. 'Have you missed me? Have you felt like I have, as if the sun has lost its warmth, as if—'

'Don't! You must think I'm a complete fool! You have a wife, the sort of woman every man must envy you. Can't you be content with that? Leave me alone, why can't you?'

The town was behind them by now as he drew up by the grassy roadside verge.

'Content? No, Jane. For ten years I honestly thought I was. Then I met you.'

'And what am I supposed to do? Throw my hat in the air and shout for joy?'

A smile tugged at the corner of his mouth. 'Don't do that, not with the masterpiece you're wearing today.' Then, seriously, 'Tell me the truth, the honest, God-fearing truth. What's between you and me is the same for both of us? Say it, Jane, just tell me ...' Did he realize how hard he was gripping her hands?

'How can I tell you if it's the same for us both. How do I know what you feel for me? I've seen you with Yvette, I've seen her with you. And you expect me to say, oh yes, yes please Matthew Bingley, I am in love with you. Well, I won't say it. I have a husband, you have a wife. And in a few weeks I shall have a baby, Ian's baby. Of course I've missed your coming to see me, I don't know many people. But it had to stop.'

Was he listening? He was certainly watching her; she felt he was looking right into her, reading her mind.

'Jane, if I never saw you again for the rest of my life,

128

nothing would alter. You're married to someone else, so am I. But we belong to each other, we are two halves of one whole, put in this world to be together . . . Romeo and Juliet—'

'Punch and Judy more likely,' she mocked, refusing to consider his words.

'You didn't give me my answer. Is it the same for you as for me?'

'Don't, Matthew, please don't. You said yourself you'd been happy with Yvette for ten years, so forgot me, be happy for the rest of your years together. How do you think we'd feel about each other if we wrecked her life – and Ian's too? Anyway, the whole thing is nonsense,' she added briskly, 'take a good look at me. Ever since you've known me I've been pregnant – and not even prettily pregnant. I've been sick and fat and—'

She saw the laughter in his eyes even before his mouth twitched with the message. Leaving go of her hands he cupped her face in his own.

'Sick and fat – and still the thought of you haunts me. Jane, Jane, say it, just once tell me the truth.'

'The God-fearing truth,' she whispered. 'Yes, I love you, Matthew. But I'm not proud of loving you. Don't those vows we made mean anything? Even to sit here together saying these things is disloyal.' She turned her head away, thankful for the restlessness of the child who stretched and strained in her. 'Just a dream, a mad, summertime dream.' And as if to orchestrate her words the sky was rent with fork lightning, followed by a loud clap of thunder. 'See, even the storm is telling us it's no use. *This* is the future for me.' She moved his hand beneath her cloak and pressed it so that he could feel the restless child.

'Dear God, if only it were me who'd given it to you.' His face was only inches from hers . . . nearer . . . who moved, did he or did she? . . . they were drawn by something too strong to be denied. Gently his mouth covered hers, then holding her close, or as close as was possible on the benchlike seat of the motor car, for both of them there was nothing but each other.

As they drew apart they avoided looking at each other, each afraid to read in the other's expression the acceptance of a future apart. For that's how it had to be. Often enough there was unfaithfulness in marriage, but theirs must never be a relationship of furtive meetings and lies. Hadn't Jane reminded him of those vows, 'Keep thee only unto him', then thinking of Yvette, 'Keep thee only unto her' as long as they should live.

The rain was beating a tattoo on the windshield of the motor car; this time it was sheet lightning that lightened the sky; thunder crashed.

'I can't turn you out into this,' he made a supreme effort for control. Later they would both remember the last precious minutes, but now they both clung to normality.

'What time are you due at the hospital?'

'What time *was* I due, you mean. They'll forgive me – I had an emergency.' He forced a laugh into his voice, it broke her heart to hear it. 'Oh, Jane, I can't bear it.' They'd parted before, on the night of the concert. But what they had said today had made it impossible for them to meet. There could be no hiding behind the pretence of casual friendship.

'We must bear it,' she breathed. 'Don't want to think ...' His arm around her, she leant against him. In a moment it would be over ... there would be nothing. 'That poor woman, bicycling in this rain.' She made a supreme effort for normality, saying the first thing that came into her head as a woman pedalled past them on her way towards the town.

'It's easing off. I'll turn around and drive to the hospital, you can wait inside while I see my two patients. Then I'll take you back to the shops.'

It would give them longer together; it would put off the moment she dreaded.

But, in the unpredictable way of English weather, the sun

found a break in the cloud and the rain stopped as suddenly as it had started just as they came towards the shops.

'Put me down along here, Matthew. I have to go to the butcher.'

He didn't argue.

'Jane, when the baby arrives – just once mayn't I come and see it?'

She nodded. Like a beggar gathering crumbs from the rich man's table, she clutched at the suggestion.

'Alice will tell you when it's born.'

Then she was on the pavement outside the butcher's, hearing the familiar sound of his motor car getting fainter, caring nothing for the interested glances of the women who, having been served, were apparently in no hurry to leave the shelter of the shop. Two of them she knew well by sight; they lived across the road from her. One a tall, purposeful-looking woman (who missed nothing and revelled in being first with any piece of news) and with her, perhaps a sister or perhaps a sister-in-law, one of indeterminable age and clearly simple. Out of habit rather than interest, Jane nodded 'Good morning', neither expecting nor receiving an answer from the first, while the second opened her mouth in an empty smile, her head nodding as if it were on a spring. Jane hardly noticed, for their reaction to any greeting was always the same. Still being served was the woman who'd passed by on her bicycle, her soaking-wet appearance evidence of her ride.

'Nasty sudden downpour,' she said as she waited for the butcher to cut her meat. Then turning to Jane, 'Not fit for a dog to be out, it wasn't. Coming down like stair rods it was when I saw you sheltering in the doctor's motor car. You wouldn't have noticed me, too occupied.'

'Yes I did,' Jane answered, too politely to give the woman the satisfaction she'd hoped for. 'You looked drenched and no wonder.'

The Mill Lane gossip-gatherer had been listening with interest. Now she gave Jane what she supposed passed as a smile and, for the first time in all the months they been neighbours, actually spoke to her.

'Shame if he was taking you for a drive, shame it turned nasty like it did.'

Jane looked from one to the other of them, aware of the silent workings of their minds, hating them for it, hating everyone. No, that wasn't true, a silent joyous voice clamoured. Nothing could take it from her ... nothing ... no one ... With a hand that shook, she unclipped her chain purse and took out a threepenny piece.

'I'll have six ounces of liver please, Mr Burgess.'

Apparently the women already knew each other. She was aware that, as the bedraggled one took her parcel and moved away from the counter, their whispers were aimed at her. She despised their small-mindedness, but it had no power to hurt her. Then one of them spoke more loudly. Purposely loudly, she was sure.

'I've been lucky, Bert is happy enough with my company. A glass or two on Saturday, but any man earns that. But every night ... I watch him set out, could put my clock right by him.'

'She's a bit of a goer, that ginger-topped daughter. Only got to look at her to know she'd be a rare one for a bit of fun.' That from the cyclist.

'Fun! Perhaps that's all it is. But I have m' doubts. More than the ale he goes there for from what I've heard. Not that Bert is what you might call a regular except, like I say, of a Saturday.'

'Men are men, not only their thirst needs satisfying. And as things are now – well, a flighty bit like that just fits the bill.'

All in loud whispers, whispers that filled the small shop.

'Come on now, ladies, rain's all but over. You want to get home before the next lot.' The butcher had heard every word and, himself a drinker at the Queen Charlotte, the meaning wasn't wasted on him. Too bad of them to behave like it, getting their pleasure from wicked, malicious gossip; you wouldn't hear a man talking like it in front of the young lady.

They moved out to the street, but as her friend positioned herself to hop on to her bicycle, the one from Mill Lane had the last word delivered with a raucous laugh.

'Fit the bill you say? Ain't the bill he'll be looking to fit.' Neither of them took any notice of the simple woman who looked from one to the other, only half understanding but wholly uncomfortable. 'Come on now, Florrie, wake up, do. We've still got shopping to do.'

Although the storm had rolled away and the downpour was over, a light rain warned them they might not have seen the last of it. As Jane came out of Mr Burgess's shop, she unpinned her hat and took it off. She knew they were watching, but her hat was more important than their silly sniggers. So she held it beneath her cloak. 'Don't want that pile of fruit to go rotten in the rain,' she could almost hear her father's laugh.

That evening she was alone when she heard a timid tap on the front door. Before she could stop it her imagination ran away with her, just as it used to in the days when she'd looked for word from her father. Now, it wasn't Amos she thought of as she hurried to open the door to her visitor. Matthew ... please, let it be Matthew ... but he's at home with his wife ... but, perhaps ... please ... I know it won't be Alice ... no one else would come ... One thought after another crowded her head as she hurried down the narrow passage. Then she found herself face to face with the simple woman who'd smiled at her in the butcher's.

'She don't know I come.' Her visitor looked furtively first one way, then the other. 'She'd be wild with me if she knew.'

'You wanted to talk to me? You'd better come in.'

Chapter Seven

What a difference she had made to his visits to the orphanage. Watching the group of tiny children gathered around Yvette, Marcos knew they were drawn to her by something more than the bag of humbugs she was passing round. Whatever her magnetism, it was felt by the children and, more, much more, it was felt by him.

'Now, you have a sucker in your mouth, so run back into your circle and sit down on the floor. While you suck, you will listen to the things Reverend Warburton is going to say to us. See, I will listen too.' And with the easy grace of a child she dropped to the ground, crossed her legs (her ankles demurely covered by the moss green voluminous skirt of her suit), and, sitting very straight, fixed her gaze on Marcos.

Sucking, scrunching, the visits of the vicar and the jolly lady with such a funny voice was the young orphans' favourite hour of the week. They'd always looked forward to the tall man with the black dress (as they thought of his cassock) coming to tell them stories, or teach them songs – only he didn't call them songs, he called them hymns and it was hard to remember the words. Sometimes a pretty lady had come with him to play the piano, and she was always kind. But she'd never brought humbugs, humbugs so big that they lasted almost all the time he was talking.

'Later on we're going to teach you a new hymn,' he

started, not seeming to mind a bit about the way they smacked their lips on the glorious sweet morsels, 'but it's no use our singing it if we don't understand what the words mean. Now, who do you think it is makes the flowers grow?'

'Mr Hobday,' an almost-old-enough-for-school voice answered. 'Outside Miss Brown's window, that's where he does them.'

'Yes, I've seen them there – and I've seen Mr Hobday working on the flower bed. He puts the young plants into the earth, sometimes I expect he puts water on them – although the water that does them most good comes from the rain. And, you know, no matter how hard Mr Hobday tries, no matter how hard any person tries, without God there would be nothing. For it's God who makes the good earth, it's He who makes the flowers to form, it's He who sends the rain to make them grow – and most of all, it's He who sends the sunshine that brings warmth to the earth. And do you know what else? This is not so easy to explain to you, but I'll do my best. I want you to imagine a tiny baby, one just new to the world. It's had no time to be tempted to do anything bad – and we all know how hard it is sometimes to do what we know is right, don't we? But that tiny baby – each one of you not so many years ago, Mrs Bingley here and me too once upon a time, is born with something of God in its spirit.' Encouraged by the humbugs, they were happy enough to listen to him, but from their blank expressions he knew there was a vast difference between listening and even half understanding. He tried again. 'A baby can't speak, can't think – and yet that – that – pure goodness that comes from God is part of it. Just like the seeds that get planted in the earth, so that new baby grows – as you're growing. And do you remember what makes the plants grow and the flowers bloom?'

''Spect it's the rain and the sunshine. But we don't grow tall if we stand in the rain.' Clearly the little redhead with her cheek bulging with humbug she was trying to make last was trying to trip him up.

'No. We grow and stay healthy because of the food we eat. Even that sweet you're sucking gives you sugar as well as a nice taste. And what makes the sugar plants grow? Rain and sunshine. Who sends us rain and sunshine?'

The redhead knew when she was beaten.

'God. But mister – um – Mr Vicar – there's a picture of him on the stairs, he looks like an old man with a verrry' (how else could she emphasize what she was saying?) 'long white beard.'

For a second Marcos looked at Yvette, not a flicker of a smile on her face yet he was sure there was mischief dancing behind her eyes as she watched him, waiting to see how he'd cope.

'Some people find it hard to understand, they need pictures of *people* – God looking like an old man in a nightshirt, angels like fat babies with wings, the Devil a sort of ogre with horns. How could we draw a picture of what I've been telling you about? We couldn't. Your soul isn't something anyone can see, it's the way we feel. It's the part of God that lives in every one of us. It's there because God loves every one of us, not just *people*, as if we are all the same; but every one of us, just as we are. But what we have to watch out for is not to let the Devil tempt us into doing things we know are mean and unkind, things that would make someone who loves us unhappy.' He knew Yvette didn't take her gaze off him. He knew that in talking to the children as he was, he was taking the coward's way. Even without looking at her he was sure that she knew the battle within his own soul. Week after week they were together, amongst children she displayed the innocence of a child. Yet in her eyes he read another message, one that haunted him. 'Almost time for the hymn, Mrs Bingley. When you're ready.'

As nimbly as any of those children, she stood up.

'Whenever it is that you are ready' (Alayne would have heard her accent as unnecessarily pronounced, but to Marcos it was just one more thing that set his pulses racing), 'then you find me willing.'

'Yes ... well ... I just want to go back one moment to what we were saying about plants needing sunshine to make them turn into flowers. So it is that all of us – you, me, Mrs Bingley, every single person – has to be like a ray of sunshine, a sunbeam. Sometimes it would be much easier to be mean and say nasty things, or even to steal from each other or fight; that's when the Devil is tempting us, trying to make a dirty smear on the soul that had been pure and perfect when we were born. Every time we fight that temptation, then we bring a ray of golden sun into the world. Now, I will sing the hymn for you; listen carefully to the words so that when we sing it together you will understand. All right, Mrs Bingley.'

Yvette didn't just play the hymn tune as Alayne always had. She was a musician. As a background to his final words as he led up to the hymn she had improvised, softly playing variations on the tune. And all the time, she had watched him. Not only watched, but let her mind have free rein. Despite his English-sounding name, his family roots had never grown in cold English soil. Italian perhaps, or from her own beloved France. But it was more than his handsome face and tall, upright figure that attracted her. Life in Brackleford was so very dull, even the men knew nothing of the rules of the games she played. They were as buttoned up as their frumpy wives. Remember the way they'd drooled at the 'run through' of the concert, but come face to face with one of them and he wouldn't have known what to do! But what about Marcos? Oh, yes he would know. Yet not once had he given her what those men in the church hall would consider to be a 'naughty' glance. She thought of Alayne's confidences and she knew, even though there was never a glance or a word from him to tell her, just how he fought the battle with his conscience. Yes, Marcos was a challenge – and she'd never been beaten by a challenge yet.

Now, taking the note from her introductory chord, he started to sing.

On the floor, with nothing left of their humbugs but a tantalizingly sweet minty taste in their mouths, the group of little girls in their ill-fitting grey orphanage dresses, listened as he sang. The verse ended, his fine baritone ringing out in the pledge: 'A sunbeam, a sunbeam, I'll be a sunbeam for Him.'

Then, repeating a line at a time, they all sang it together. Unsure of the tune, sometimes getting the words wrong, but there was no doubt the little girls were full of good intentions. His lesson had not been in vain – at least for the time being! Clearer than all their voices, Marcos heard Yvette's husky tones. A sunbeam ... the glory of love is the glory of life ... it wasn't the words that spoke to him, those husky tones needed no words. Against his will he turned to look at her. The children were forgotten, Alayne was forgotten ... the glory of love ... A sunbeam, a sunbeam, came the unmusical childish voices, pure, off key, innocent.

Another ten minutes and they were out in the street in the midst of busy mid-morning Brackleford. The storm had gone; the wet road shone in the sunshine; steam rose from the dripping awnings.

'Are you in a rush? If you have time we could take the tramcar to Millsham. I have music of some songs—'

He didn't want to listen to her telling half truths in her effort to persuade him, better not to hear than to pretend.

'I've nothing to rush for. Alayne is at the workhouse. She is incredible in all she does. Today she was shopping on the way, then she's working with the women in the kitchen, encouraging them to make a good wholesome meal. Then – and this is what makes her so different from most of us – instead of going home and sitting at her own table, she will stay and share the meal with them.' Standing very still, he looked directly at her. 'We talk of saints – but what can anyone do more than give all that they are, every hour of their time, to caring for others?'

'But yes, do I not agree with you, Marcos? Alayne is a

truly *good* woman.' Then, a chuckle bubbling up from some inner joke: 'Me? I am more mortal. No man will ever liken Yvette to a saint, not so much as a minor saint. If I am to be a sunbeam, then I fear my warmth will never be felt by the poor souls in the workhouse. Quick, across the road, here comes the tram.'

No more was said until journey's end at the terminus at Millsham. Then, setting off by his side, she told him, 'Knitting for the poor, helping the workhouse people, your beautiful Alayne she is a golden sunbeam, she casts her light on so many. My ray of light does not shine on those things. But it has warmth. There are many ways of finding happiness. *N'est-ce pas?*'

'You bring happiness to those poor little souls in the orphanage.' He clutched at his fast-disappearing hold on normality.

'We do, don't we?' Surely there was nothing of the seductress in that open, laughing smile she gave him? 'You and me too. That is because we are enjoying ourselves. And surely that is the warmest sunbeam of them all.'

Jane led the way along the passage into the living room, her visitor shuffling behind her.

'Like I said, she'd be that wild,' the poor woman repeated. 'But I ain't gonna listen to her saying things like that about Elsie. It wasn't right what she said. You heard her – that's why she said it, so that you would hear.'

'About Elsie? Elsie who?'

'If she walked by she'd see me through the window. She's gone off to see her dad, down Foundry Lane he lives. Said she'd be gone all evening, but if he's out then back she'll come and find me not there.' For all her anxiety, the woman's round face remained blank; the only sign of her nervousness was the way she twisted her white and newly ironed handkerchief in her hands. The sight of that clean handkerchief touched Jane with pity. Didn't it show how the poor, muddled soul had seen her visit as important.

'If you'd rather, we could go and talk in the kitchen. Then no one can see. I don't know your name. What can I call you?'

'Florrie.' Already she was backing towards the kitchen, her mouth falling open into a smile.

'You wanted to tell me something. About Elsie, was it?'

Florrie set her head nodding.

'Bit of a goer, that's what she said, you heard her. The ginger-headed one, anything for fun.'

'But I don't know Elsie. I don't know anyone with ginger hair even.'

'No, course you don't. It's him what knows her. He's no good to her, he don't make her happy. She shouldn't have said those things, they were lies. It's me what knows Elsie, not her. Just because I don't think quick like she does, she reckons I don't know what she's on about. But she can't go about saying things like that about Elsie. She's a good girl. Little love she always was.' This time when her mouth opened into a smile, the vacant expression was overtaken by a look of real love. 'When she was little they used to let me take her out. Oh, but she was – she was—' Lost for the right word, she looked helplessly at Jane.

'You really loved her,' Jane prompted. 'Is she still a child? No, she can't be . . .'

'You heard what Dorrie said about her, you know she's a woman now. But she's still *good*, it's wicked to say she's a goer as if she chases after the men. That's what our Dorrie meant. She ought to be struck down, talking like it. Always ready for a laugh, always ready for a bit of fun, that's how Elsie is. Oh, I can't tell you – I just ain't got the words to tell you what a – a – what a darling girl she is. Looks after George good as gold too.'

'You musn't worry about what your sister – is she your sister? – said about her. I didn't even notice, I was thinking of someone else.'

The round head nodded excitedly. 'Thinking about that nice doctor with the motor car I wouldn't wonder.' There was nothing malicious in the statement. In fact Florrie appeared rather pleased with herself that she had contributed anything so intelligent to the conversation.

'Thinking about what I had to buy for dinner,' Jane corrected her, less than truthfully. 'I'm sure you know more about this girl Elsie than your sister does anyway.'

'She's good as an angel. Well, if she wasn't she would have sent him packing when he went off to see to things for his mother, then came back saying he was marrying you.'

The pieces of the jigsaw fell into place. The hours Ian spent at the Queen Charlotte, the way he went off so readily each evening, so often coming home moody and depressed.

'You thought he was going to marry Elsie?' Treading carefully, Jane's manner was friendly, gentle.

'Course I did. My little Elsie, she always talked to me. Mostly there's just a lot of men there at the pub, and she don't get much time to make friends, her with her pa to look after and that bar to help with. But me, she knows I'm always there to listen. Chatter away, she used to. She knows I never tittle-tattle, she knows I like to listen to her and – well, she's my same little darling. Too good for him, too good for any of them. And she could have had plenty more, but never cared about anyone but him.'

'Ian?'

'Course I'm telling you about Ian. So you know now. I've said what I came for. You know that Dorrie didn't have no call to say things like she did about Elsie. A bit of fun, oh yes, if ever a girl loves a laugh it's my Elsie. But a goer? That was a wicked thing to call her.'

'You think she still loves Ian?'

'She don't change like the way of the wind, not Elsie.'

'Does she still talk to you, Florrie?'

'About her and him?' Her pale blue, round eyes filled with tears. 'Cried she did. Walking down there by the mill stream we were. Cried ever so, made me cry too. Wicked things he did letting you steal him off her, he should have

141

known it's not money that matters, it's love. If they'd got wed a bit sooner, then she would have gone with him to see to his ma's things, then he wouldn't have got – got – what did my Elsie call it – yes, I remember – bewitched, that's it, bewitched with your fancy ways.' Proud of her effort, she carefully refolded her twisted handkerchief and put it in her pocket. It seemed, her mission accomplished, she was ready to leave.

'And what about now?' Jane felt mean, leading the poor simple woman on to talk, 'Is he still bewitched? Did Elsie tell you that?'

Florrie looked puzzled. The conversation seemed to have left her behind.

'With me,' Jane smiled gently. 'Is he still bewitched with me? What does Elsie tell you about now?'

'I said. She cried fit to hurt herself. Even when her ma died, or when he told her him and you were getting wed and going back to that place you came from, even then she never cried like she did that day by the stream. She's brave, brave as a lion. When he told her he'd changed his mind about her, she held her chin up like a soldier. But now all that's changed. It's her he wants. Love, that's what he calls it. But she's a good girl, I told you. Poor little soul she is. Every night when I kneel and say my prayers I ask that she'll be happy. Doesn't seem to do one bit of good.' Two big tears rolled down her cheeks.

'You're a good friend to her, Florrie.' Jane wanted her gone and yet she was torn with pity for Florrie's innocent, outspoken love for Elsie Hamley, probably the only person who made her feel necessary. 'We won't tell anyone that you've been to see me – not Dorrie, not Elsie, not Ian. It'll be our secret. But I'll remember what you said and, honestly, I shan't give a thought to what Dorrie said about her. It's you who are her friend, you who know all about her.' The folded handkerchief had been brought out of Florrie's pocket and had blotted away her tears; now, hearing Jane's words, they were forgotten. 'Florrie, you'd better go, I'll look out and make sure the coast is clear if you like. And thank you for telling me.'

Florrie's head nodded vigorously; she looked at Jane with her vacant, unblinking stare while her mouth opened in a beam.

'Wicked of her it was to say things like it. But now I told you.'

The street was empty. Jane watched as she plodded across, ducking under a line of washing that had been hung out the previous afternoon by the occupant of No. 9, had dried in the night, only to be soaked again by the morning's storm and, wet or dry, was going to hang for another night. Then she closed the door and for the second time that day slumped to sit on the second stair.

How much could she believe? Florrie was a simple-minded woman whose love for Elsie Hamley wouldn't allow her to see any wrong in her. For herself, it mattered nothing what sort of a woman Elsie was. But how much did she want to believe? Bewitched by her, bewitched by her lifestyle, expected by marrying her he would be sharing it. Had he ever loved her? Loved her for herself? And what about her? Had it ever been *love*, real love, she'd felt? ('Two halves of one whole,' she seemed to hear Matthew's voice.) Leaning back, her elbows on the third stair, her eyes closed, she made herself remember those first weeks with Ian. Him kneeling over her, both of them naked, both of them driven by intoxicating desire. Both of them? Or had it been only her? Would his sexual appetite have been any different had she been some other woman? Willingly, eagerly, she had let him arouse her passion until she had cried out for more. Night after night she had gloried in the frenzied journey of desire and fulfilment; she had believed it had been the same for them both, that for both of them there had been nothing but each other. Before he'd come to Deremouth had he carried ginger-haired Elsie to those heights of rapture? And now? What was he doing each evening at the Queen Charlotte? Had he ever been there out of friendship for her father, or right from the start had it been Elsie?

Opening her eyes, she sat up straight, her hands returning the pressure of the precious child that moved within her. ('I wish to God it were me who had given it to you,' again that voice.) If only it were ... if only ... Then, she pulled her mind back to the reality she had to face. What if at this very moment he was with Elsie, rampant, driven by desire – did she care? She faced the truth – and she wasn't proud. Whatever Ian did, he had no power to hurt her. So, whose fault had it been that he had gone back to his one-time love? For weeks, for months even, she had been so determined to make her marriage a success; but, if she'd still loved him, would it have been such a conscious effort? The baby would bring them close again, wasn't that what she'd been telling herself?

Her mind was racing ahead. What was she doing here, there was nothing of *her* in this miserable hovel. Oh, there could have been. If only her dream had had substance, poverty wouldn't have defeated her. What if she'd never met Matthew – two halves that make one whole – supposing her life had been nothing except the poverty and drudgery that was her share of the union of marriage? Perhaps she would have accepted. But Matthew could have nothing to do with the decision she was making as she struggled to her feet and started to climb the stairs. There can never be any future with Matthew, stop thinking about him, stop remembering, stop dreaming. Just be calm, you've made up your mind, take it one step at a time. No future with Matthew – no, and certainly no future with Ian. The baby – Ian's baby – no, the baby is mine, just mine, part of me. Soon it'll be here, warm, dependent. I won't fail it, I swear I won't.

He won't be back yet. What's he doing now, I wonder? Begging poor Florrie's Elsie to take him to her bed? How much do I care? Truly? As if she'd get nearer the truth if she asked the question of her reflection, she stared at the woman in the bedroom mirror. I care that I was fool enough not to see he saw me as a foothold into an easy life. Dad knew – and I wouldn't listen. But of course I wouldn't. And now? I can't go back there and say he was right and I was wrong. It's Dad's fault I can't go back. Why couldn't he have loved me enough to be there for me now? He didn't have to accept us back in Deremouth, he didn't have to come here if he didn't want to; but, if he'd cared enough, surely he could have answered my letters, surely he could have written to say something about my baby? It was the last that hurt more than anything. Her baby, his grandchild, yet he still maintained that stubborn silence.

The cabin trunk that Dulcie had sent to her was kept under the bedroom window, covered with a worn blanket. As she'd let her thoughts ramble, she'd pulled off the blanket and opened the lid. Now, from where they hung in the cupboard, she took the clothes she could no longer get into and packed them. Then, for more immediate use, just as she had when she left Maybury House, she packed the hamper she would carry. Tonight she would go to Alice. Tomorrow her mind would be clearer: by then she would have a plan. Tonight she knew only that she had to get away from this house she'd come to hate. Never again would she lie in bed hearing him come home from 'helping George', sometimes hardly saying a word, sometimes turning to her to find satisfaction for the sexual hunger that she suspected had been aroused by Elsie. Over the last few weeks he had been careful of the baby, *his son*, but there had been other ways of reaching his goal and sending him to sleep. Well, tonight he'd find her gone, his bed would be empty.

Her packing was nearly done, when although it wasn't even ten o'clock, she heard the front door slam. He was home! Facing him with her decision hadn't been part of her plan and, realizing it, she was ashamed. Head high, she walked down the stairs and followed him into the living room.

'You're earlier than usual.' Just so many words, something

to hide behind while she found her courage.

'Well? Any objection?' She knew the signal: he was looking for an argument. So often she'd blamed herself when he'd come home in these moods, always conscious of her failings. Tonight her eyes were opened. She was only a part player, the woman who had bewitched him with wealth she didn't possess.

'No, I suppose I'm glad. I can tell you directly. Letters are a coward's way.'

'What the hell riddles are you talking now?'

'I'm going away. Don't pretend you'll miss me—'

His expression was changed by the hope that had been dormant so long.

'You're telling me your old man has sent for you? After all this time is he wanting you to go back to have the baby born there? So what about me? Why just you? I'm your husband.'

It sickened her to see his outward change of mood as that old hope flickered into life.

'I'm going, Ian. I'm leaving you. And I haven't heard from Dad, that's not why I'm going.'

In an instant hope was gone. What she saw in its place was ugly. She'd seen it happen to him before, as if he were possessed by some inner devil. The corners of his mouth were twitching as he lost control.

'Just you listen to me,' his voice was getting louder by the word, 'you're going *nowhere*. Your job is to give me my son, you hear me. Then it's to look after him. Why the hell can't you behave like other women? What sort of a wife do you call yourself? Fancy yourself too good, is that it?'

'Oh, why can't you be honest for once? Marriage should not be like this. What have we in common? Nothing. If we had, you wouldn't go every night to the Queen Charlotte. You've more in common with Elsie Hamley. Why didn't you marry her? Tell me the truth. No! You've lied to me too often. I'll tell you. Even in Deremouth when you

146

pretended it was *me* you wanted, it was a lie. What you wanted was what you believed I had. Then you found I had nothing – nothing but a stupid, girlish infatuation. Well, no one could live this life and keep any girlish illusions—'

'You bitch!' Breathing heavily he lunged towards her.

'Don't you dare touch me.' Instinctively she held her hands as if to protect the baby. 'If you hurt my baby—' He was shaking her so that her words were hardly audible. 'You're not sane!' What made her say it? Was it the wild look in his eyes? Was it the memories that haunted her of other scenes where he'd ended sobbing for forgiveness? Or was it sheer fright that made her say the first thing that came into her head?

'Bitch! Bitch!' With his left fist he punched her chest, with his right hand he hit her head so that she reeled under the force of the blow. Then again, this time his right fist sent her stumbling backwards.

'I'm master here!' She heard his voice as if it were coming to her from far away as her legs gave way under her and she crumpled heavily to the ground. 'You hear me ...'

'No, no ... going ... going away ...' Did she actually say the words, or did they get no further than a silent prayer in her heart? If in saying he was insane she had expected to goad him into finding his control, then immediately she saw her mistake. She'd collapsed on to her knees. Now brutally he pushed her backwards so that she was lying on the linoleum-covered floor. She saw what he was doing, she made a supreme effort to scream at him, to stop him, but as he unbuttoned his trousers and forced her legs apart she fell from hell into unconsciousness.

Ian cared nothing for her sudden silence, he didn't seem aware of it. That evening in the sitting room above the bar, Elsie had held his head to her soft, white breasts. Driven by desire he'd moved his hands up her leg, he'd felt the plump flesh beyond her stocking tops; she'd guided him to touch her, she'd sighed and moaned with delight as his fingers

147

had probed. Only then had she pulled back. He seemed to hear her voice echoing in his head, telling him she wanted him more than anything in the world, she wanted to be his, she wanted to be the woman who bore his child. Passion roused, terrified of pregnancy, they had looked at each other in frustration and misery. Then, hating Jane for the hold she had on his life, he had left Elsie still rebuttoning her blouse and straightening her clothes. Tonight they couldn't bear to be together and they couldn't bear to be apart. So, with his eyes closed, all his weight on unconscious Jane, his fantasies were of Elsie. Thrusting deep, he wanted to reach the son, the son that should have been his and hers. When he'd pushed Jane backwards to the ground and forced himself on to her, he had been following animal instinct that gave him superhuman strength. But in less than a minute it was over, reality brought him back to some sort of sanity. Lying heavily on her, his body shook with sobs.

'Shouldn't have let me,' he blubbered accusingly, 'might have hurt the boy. Oh God, don't let us have hurt the boy. Wake up, can't you. Jane ... Jane ...' He rolled off her, suddenly frightened by her deathly pallor, by the trickle of dribble that escaped her mouth and ran down the side of her face. Supposing she's dead? 'Jane! Wake up, Jane! Think of the boy. You were going to take him away from me. Bitch.' Talking to himself, gulping on the sobs he could no more control than a few minutes before he could have stopped himself from raping her, he stood looking down helplessly at her still form.

Help, that's what he needed. He must go to a neighbour and get help. Yes, but what if they knew he'd forced himself on her? With his returning sanity came cunning as he decided on the tale he'd tell. He straightened her tumbled skirts and put a cushion under her head.

'Evening.' His next-door neighbour answered his pounding knock. 'What's the trouble old son?' For clearly something was very much the matter.

'It's my wife. She fainted. Went down a hell of a crack.

I've put a cushion under her head, tried to bring her round. Can't. Must get a doctor.' Supposing the doctor said she was dead! No wonder he blubbered as he blurted out his story.

'Steady now, lad. I'll come and take a look with you. And Jess, she'll come. Near her time like she looks to be, I expect your missus would rather have a woman there to help her.'

Jess came willingly. The fact that tomorrow she would have a tale to tell might have influenced her, but beneath that was a natural kindness for one of her own sex. Perhaps she ought to help Mrs High and Mighty to bed; she wouldn't be surprised if by morning the baby was here. But one look was all it took for them to know, Jane was no case for the local midwife. Mrs Clampitt had seen many babies into the world, but she needed the mother's help to do it. This soon-to-be-mother looked as if she was about to lift the veil and disappear into the next world.

The neighbour wheeled his bicycle from the front passage where it lived and pedalled as fast as he could to the doctor's house in the Market Square. He gave his message to the maid who opened the door to his urgent knock.

'Dr Smedley's been called away. Best you come in. I've been told that if a doctor is needed I have to call on the telephone. Doctor has a telephone here in the hall, see?' Full of importance at her knowledge in using the instrument she lifted the earpiece and turned a handle to alert someone at the exchange, then in loud precise tones asked for Brackleford 204.

'This is Dr Smedley's house speaking.' She nodded as she said it, as if to give emphasis to the importance of her call. 'There's someone in trouble at No. 4 Mill Lane.' Each syllable was shouted into the speaker. 'Had a fall, lying unconscious. Man here says doctor is needed quickly.' Then, replacing the earpiece she turned with a smirk of pride. 'There now, that should get it sorted.' And Jess's

149

husband, Claud, felt something of the same satisfaction as he rode back to Mill Lane.

While they'd waited for the doctor Jane lay motionless, her quick shallow breathing her only sign of life, only once crying out. The other three listened for the doctor to arrive and, when he did, Jess had a feeling of satisfaction of her own. That the one to be sent should be Matthew Bingley would add colour to her account in the morning. But, she found, that was only the beginning. The best was still to come.

As he held his stethoscope to listen first to Jane's heart and then to the baby's, Jane opened her eyes.

'Matth . . .'

'You're going to be all right, Jane. I'm going to take you to hospital.' Whispering to her, just to her. Whoever heard of a doctor behaving like it. It was her husband he ought to have been explaining things to. Instead of that he and Jane might have been the only two there. And not once did she take her eyes from him. And that poor husband of hers, shaking like a leaf, being ignored by the pair of them. 'The baby's on its way, I'll take her in my motor car, it'll be quicker than waiting for the ambulance. Help me lift her.' This to Ian as he gathered Jane into his arms and, still kneeling, raised her from the ground. Only then did he pass her to Ian, hearing her whimper of fear and protest. Immediately he was on his feet. 'Back to me,' he ordered. 'Get me a blanket or something to wrap around her.'

'Oh, dear me, just look at that!' Jess pointed to the wet patch on the floor. 'Baby's on its way,' She'd had four herself, she knew the signs. 'Poor soul, falling like that must have started her off. With the waters gone, baby can't be long.'

Still holding Jane, Matthew sank to sit on the arm of the chesterfield while he waited for Ian to come back with the blanket he'd stripped from their bed. She was heavy, but he'd seen the look on her face when briefly he'd passed her to Ian.

A sudden gasp from her, a tensing of her muscles, then her eyes were wide open.

'Matth-ew. Ahhh, oh . . .'

'It's all right, it's the baby starting,' he rocked her gently. 'Just grip my arm when it hurts. Once I get you to the hospital it'll soon be over.' His soft voice was aimed at giving her confidence. Then, to Ian, 'Go ahead of us to the automobile, hold the door wide open so that I can get her in without hurting her.'

'What about me? I want to know about the—'

With Jane wrapped in the blanket and deposited on the front seat, Matthew was already cranking the engine into life. Only that morning he had assured her that three could ride on that seat, but not now.

'Plenty of time for you to get to the hospital. Say you want Ward D. Any nurse will be able to tell you how far she's got.'

Even as he spoke he started the car forward. At a sound from Jane he reached out his hand to her, felt her vice-like grip, felt her nails cutting into his palm, heard her deep, gasping breaths. Then, gradually her grip slackened, the pain had eased.

'It's stopped hurting,' she told him as he drew up in front of the gaunt hospital building. 'I can walk in.' It may have stopped hurting, but he knew from her voice just how frightened she was. Never had she known anyone who'd been having a baby and even though children swarmed the street to play in Mill Lane, none of their mothers had told her anything to prepare her. Was it natural to hurt like she had, so suddenly? And why was her skirt soaking wet? 'Has something gone wrong? Matthew, I don't know what's natural? I don't know what to expect.'

'Nothing has gone wrong, darling. It will hurt you, hurt worse than anything you've ever felt. But not for long. Then it'll be over and you'll have your baby.'

Her mind hung on to that one word, 'darling'.

*

The only sound in the hospital corridor was the hiss from the gas light. For hours Ian had waited, hours that seemed like eternity. His ears were alert for the sound of a newborn baby. Then, out of the dusky shadows he saw the white-clad form of a nurse.

Immediately he was on his feet.

'Is it over? Why did she take so long?'

'Had a hard time has she? I've only just come on duty, I don't know anything of the case. But they sent me to say the sister needs to have a word. Follow me, I'll show you where her office is.'

Up one corridor, down another, his boots ringing out on the stone floor as he followed the rubber-soled, stiffly starched figure. Other women had babies, had them at home sometimes without so much as a midwife. Why couldn't Jane be like everyone else? All these hours, even though it had seemed the boy was well on his way before she even got here. Was Jane so frightened of pain that she couldn't find the courage to help the poor little bastard into the world? And why should the sister want him? Did she deliver the news to every new father? But in his heart he knew that wasn't why he'd been sent for. Jane ... she'd made fuss enough these last months, hardly eaten enough to nurture the boy, always tired, often sick.

'Mr Harriman,' the elderly nursing sister smiled kindly at him, at the same time dismissing the nurse. 'I'm afraid I have sad news for you ...'

Chapter Eight

Like a man in a trance, Ian walked down the four steps
from the main entrance of the hospital, out into the silence
of night. Day or night, streets empty or crowded with shop-
pers, he was aware of none of it. Never in his life had he
experienced such a feeling of rage, hatred and despair,
something of all of them. There was nothing sane or
reasonable in his emotions. As he walked blindly towards
Mill Lane he moaned like a sick animal.

His boy, his son . . . even in that she'd cheated him. But
then, hadn't she always?

'Let me see him! He's *my* son, you can't stop me seeing
him.' He hadn't realized what a giant he had appeared as he
stood glaring at the sister, his stance defying her to thwart
him. 'You say he was stillborn. But he was moving, he was
strong. What have you done with him?' He hadn't even
known that his voice had risen dangerously.

'It was a breech birth, and the child was in a hurry to get
born. Unfortunately he was strangled by the umbilical cord.
It's rare, but I have known it happen before. I am truly
sorry.' The sister recognized trouble when she saw it
coming, and she knew there was no way of placating 'the
poor, distressed man'.

'What have you done with him? I'm going to see him.
You can't stop me seeing him.'

'I'll have a nurse see to him. While you're waiting you

can have a just a quick moment with your wife. But only a moment. She needs to rest, but she may do that more easily once you've shared the disappointment.'

'I want the boy. I'll wait here.' He remembered being left alone, slumping into a chair. Never had he known such desolation. How long he waited he had no idea, but at last a nurse had fetched him and he'd been taken to a cubicle where, lying on a couch which had been covered with protective paper, had lain the perfectly formed, lifeless baby who'd been born before his time. His skin and lips were so pale they seemed tinged with blue; this was his son. He'd heard the sound of the door closing behind the retreating nurse. He'd touched the minute hand, a hand with no warmth. He remembered seeing a drop of water fall on the tiny naked chest and, as he'd wiped it away, realizing it was his own tear. Then, he'd turned and left.

'I'll take you to your wife.' The nurse had been waiting in the corridor with her instructions. Had he even answered? Probably not. All he could remember was the sound of his hobnailed boots on the stone-flagged floor as he'd retraced his steps back to the corridor where he'd waited for what had seemed eternity, waited eagerly, never doubting. 'The boy,' he'd said so often – and always Jane's reply had been the same, 'Or the girl.'

Something between a smile and sneer crossed his handsome face. 'Serves her right, the bitch. Serves her bloody right.' He said it aloud, but there was no one in the empty street to hear him. At the sound of his voice a sob caught his breath. 'My boy. She couldn't even do that, couldn't even carry him till he was ready.'

Blindly he walked through the sleeping town, the silence only broken by his hobnails ringing on the pavement and his occasional whimpering moan. He came to the Market Square, eerie in the starless night, the ray of light from a single gas lamp emphasizing ghostly shapes of the fountain flanked by two iron seats. What was he doing here? He must have walked the length of the High Street, gone past the end of Mill Lane without so much as noticing where he was. He ought to go home. Back to a house that was empty of hope. Remembering the scene when he came home from being with Elsie, remembering how Jane had said she was going to leave him, remembering his fear that she was taking his son away from him, he heard his own rasping sobs. No one knew, *no one*, not even Elsie, knew how his thoughts and hopes had focused on his boy. He couldn't remember his own father, but he'd known exactly the bond that would exist between the child and himself. Jane wasn't important – had she ever been important? She'd impressed him with all her fine living and when it came to the point she had nothing. She'd thrown herself at him, inveigled him into marrying her when her father had thrown her out! Now what had he? Nothing. Nothing except a marriage that tied him to a woman who'd been responsible for his losing his son.

'There will be other children,' that damn fool sister had told him. Other children, with Jane! Months of watching her stagger about as though she hadn't the strength to live. And for what? He ought to have married Elsie, jolly, warm, loving, generous Elsie. If he'd given her his child, then none of this would have happened. But what chance was there of that? He was married, he was trapped. No son, no small replica of himself, no lad to teach and train. 'This is my son.' How often he'd imagined himself saying it, a boisterous dark-haired child at his side. Did all men feel like that? No, what he'd felt had been different, special. Elsie had always been there for him, she would be a natural mother. Think of her only this evening – could it be only hours ago? He'd begged her to let him make love to her. But even though he knew she loved him, even though she'd wanted it as much as he had, yet she'd refused. He had a wife. Bloody fool he'd been, why hadn't he married her instead of chasing after the bait Jane had held out for him?

He'd go and find Elsie now, he'd tell her what had happened. He even stood up from the iron seat ready – and then the church clock chimed and struck. Three o'clock. If he went there, George would answer the door to him, George wouldn't leave him alone with Elsie. Think of her, her hair rumpled from sleep, wearing just a nightgown, her eyes warm with love and pity, her plump white arms held out to him ... she would hold him, she would comfort him. But there was no comfort for him, there was nothing but the rasping sound of his own crying. He must go home. Tomorrow the neighbours would want to know about the baby – he'd have to tell them. 'I'd wanted him so much,' he heard his voice as pathetic, the sound adding to his grief.

The constant sound of water from the fountain had its effect. Unbuttoning his trousers, with a shuddering sigh of relief, he urinated against the surrounding wall of St Stephen's graveyard. Did they leave the church open at night? If they did, he could go in there, he could sit on his own and wait for the dawn. Was there really a God who understood? If there was, then surely He would show pity. And even if the whole thing was a lot of lies designed to make people accept the rotten deals life handed out, then he had nothing to lose.

He walked up the path toward the stone building and then he stopped, surprise even silencing his blubbering. From the far window of the church, surely that was a light shining. Did they leave it on all night, a refuge for miserable souls like him? He went up the steps to the porch, then very quietly lifted the latch and pushed open the heavy door. It was as if the single candle had been lit especially for him. Putting his feet down as quietly as he could he walked up the aisle. This was where he and Jane had been married. She'd lied to him even then, she'd told him her father would be there waiting for them. What if tonight his son had been born, healthy, strong, just as he'd imagined? Surely then his grandfather would have wanted to know him.

His mind rushed off at a tangent. What was the good of coming here to tell God about his misery? If there was a

God at all, wasn't he supposed to be omnipotent? So it was *His* fault, He must have done it purposely.

Jane had experienced Ian's uncontrolled hysteria, recently so often the culmination of his frustration and rage; but never had he wept as on that night. Perhaps that's what prevented him realizing that he wasn't alone, until Marcos came down the step from the chancel and, with hands outstretched, walked towards him.

'You are in trouble,' he said kindly. 'Would it help you to talk, or would you rather I left you alone?'

'No one to talk to.'

'Why don't you try me?'

For hours Marcos had sought solace for his own troubled soul and had found no comfort. Now, faced with another person's despair, he was ashamed of his thankfulness; his own anguish was nothing compared with Ian's grief. The realization only increased his self-abasement.

Somehow Ian found himself sitting next to the priest in the front pew. The single candle in the chancel was flickering, its light giving Ian a feeling of unreality. His surroundings were unfamiliar, for except for his wedding he'd never been inside the church; and what was a priest doing here in the middle of the night? He took out a would-be-white handkerchief (an example of Jane's less than housewifely attributes) and mopped his face.

'You and your God! The boy – my son – I saw him – small. She did it to spite me.'

'You wife's had the baby? I saw her only this morning. What's happened to her?'

'Oh, *she's* all right. Must have your bloody God on *her* side.' At the way he said it, Marcos was shocked, hurt. The doubts that had bothered him when Ian had brought his solitary bride to be married were rekindled. With a conscious effort he tried to put them aside, to listen with compassion. 'He was alive, you know. When she went into hospital the boy was alive, he was moving, he was strong. But he never breathed. Never lived. Nine months, other women manage.

157

But not her. She couldn't even carry him until he was ready for the world.'

'Tonight I can't expect you to be consoled. Can we pray together for the boy's innocent soul, and ask that you will find the strength you need to help your wife who has suffered so much and is faced with this sadness.'

'Her? She never wanted the boy – not like I did. "The boy" I used to say – and always she gave me that superior bloody smile and corrected me, "or the girl".

'And tonight she has neither. But the child is delivered, she will recover. This night will pass—' Oh please God, let this night pass, show me the way. Never known such joy, loving her there was nothing, nothing but the moment. Was that a sin? I can't get her out of my mind. The way her eyes light with laughter, the way she speaks. 'Ee iis a good man, my oosbond, the so boring doctor. Me, I am not of the saints, life it is a giift, not to enjoy iit iis the sin. *Comme ca?*' A good man. And Alayne, dear, pure Alayne. Dear God, forgive me. But is love, real love, a sin? I've never been so alive, just to be with her, to be part of her zest for living . . . is that a sin? Lust is a sin of the Devil – but that wasn't lust. Loving her was – was like a glimpse of paradise. And for her too, surely it must have been the same. She is like a tornado, remember the way she cried out. God made man and woman for the joy of each other – was it a sin? Tomorrow I shall see her again . . .

He pulled his mind back to Ian, who sat staring ahead into the shadowy darkness, his face contorted now, not with tears but with anger.

'. . . That's what she wanted me to think. She and her precious daddy, she only had to ask for anything and he gave it to her. Until it was *me* she wanted. Not good enough for her, not smart enough, that's what the old sod thought.' He peered closely at Marcos, his eyes screwed up as if he were recognizing him for the first time. 'It was you who married us. She said her old man would be here at the church. No one bloody here. I should have pulled out then,

158

I should have seen she'd been lying. But I kept hoping. She wrote to him, but all he did was send her a trunk filled with her clothes.'

'I'm sorry,' Marcos spoke quietly, 'for all of you. How hurt she must have been – and he too. He must have been hurting himself as much as he was her.'

'What about me? Don't I count!'

'Of course you count. But you had her love. She forsook him for your sake.'

'What sort of a wife do you think she is, eh? *Eh*!' He leant even closer as if he were forcing the question home. 'All right in bed, or she used to be. But no more. After what she's done, I don't want her. He was alive you know, I could feel him moving in there. My boy ... Even the animals in the field drop their young. But her! Her old man spoilt her, fancied she was too bloody precious. I tell you, she made an invalid of herself for weeks, months. Then she couldn't go through with it properly, couldn't bring him into the world. Shouldn't have married her. Needn't have done, you know. Ought to have got wed to Elsie. She's the right one for me.'

Marcos didn't want to hear. It wasn't the first time he'd listened as one or another of his parishioners had poured out their troubles and griefs, had burdened him with their guilt, had been guided by him to seek forgiveness and had gone home feeling cleansed. But Ian hadn't come for absolution, he'd come for sympathy.

'The two of you started your marriage with trust and hope. No one's path is always smooth. Trust each other, remember your vows, pray for strength – and out of this sad night will come a deeper understanding.'

Out of this dreadful night will come deeper understanding ... remember your vows ... what was he saying? And what right had he, a man who'd sinned as surely as any other, to preach? Dear God, forgive me. Help me to find my way. Yvette had made vows too, and her doctor husband. Guide me, help me ...

159

'Oh, I understand well enough,' Ian was saying. 'I understand that Jane cheated me, yes she did. Never short of a bob, she wasn't in those days. Have you ever been hard up? Do you know what it's like to be frightened to buy a pint of ale because you wouldn't have enough in your pocket to feed yourself till the next pay day? No, you bloody well haven't. But Jane, all her fancy clothes – she even used to drive herself to her old man's brewery in a posh motor car. Drive it herself! She fancied *me*, set her cap at me. If it had worked out like she said, we'd have been set fair. A good house in Deremouth, her running the brewery with her old man – but not for long. Time he packed it in, I could have taken it on with Jane to show me the ropes. Why couldn't he see it? Never had a son – but he could have made a son of me. Silly old bugger. Well, let him stuff his brewery. He's lost Jane now – and serves him right. But, see, if it had gone the way I expected, I'd not have gone back to Elsie.' He seemed to be speaking his thoughts as they formed. 'Her and me were all set to be married, then my old lady died and I had to go to Deremouth to get rid of her things. If your God is so clever, what did he let me get mixed up with Jane for? I ought to have married Elsie. She'd not have lost my boy. She loves me right enough, but she won't let me touch her, won't let me have her. Because I'm tied to that bitch, that's why she keeps her legs closed.' He caught hold of Marcos's arm. 'But listen, Vicar, I swear to you – and that God of yours if he exists, he can listen too – Elsie and I would be all right together. She and I are proper mates. Nothing gets her down, never seen her without rosy cheeks and a smile. Warm, that's what Elsie is. You know what I mean? Nothing makes her happier than seeing I'm all right.'

'But she remembers the vows you made to be faithful to Jane.' Marcos cringed with shame at the tone of his voice. What a sanctimonious fraud he was! But surely, what he said was the truth. And wasn't he a greater sinner even than this snivelling rogue who seemed to have no idea of the wrong he did his wife. God of love, God of mercy, hear me, speak to me, help me.

'Elsie remember my vows? It's not that that stops her. Frightened I'll get her pregnant. I tell you, I swear it's the honest truth, I wish that ruddy God of yours had seen fit to take Jane when He took the baby. There, now I've said it. If saying a thing here in your church makes any difference, then you can count *that* as a vow. I wish He'd taken her. Then I could have married Elsie like I ought to have done. We're right for each other, Elsie and me – Jane and I have nothing, *nothing*. And kids, we'd have kids, Elsie and me. Instead of that, even if Jane leaves me like she threatened, that doesn't get her off my back. Where would I get money for divorce courts? They're for the rich, not for poor bloody workers like me. Instead of the boy – poor little bastard, I saw him you know, I touched him – instead of him being taken without a chance of a life, why couldn't it have been her?' Bringing his face within inches of Marcos's, his smile appeared satanic in the flickering candlelight. Perhaps he meant it to. 'Go on then, Vicar. You with your smooth talk. What are you going to say to that?'

'Forgiveness isn't in my hands. Forgiveness comes from God, not from me. I'm going to leave you here –' Coward, coward, Marcos's conscience screamed at him '– just open your heart. There's no other way to find the peace you seek—' But didn't I open *my* heart? So why haven't I found peace? Was it a sin? A sin against Alayne and her trust, yes. But a sin against love? No, it could never have been that. Love consumed me, love drove me, love, pure, perfect love beyond all words. His thoughts running ahead of him, he got up from the pew, eager to get away and leave Ian to find his own salvation.

'Forgiveness? Why the hell do I need to be forgiven? It's Jane ought to ask for forgiveness. I told you, she tricked me, made me believe life would be a bed of roses. Now what have I got? Nothing.' Ian got to his feet, glaring around him, hating the church, hating the vicar, hating the cruel trick fate

161

had played him. 'If you get comfort out of all this hokum, then good luck to you. But you won't get *me* listening to your rubbish. Remember this, Vicar,' with eyelids swollen from weeping, he loomed over Marcos. 'Kid yourself what you like. When the chips are down, we have to make our own lives. If you think I'm going to grovel for forgiveness, Jane's or your Almighty's, then think again.'

With his hobnails ringing on the stone floor he disappeared out of the area of pale light from the fast-guttering candle. Marcos heard the church door close behind him. The light went out; there was only stillness.

It was about half an hour later when he let himself into the vicarage and, carrying his boots so that he wouldn't disturb Alayne, crept up the stairs. As he reached the landing her door opened and she stood there holding her bedside candle.

'You've been with poor old Mrs Dance. Has she gone?'

He shook his head.

'No, I've been in the church for hours. You remember that wedding when you had to sign the register, the Harrimans? They have been having trouble,' (no need to upset Alayne by telling her about the loss of the baby), 'he came to the church looking for help. He was there a long time.' How could he tell half-truths and hide behind other people's misery? He'd been no longer than half an hour with Ian Harriman; what of the preceding hours? If his evening with Yvette had carried him to paradise, then his humility dragged him down to hell. But Alayne, standing in a pool of golden light from her candle, didn't notice.

'Marcos, I haven't been to sleep. I wish I'd come to the church. That's where I ought to have given my thanks instead of here kneeling by my bedside. I've waited all these weeks, frightened to hope, frightened to believe. But it's more than two months now ... don't you understand what I'm saying?'

'Two months?' His mind seemed incapable of following her.

162

'I'm two months and thirteen days late. Remember that night at the end of April?' She put her candlestick on the landing table and moved to him, her arms around his neck, her lovely face aglow with such happiness he could hardly bear to look at her. 'Perhaps it's a good thing I didn't know you were in the church. I would have come so that we could have given thanks together. But if you had poor Mr – what did you call him? – it was right that you gave all your thoughts to him.'

'That night in April? Three months and a week ago ...' Words, just words while he held her tenderly against him and tried to digest what she was telling him.

'All these years I've fought to make myself accept that being a mother wasn't what was wanted of me. Remember how we used to try, to hope, to pray, to try. Then I was shown a different way of serving. That night I couldn't help myself, I really did beg to be given another chance, but I begged it without faith. I was sure I was barren. But, Marcos, it's really happened.'

'Are you sure?' His emotions in hand, he tipped her face towards his. 'You seem so well, you've been so full of energy.'

'But of course I am. What is more natural than having a baby? And, yes, I'm quite sure. I sent a note to Dr Bingley and he came to see me this evening when he'd finished seeing the people who go to his surgery. He examined me. He said I could be three months, but of course I know just when it was. Ten weeks ago last Friday, the night of the run through of the concert. You haven't said you're pleased. Marcos, you *are* pleased, aren't you?'

'I'm more than pleased,' he said softly. Pleasure was nothing compared with the wave of thankfulness that flooded through him. He had sought for guidance, for a sign to point the way. 'I'm thankful.'

He was ashamed of the love he saw in her eyes, made bright by the flickering light of the candle.

'You cared so much,' she whispered, 'yet never once did

you belittle me for my barren state. I'm so – so – blessed. Let us kneel together just as I have while I've waited for you, together let us give thanks. For Marcos, this must surely be a miracle.'

He went with her to her bedside, he knelt at her side with his head in his hands. He gave thanks for the way being made clear to him, for dear Alayne's happiness. And he begged for the strength and courage to turn aside from that other miracle of love.

Jane gave herself over to the nurses' care. They bound her aching chest uncomfortably tightly, telling her that was the way to stop the milk; they bound her stomach, telling her that would help her get back into shape. And so she lay in the long ward, the foot of the bed propped up to stem the haemorrhaging and a feeling of numb desolation in her heart. The nearest she came to privacy was when, about every two or three hours, one or other of the nurses closed the curtain around her bed while she attended to her, if that could be called privacy. The only visitor to be permitted would be Ian. He didn't come and neither did she want him. They'd lost their child but, to Jane, the grief was hers alone.

'She's in the last bed but one on the right, Doctor.' She heard the brisk voice of the nurse but took no notice, it didn't even register on her, as she lay with her eyes closed, that hers was the last bed but one on the right. It wasn't until the rasp of the curtain being drawn around her alerted her that she realized she was the patient who was to be seen. Last night, amidst the agony and horror, she'd been aware of an elderly doctor. Surely he wasn't going to examine her ... instinct told her not to open her eyes, perhaps he'd go away.

'Jane ...' No more than a whisper, but in that second she was back amongst the living, her hand reaching out and being taken in Matthew's firm grasp. Then he was on his knees by her side, she was held close to him, his nearness breaking down the barrier that had held her pain at bay and letting her tears flow. 'My poor Jane,' he whispered against her rumpled hair.

'They let you in?' A silly question, and spoken in a whisper that was barely audible even though he was so close.

'I said you'd been my patient. My precious love.'

'I wanted my baby so much,' she gulped, 'someone of my own. Someone who'd always be there, someone I wouldn't be frightened to love.' Even as she said it, the ghosts were there. How proud her father had been when he'd first taken her to the brewery, how pure and uncomplicated their affection had been for each other. But had it? Had he really loved her for herself, or simply as a possession? And what was she saying about the baby she'd wanted so much?

'Never be frightened to love. Oh, Jane, what a mess. I want to give you the world, I want to give you all that I have, all that I am.' It was so quiet she might almost have dreamt it.

She shook her head. 'Can't,' she breathed. 'I shouldn't listen.' She felt his lips on her forehead. Even in her misery, she'd never felt so loved.

They heard the brisk, rubber-soled tread of the nurse. Their moment was over. By the time the nurse drew the curtain aside and came to join them, Matthew was off his knees, closing his bag as if he'd been using something from it. Jane was once again lying with her eyes closed.

'You're looking after her well.' Jane heard the smile in his voice as he spoke to the nurse. 'She couldn't be in better hands.'

'Dr Huntley saw to her last night,' the nurse said, hoping to hear more. She'd been told that Dr Bingley had carried the patient in but hadn't stayed to help with the confinement.

'Yes, I was told he was here. I'd already been called to another patient.' He lied of course. He had left her to Dr

Huntley because he had believed Jane wouldn't have wanted him to deliver her premature child. And now that it was over, he thanked God it hadn't been he who had been unable to give it life.

'How long do you want us to keep the bed on blocks, Doctor?'

'I think you should wait until Dr Huntley tells you. I don't want to interfere at this stage.' Then, with a conspiratorial smile that made the nurse's cheeks warm with pleasure, 'But when I'm this way, you'll let me in to see her, won't you.'

'Of course you'll come in. But as things are –' (which Jane knew was her tactful way of saying 'with no baby') '– I expect she'll be sent home soon.'

'Very likely. Goodbye, then, Mrs Harriman. I'll call again in a few days. See you eat up your meals, you need building up.' His voice was cheerful, encouraging. This was Dr Bingley, admired and respected by all his patients.

'Thank you for coming, Doctor.' From her tone she was no more than just one of them.

Twice more he came to see her during the days she was there. On each occasion the curtains isolated them in whispered privacy, and each time he left her Jane was even more frightened of the future. She couldn't live with Ian again; she couldn't live at all if she didn't find work. In Brackleford? Doing what? Time and again, of its own accord, her mind leapt back to Deremouth and the brewery. Close her eyes and she could be there amongst the heady smell from the mash tuns, she could hear the coopers hammering, she could see the dust dancing in a beam of light that shone from the high window to fall across her father's desk. And time and again, those thoughts would be pushed from her mind by desolation that, catching her unprepared, would swamp out every other feeling. But she wouldn't give in, always she fought and overcame it. Of course she was capable of earning her living, she'd been capable of running the brewery so it was ridiculous to think she couldn't find work. But here in Brackleford? Remembering how ignorantly confident of her future she'd been when she'd arrived, she hated the town. Yet Matthew was in Brackleford. Matthew, respectably married, respectfully admired, think what malicious pleasure people would find in knowing he was having an affair. For that was all it could ever be – an affair.

So you have no one; the voice of self-pity was quick to find a chink in her armour. If you'd had your baby you wouldn't have been alone. Perhaps it was to punish you for wanting to break his marriage (for that's what you did want – what you still want) that you lost your baby. If only they'd let me have a visitor, if only I could talk to Alice. But I couldn't tell her ... would I need to tell her, doesn't she know already? Confused and wrapped in a misery she fought against admitting to, she drifted through the days.

Then, with no prior warning, the nurse came bustling down the ward, making for her bed.

'Good news, Mrs Harriman. Dr Huntley says you may go home. You'll need to rest for a while longer, but you can do that as easily at home as here,' then, drawing the curtains to shut out the rest of the ward and speaking quietly, 'better, I dare say. Surrounded by sick people – except for Mrs Jones and her wee babe – that's no way to get yourself back in step again. So let me give you a hand with dressing. You've been getting out of bed, I know you have, I've spied you. Naughty girl. But a good thing you have or your legs would be feeling like jelly.' Jane was going to miss the brusque kindness of this middle-aged nurse. 'My word, but there's nothing of you. Some women stay plump for months, but you, oh dear me, but what a skinny thing you are.'

'I always have been. Until—' But it was over, she mustn't think of it, she mustn't listen for the sound of 'Mrs Jones's wee babe' when it was brought in to fed; those were things she *mustn't* do. But she was going home. To what?

Not to stay. Quite definitely she knew that whatever else she decided, nothing would make her stay in that little house so full of the memories she wanted to escape.

'How will you manage?' the nurse said anxiously. 'You don't have to go this minute, you could wait while we get a message to your husband – or a friend.'

Her worried expression was the boost Jane needed. She smiled with a confidence she was far from feeling.

'The tram stops right opposite the hospital and again at the end of Mill Lane. And I've no luggage. In fact – I haven't even the ha'penny for my fare, now I come to think of it.'

'I'll give you that right enough. Can you get in when you get home? Will the door be locked?'

'No, I'm sure it won't. We've never bothered to carry a key, it's easier not to lock the door.'

'Well, if you're sure you'll be all right on your own. It's only a fortnight though, some women lounge in bed for six weeks.'

'Life's too short to waste six weeks,' Jane forced her laughing reply. Yet, suddenly, standing on her own two feet, wearing clothes that had become far too big for her, she found there was truth in the remark. Ahead of her was a hurdle she intended to jump; whether she would land on the other side she had no idea but, whatever she found herself faced with, she was resolved not to let it beat her. Deeper than that she wouldn't let herself delve. It was easier to look ahead with forced confidence than it was to look back.

The tram took her to the end of Mill Lane. If she'd imagined it would feel like a return home, then she was mistaken. It seemed a lifetime ago when she'd struggled through each day, humiliated by her own inadequacies, shamed that she could so soon have replaced the love she'd believed she'd felt for Ian with something more akin to loathing. Their baby . . . all her resolve to make something of her marriage had been rooted in the love they would share for their baby. Letting herself into the dark passageway she closed the front door and leant against it as she had so often as she'd listened to the sound of Matthew's motor car growing fainter. But today she wasn't thinking of Matthew – or, if she was, it was only in the subconscious recesses of her mind. There was no baby ... if she'd needed a sign, then surely taking the baby from them must have been it.

Even before she'd been carried into the hospital, her mind had been made up. She caught her bottom lip between her teeth, aware of a great surge of relief. For a woman to leave her husband, to break the vows she'd taken so solemnly, was almost unheard of. Love might die, oh yes, vows to love, honour and obey, they might be broken in many and many a home; but wives kept their side of the bargain, they ran the home, cooked, cleaned, did all the things she had done so badly. Well, that wasn't for *her*. So, what was for her? She would leave Brackleford, that was the only sure thing she knew. Moving down the dingy passage, she looked into the living room, surprised to see it was not only tidy, the table shone, the cushions were plumped. In the kitchen the curtains looked washed and ironed, the brass tap had been polished. Perhaps Ian had given up renting the place, perhaps it belonged to someone else.

Half expecting to see the bedroom cupboard full of someone else's clothes, she went upstairs, her first thought going to her underwear drawer. What if he'd turned everything out, what if he'd found what she had hidden there? Relieved, she saw her own undergarments; at a glance she knew he hadn't rifled amongst them. The few valuables Dulcie had put in with her trunk of clothes were still there: a diamond brooch that had been her mother's, a gold fob watch she'd often been tempted to wear yet some cunning instinct had made her keep it hidden. Taking off her wedding ring, she wrapped all three items in a clean handkerchief and stuffed them into the draw-string bag she always carried. Now for her clothes. Stripping off skirt and blouse that hung loose on her, she draped them across the bed, adding one more skirt she'd also tried to remodel as her figure had changed, then she took her russet brown dress.

'Let it fit, please let it fit,' she muttered as she thrust her arms into the sleeves. This was the dress she'd worn the day her trunk had arrived; to her it seemed symbolic that she wore it again as she moved towards wherever the next stage would take her. It did. Looking in the long, speckled mirror it was impossible not to smile. Next she unpinned her long hair and brushed it, the action seeming to brush away the past she wanted to leave behind.

All that done, and feeling absolutely no shame for her vanity, again she admired her reflection. She took her remaining things from the cupboards and drawers. She filled her hamper so full that she had a job to force the lid on it and put the rest into the trunk, her plans already taking shape. Alice would keep her secret, Alice would look after them for her.

There, it was done. Leaving the bed with its rumpled state made worse by the shapeless garments she had discarded, she dragged the trunk to the head of the straight stairs. One tread at a time she hauled it into the passageway where, with her hamper on top of it, she left it. Feeling more exhausted than she cared to admit, she went back to the High Street clutching her draw-string bag.

Jo Higgins, the pawnbroker, was used to women bringing trinkets to him, as often as not redeeming them again after the next pay day. But he was experienced enough to know that what Jane laid before him were very different.

'I don't want the constabulary coming calling, miss,' he told her, having noted her ringless hand.

'The constabulary? But what has it to do with them?'

''Tis to be hoped, nothing. These things are your own, are they? Don't misunderstand me, miss,' for at a second glance, he felt uneasy about his accusation. That hat must have cost a pretty penny, and the clothes she wore, they smelt of money.

'Oh, I see. You think I stole them. Well, they're all my own. I promise you they are. The brooch belonged to my mother, the watch I had for my twenty-first birthday ...' Her voice tailed into silence. The pawnbroker knew the ring would be the easiest to sell, but that brooch was worth a deal of money, of that he was sure. If he was lucky, give the young woman a year and a day and if she hadn't been back to retrieve it and pay him his loan and the interest, then it would be his to get rid of in the right channels. Best for him to ask no more questions, just to pay her enough to satisfy her (and she must be on hard times or she'd find somewhere more suitable to get rid of her treasures), then put the brooch and the watch in his safe for twelve months.

'I'll just need your name, miss, then you hang on to the ticket. You'll need it if you come to redeem your things.'

'My name is Bradley, Miss Bradley.'

'That'll do me.' He unlocked a tin and carefully counted out the money, two guineas for the brooch, a guinea and a half for the watch and seven and sixpence for the ring, pleased that she accepted without question. It was so long since she'd handled such wealth that she left the shop telling herself that her troubles were behind her.

Outside the railway station she found two vehicles waiting, a hansom cab and an autocab. She chose the first. For one thing it would be cheaper and for another it would create less interest in Mill Lane. As the hansom took her along the busy thoroughfare, memories crowded in on her and almost destroyed her self-imposed determination. The sound of a motor car in Mill Lane, the sound of his voice, the rightness of being with him. Rightness? How could it be, when he had a wife? And more than that, he had the affection and respect of the people he served in Brackleford. If she loved him – *if*? There was no *if* – she was only half a person when he wasn't with her, two halves of one whole – she had to leave him. He'd been content before she came into his life ... Would he call at the

171

hospital today and find her gone? If he did, then he would come to Mill Lane. Don't think about the sound of his engine stopping, the door slamming, don't think about his anticipation that he would find her there waiting. But she wouldn't be there, she'd be gone, gone and he wouldn't know where.

The driver was fortunately brawny and he manhandled her trunk while she put the hamper on board and climbed up after it. Five minutes later she was knocking on Alice's door.

Alice's welcome was almost her undoing.

'My poor child,' she said as she loosened her from her warm embrace and the hansom cab rolled away, leaving the trunk inside her front door. 'You did right to come to me. I thank God you've made the decision. If he comes here looking for you—'

'No, Alice, I'm not staying in Brackleford. It's not just Ian. I have to go away. It's not Ian I'm running away from, I think it's myself. If I stay I shan't have the courage to – to—'

'My dear, you don't need to tell me. It's Matthew, isn't it?'

'We have no right to care about each other. But if I stay here, then neither of us has a chance. And Yvette, what about her? But the truth is, I don't think about Yvette, it's not for her sake I'm getting out of his life. It's for his own. Step outside the conventions and people can be cruel. He doesn't deserve that. He's respected now – but if the gossips got to know about him and me, how long would that respect last?'

'Damn the gossips.' Alice glared defiantly. 'Haven't you suffered enough in losing your child?' There, it was said. To endure a difficult pregnancy such as Jane's, and at the end of it have nothing, Alice could find no words of consolation. Her brusque sentence took Jane by surprise, bringing quick tears to fill her eyes.

172

She nodded, frightened to trust her voice. But she blinked the tears away and squared her jaw.

'I'd made up my mind to go away; I told Ian so the night I lost my baby. But, if the baby had been born strong and healthy, the boy Ian had so wanted, then I don't know if I could have done it. It's almost as if this happened purposely. My fault? I don't know. I'm so confused. But Alice, there's one thing I do know. I think you taught me, when you told me about your Gerald and how he'd beaten those cruel boys. Love is the strongest thing in our lives, every one of us. So I can't stay here, I can't wreck Matthew's life.'

'You want me to keep your trunk until you have an address for it to be railed to, is that it?' Practical Alice helped to put emotion behind them. 'Well, my dear, you know you can rely on me. And if that husband of yours comes knocking on my door, I know nothing. But I'm going to miss you. Don't like to think about it.'

'I shall go to London,' Jane said. 'Like Dick Whittington, I shall hope to find the streets paved with gold. And when I find work and somewhere to live, you shall come and stay with me. Just think, Alice, you and me in London. Have you ever been there? I haven't.'

'Once I did. Before all our troubles started. Gerald and I took Terry to see the procession when the Queen died. So secure, that's how we thought we were ... Live for the day, Jane. Snatch your happiness.'

'No,' Jane turned away, 'no, Alice, no. It's what he'd say too, I know that. But I can't do that to him. Today is a new beginning. I'm going to prove I can stand on my own two feet.'

Chapter Nine

Autumn 1906

Leaning back in her compartment Jane closed her eyes and listened to the message of the train as it sped over the sleepers: a new beginning, a new beginning, a new beginning. The steady rhythm didn't vary. And so it *must* be, not just a new one, but one full of promise. She wouldn't let herself consider anything else. Whatever shape the future took, she alone had the shaping of it. When her thoughts turned – as they did every time she ceased consciously to keep them away – to the baby, to Matthew, even to Ian and what she saw now as her ignorant trust, then she pulled them back in line. She would find work, she would prove that she could earn her own way. She wouldn't even consider that she might be held back simply because she was a woman.

By the time she reached Waterloo it would be evening; her first challenge would be to find somewhere to stay. A new beginning, a new beginning: the sound was soporific; given a more relaxed mind it would have taken no time for her to lose the battle for wakefulness. Twelve hours ago officially she had been confined to a hospital bed, still at the stage when she watched for unattended moments to walk up and down by the side of it rather than let her legs turn to jelly. So much living had been crowded into the few hours since she'd been given her freedom that it was small wonder she felt drained and exhausted.

Had he been to the hospital today, expecting to find her? The question found a chink in her armour. Be glad you've gone from it, be glad for *his* sake. Remember the silent glances you've seen between the nurses. Of course they wondered at his being so attentive, always pulling the curtain around your bed even though you were there as Dr Huntley's patient. Nothing spread faster than malicious gossip. I must never let that happen to him. But what about me? Better to have stayed in Brackleford, better to have a life that revolved around listening for the sound of his motor car, the high points of being with him and the desolation when he left to be swallowed up in that other life. But supposing gossip about him spread, cast a shadow, altered things for him. I couldn't do that to him. So I'm right to go. For his sake ... for his sake ... the rhythm of the train sang the chorus. Only then did she realize that in all her heart-searching she hadn't once considered his wife, the woman they'd been deceiving. Neither had she imagined Ian arriving home (to that house no doubt so highly polished by the woman poor simple Florrie had told her about) to find the cupboard and drawers empty of her clothes. Leaning back and closing her eyes she pressed her hands against her flat stomach. She felt empty, empty of love, empty of hope.

But she fought back. It's up to me ... it's up to me, then as the train lost speed ... I won't be beaten ... I won't be beaten ...

The train stopped, there was the sound of one or two doors slamming but no one came to share her compartment and for that she was thankful. Not that it was usual for fellow travellers to chatter, but it was a chance she'd rather not take. She felt like an actress who hadn't had time to grow into her role. Jane Bradley ... well, for most of her life that's what she'd been. But the Jane Bradley of a year ago was very different from the woman who was leaving her husband, who had lost her child, who was running away from the one person she wanted above all else. With gathering speed they covered a few more miles, then she noticed they were slowing again. But why? There was no sign of habitation; on either side of the track were fields.

And then she saw a building that brought her to her feet. She had no doubt at all of its purpose, it was a brewery. Juddering and hissing the train stopped by a wooden platform carrying a painted sign telling her she was at Addingford Halt. She didn't stop to think, she let instinct be her guide as she reached for her hamper, then opened the window and shouted to the signalman who was already holding his green flag poised and with his whistle in his mouth.

'Wait!' she yelled. 'Don't start. I'm getting off.'

'Nearly missed your chance, lady. Here let me take that.' He reached to lift the hamper on to the platform. 'Anything more?'

'No, just me and that.'

'Then off she goes.' He blew his whistle and waved the all clear up to the driver then, nodding in satisfaction, kept his eyes on the train as it jolted and juddered back into life and moved off leaving them in a swirl of smoke. Then he turned to Jane as if she were a visitor he'd been waiting for. 'Wasn't expecting anyone would be wanting Addingford, not this late in the afternoon. No one ever gets off from that one. It just has to pull up while I put the postbag aboard. Visiting here would you be?'

And she saw now that, beyond the railway halt, there was what looked like more than a hamlet but less than a village.

'In a way. I have to call at the brewery.'

'At Watford's? I dare say you made enquiries about the times to get back home again. You'll have to make it a quick call if you want the quarter past five, and after that there's just one at half past seven. Or would you be going on to Waterloo?'

'I hope I'll not be going anywhere,' she smiled, forcing confidence into her voice. Surely she'd been brought to

Addingford for a purpose. If she'd let herself be lulled into sleep and sped on to Waterloo, then she wouldn't have known about the brewery. So she refused to consider anything except that this isolated railway halt was part of some great design. 'Is there a station master here? I want to ask him where I can leave my hamper.'

'That'll be me. Guard, station master, ticket seller, ah, and sweeper too. I come in in time for the first stopper of the day just after eight and I stay to see the last one out at half past seven. I'll put it in the ticket office safe enough, and you get it when you've done your bit of business at Walford's.'

'To be truthful, I'm looking for work, and I know about brewing. That's why I'm here.' Jane surprised herself in talking to a stranger.

'Oh ah,' her new friend absorbed the statement. 'It's always been a family business, I've known Watford's since I was knee high to a grasshopper as you might say. The old gentleman only had the one son, four or five girls but when it comes to going into the business then, of course, it was the son he looked to. But it wasn't to the young chap's liking I dare say. Upped and offed – where was it now? – somewhere across the ocean. So now the old gent, he's had to take a manager. No use waiting until he gets his call to go up yonder, then leaving the place with no one knowing how to set about things. So what would you be hoping to do, miss?'

She smiled, more confident by the second. 'That'll be up to Mr Watford. I've had lots of experience.' She was even imagining the manager deciding it wasn't the job he wanted and she being there ready and willing. 'Just one more thing,' she asked her uniformed friend, 'do you know of anyone around here with a room to rent?'

'Get yourself a job first, missie, then you come back here and I'll see what I can do for you. Nothing round here that either me or my missus don't know about. Might be tempting fate to think of somewhere to lay your head before

177

you've fixed yourself up with some work. A brewery though – that's a mighty funny place for a young lady like you to be seeking employment, I'm jiggered if it isn't.'

Funny place or not, to Jane it felt like going home just to walk into the large red-brick building and breathe in the familiar pungent smell. Standing alone she closed her eyes, giving rein to the daydream.

'I saw you come in,' a voice from just behind startled her. 'I'm the manager here.' Then, when Jane turned round and from the cut of her coat and the style of her hat, the man recognized that she wasn't a wife of one of the workers, he added more courteously, 'I don't believe we've met. I'm Richard Foley.'

Jane knew she was being unfair, but her first impression of the manager wasn't promising. He was a well-built man with florid complexion and thinning sandy hair. Clearly his moustache was waxed and groomed with care, while his sideburns grew with vigour she was sure had never been the case with the fine hair combed so carefully to cover his almost bald patch. His suit was gingery check and, in full flower in his buttonhole, he wore a yellow rose.

'I'd like to speak to Mr Watford. Is he here?'

The manager frowned. Was she a family friend? Or perhaps a client?

'No trouble, madam? Nothing wrong with any of our supplies?'

'It has nothing to do with your orders. Would you mind telling him that I'm here. My name is Bradley, Miss Bradley.'

'Well, Miss Bradley, I'm sorry. You couldn't have come at a more unfortunate time. Mr Watford was here this morning, but he's gone home now. If you're acquainted with him, you know that he's getting on in years; he never comes in for more than an hour or so at a time. I hope you haven't made a long journey specially. You came by train I believe, I saw you walking from the railway station. I can't suggest you go on to see Mr Watford at home, for clearly you have no carriage. So, perhaps you'd care to come to my office and wait until your train is expected. At least it will be more comfortable than the railway platform.'

'If he's not here, then I'd better tell you what I've come for,' she said as she let him usher her up the short flight of wooden stairs and into his office. 'I need to find work – and the one thing I know about is brewing.'

'What will you ladies think of next?' Throwing back his head he laughed, laughed *at* her. 'What would a girl like you know about brewing?'

'As much as you do I've no doubt, and probably a good deal more,' she retorted, honesty overcoming the need for tact. From the moment she'd set eyes on him, she'd disliked him. She knew she ought to behave differently, she was destroying all her chances of employment but, when it came to brewing, she wasn't prepared to be talked down to. 'My family are all brewers.' And that's the truth too, for the family was just Dad and me – and Grandfather before him, she thought. 'I've grown up with the trade. The only thing I don't know about ale is the drinking of it.' Which is something you're certainly familiar with, if the colour of your face and nose is anything to judge by.

'What did you say the name was?'

'Bradley. But we're not in this part of the country.'

Leaving her standing. Richard Foley sat behind his desk, eyeing Jane up and down with an expression of appreciation so blatant that she saw it as insolent.

'And you want work,' he mused.

'I'll come back tomorrow. You say Mr Watford comes in in the mornings.'

'Did I say that? I said he was here this morning. But staffing is my responsibility. I shouldn't wonder he gets himself brought in here for an hour or two when he gets fed up with being at home surrounded by those spinster daughters of his. I said when I introduced myself, I'm in charge here.'

'I see. Then I dare say we're wasting each other's time.'

She was sure he was no more drawn to her than she to him.

'Did I say that?' He raised his light pale gingery brows. 'As it happens I have a vacancy.'

'Yes?' Perhaps she'd misjudged him. 'I promise you won't regret it. I've been used to dealing with every aspect – from the maltsters right through to delivery of the barrels of ale—'

'So you'll know about account books.'

'Why, yes, of course. No one can run a business without understanding the account books.'

This was her first day officially out of bed and weakness came over her with no warning. She felt as if her whole body trembled, she wondered that her legs had the power to support her; the walls seemed to crowd in on her. Without waiting to be invited she sat down, facing him across the desk.

'You need not make yourself too comfortable.' Did she imagine it or was that mockery she saw in his light blue organ-stop eyes? 'I've said I'll give you work. You can assist Mr Hopkins in the accounts room. Got beyond his job, it's time I sacked him. But Mr Watford won't listen to a word against him. I'll pay you fifteen shillings a week, your hours will be eight-thirty until six and eighty-thirty till one-thirty on Saturdays. You may report to Hopkins in the morning, I'll tell him to expect you.'

She nodded, frightened to speak in case her voice was as wobbly as the rest of her.

'That'll be all. You may go.'

She ought to refuse the offer, she ought to argue that work as an assistant book-keeper wasn't suitable. But she couldn't. Her thoughts weren't clear, it took all her willpower to keep her gaze steady. Fascinated, she watched as one of the outer petals of his overblown buttonhole gave up its hold and fluttered to rest on his rounded stomach.

'You can see yourself out.' Richard Foley nodded a curt dismissal.

She stood up, making sure she was erect, making sure her

head was high as she left his room even though the floor seemed to be moving uncertainly beneath her feet. Gripping the handrail she went back down the wooden stairs and into the vestibule where he'd first spoken to her. Leaning against the wall she breathed slowly and deeply. When a person feels faint, help can come from breathing fresh air; Jane's help came from the atmosphere of the brewery, the sound of the men working with the mashing tuns, the smell of the wort.

Her mind was clearing, disappointment giving way to determination. What did it matter if she had taken an instant dislike to the florid and flamboyant manager? He wasn't important. A new beginning . . . a new beginning . . . and so it would be. An assistant book-keeper wasn't what she'd been fool enough to let herself dream. But everyone had to start somewhere, no one could expect to have a golden future handed to them on a plate.

So thinking, she pushed herself away from the wall, straightened her hat, squared her shoulders and started back to the railway station.

'Well, missie, and how did things go? Did you get the work you were after?' It was silly to let the station master's kindly enquiry knock her off balance. Biting the corners of her mouth she stooped to make an unnecessary adjustment to the buckle on her shoe.

'Mr Watford wasn't there, but I saw the manager. I'm to start work tomorrow helping the book-keeper.'

'Old Silas Hopkins, that'll be. You'll be all right with old Silas, missie. Now, about a place for you to stay. I couldn't think of anyone – not like as if we're a town, there aren't that many houses in Addingford. So I slipped home to have a word with Agnes – that's the wife. She's not averse to having a lodger. Never done it before, but we've got a room not slept in and while she's cooking supper for me she says she might as well do it for you too. Bring her in an extra bob or two, and you'll get fed better by Aggie than you would if you got yourself a room with an oil stove to cook on. So, what do you say?'

'I say, yes, yes please. And thank you.'

'It's just along the road, I've got the name painted on the gate. "Haphill" that's what we call it. Her idea it was. H, that's for Hugh; my name you see. The A, that's for Agnes. Phillpott is our surname, so that's how she got the P and the "hill". Funny thing to call it, I tell her, when it's flat as a pancake. You hop along there, m'dear, and make yourself known. Can you manage your hamper? I dare say you want to get your things unpacked.'

And so Jane started on her new beginning.

'You say she isn't here? But where else could she have gone? I went straight to Mill Lane as soon as I heard they'd discharged her. Perhaps she's gone back to her father.' Matthew looked helplessly at Alice. 'You're not hiding anything from me?'

'Come inside, we can't talk here. Matthew, my dear, I'm in the middle of the two of you. She told me she was going to London. More than that I don't know. No, that's not true. She told me it was because of you that she wouldn't stay in Brackleford.'

'I had a note, she must have handed it in at the Elm Road surgery on the way to the station. She said nothing – nothing of the things that matter.'

'Then, sit down and let me tell you. She's running away from you because she cares too much to risk hurting you. What was it she said? I can't wreck his life, that was it.'

'As if her going away doesn't wreck it! Alice, I don't need to tell you about Jane and me.'

'Neither of you needed to tell me, I think I've known what must happen since that first afternoon you met her here with that great gash on her head. Thank God she's left him. She was going anyway, she'd made up her mind. Now, the baby lost, nothing could have kept her with him. But that's not why she's left Brackleford. She's gone because of what the gossip would do to you in a town where you are respected.'

'As if I care—'

'She said it was something she'd learnt to understand – that love is the guiding force in all our lives. And it's love for you, my dear, that has given her the strength to set out and make a new life for herself.'

'And you promise me you don't know where?'

'I swear I don't. She told me she was catching the train to London. And, Matthew my dear, all we can do is say "May God go with her".' She meant it with all her heart. But she was glad that she'd managed to drag the trunk into the back lobby out of sight until she had a forwarding address.

'You are looking full of trouble. Why is it you cannot shut the door on other people's pains and illness when you shut the door on that gloomy surgery?' Yvette looked petulantly across the table at Matthew who was toying with his meal, his mind somewhere far away. 'Why do you not give thought to your so poor wife, the dullness of her days?'

'Umph? Dullness? What made today so dull?' For although Yvette thought his occupation tedious and made no secret of the fact, she usually found something or someone to add a sparkle to her own days.

'It is the little girls at the orphanage.'

'The orphanage?' He made an effort to haul his thoughts away from the gas-lit London streets, the image of Jane, weak and weary, knocking on doors to try to find a vacant room. She had no money (for he knew nothing about the treasures left at the pawnbroker's), how had she even paid for her ticket? Perhaps Alice had helped her. But these days Alice had so little ... What if she couldn't find a bed? What if, alone on the streets, she was accosted?

'Why should you remember that I go there to play the pia—?'

'But of course I remember.' He dragged his mind back to Yvette. 'You help the vicar. But I thought you enjoyed the children, you've often talked about them.'

'That is it!' Her accent grew stronger with each word. 'I do not know how it is I can stop going there? They run to me, they are like bees swarming around their queen. And what happens to the bees if the queen leaves them? I cannot do it. And that is why I am disconsolate. The vicar, Marcos, he was my friend. I think I frightened him. The women of your country, they are cold and make no demonstration of fondness. His wife is – how he calls it? – she is a saint. But a saint must be so dull, so hard to have any fun with. The vicar, he used to look at me like a child looking at a greatly tempting confection, so much wanting to taste yet knowing it is not his own.'

'My dear Yvette, you can't be asking me to believe that you can't handle a man of the cloth?'

She shrugged. And, for the first time that evening, she even laughed. 'But did I tell you that? There is no man I cannot handle.'

'So, was this glorious confection too much for his digestion?'

'You are mocking me.' The smile had gone as quickly as it had come.

Matthew leant back in his chair, surveying this wife of his. Perhaps he should never have married her and expected her to conform to the rules of small-town society. Her own life had been so different. Looking back to those early days in Paris, he had been as smitten by her as had so many before him – and so many after. He had no illusions. After ten years of marriage, he was still tolerantly fond of her even though their lives moved on different planes. In their shared bedroom they slept in separate beds and, although she welcomed him into hers, for years he'd known that for neither of them was the ensuing love-making more than an outlet for sexual need. Getting into his own bed afterwards, the thought often came to him that so he might have felt after a visit to a good-natured prostitute. That there were other men in her life didn't even touch him. He knew that their home was a more cheerful place for her presence; the two maids idolized her. That their marriage was unusual had never bothered him, neither had he ever been prepared to give her the constant flattery and attention she thrived on. While he'd been content to accept a relationship that made no demands on either of them, his much more real concern had been for Anton, her son. Remembering his own childhood, two parents for role models, a home where undemonstrative affection and faithfulness had been taken for granted, he felt that both he and Yvette had failed the child. When he'd suggested sending him to the same boarding school he'd attended himself, Yvette had made no protest. At the time she had been engrossed in a friendship with an artist who had moved into the area, a friendship about which Matthew had asked no questions and felt no interest. His own experience of boarding school had been good, he'd enjoyed the companionship, he'd proved himself as an oarsman, his interest in medicine had been nurtured and his way ahead made clear. And that's what he wanted for Anton, a child who seemed to fit comfortably nowhere.

All this flashed momentarily through his mind as he studied Yvette's unusually petulant expression as she waited for his answer.

'I'm not mocking you at all. I'm just puzzled. If you are capable of handling the vicar, then why the problem with the orphanage?'

'I am angry with myself that I cannot walk away and leave those little girls. In the beginning, being with Marcos was fun, yes, it really was. I'd known no one like him. Perhaps that is how it is with all men, each one different. But Marcos ... oh well, that was in the beginning. But perhaps it is as you say, the confection was too much for his feeble digestion. He has become so – so – *righteous*, is that how you would call it?'

'I shouldn't wonder.'

'And I do not understand the reason. There is no gaiety in the people of this so sober town. I never had this trouble in my beautiful Paris.'

'In Paris you were not the wife of the local doctor.'

She gave an exaggerated sigh and looked to the ceiling as if for understanding that was beyond her.

'Being a wife, why is that supposed to mean life has to be so solemn? Is it a sin for a man to seek joy in his life – a man or a woman either? Would you have me sit in my home from morning until night? But of course you would not. And I will not. Matthew, you and I, we have a good arrangement, is that not so?'

'I've never complained.' And until he'd met Jane he had found a detached amusement in her dalliances. Although he'd never consciously thought about it until now, could it be that he'd secretly taken pride in the fact that men found her irresistible? Yvette needed admiration and excitement as surely as she needed food and drink. He had supplied her with the second, but after the first few months in England he had known she looked elsewhere to find satisfaction with the first. They'd come to understand and accept each other. She made no secret of the fact that she thought his life dull – and hers too, except when she found ways to bring it colour.

'If I ceased to play his hymns for the little girls, his wife would find the time to help him. But not for long; that is another problem.' Then, her expression changed as suddenly as the sun appearing from behind a dark cloud. 'She came to see me. When I saw her come up the path,' she chuckled, 'I thought she must have come to tell me I was – how do you say? – a bad lot for tempting her holy man with such sweetmeat. But, no. Perhaps it was too soon for it to have troubled his so feeble digestion, for he had hardly had time for his conscience to have reminded him of the sins of stolen fruit. I thought what a joke it would be if he arrived while she was here; for I was expecting him to sing some songs with me. Perhaps being a holy man his conscience works quicker than mine or yours, for he never did come. But I was telling you about his wife and why I cannot give the piano playing to her. She came to give me her news. She was so happy,' (it sounded more like 'arppy' as Yvette warmed to her story), 'she said she had no one to tell except me. She has friends amongst her oh so good ladies who come to the vicarage to sew and who do their good works, but to them she could not speak of things so intimate.'

She laughed without malice as she remembered the group who'd listened aghast as she'd sung of 'The Glory of Love'. 'But to me she could tell it, we have talked before. She is to have a child. She conceived it on the same night as I sang my 'Glory of Love' song. She told me. Such a happening as a visit from her husband was rare. And yet, Matthew, they hold each other in large esteem. People are so strange. Have they no warmth in their blood, these countrymen of yours? She and Marcos alone know of the child – and now me – and I have told it to you.' It didn't occur to her that she was telling him what he already knew.

He tried to concentrate on what she said, but in his mind was an image of Jane. She wasn't fit to be trailing around a strange city looking for somewhere to live; she wasn't fit to be looking for work. If she'd borne a healthy child, then nature would help her, but she had nothing ... no one ... but that wasn't true – she must surely know that wherever she went, whatever befell her, his spirit was with her. Yvette wasn't aware of the journey his thoughts had taken. Blithely she continued her tale. 'To see her face you would think she had been visited by a holy spirit. Perhaps that is what she imagines, perhaps she believes the oh so good vicar has blessed her.' Her mood of gloom had gone, gone just as surely as had any desire she'd had to tempt the handsome priest. She bore no malice that having tasted of that glorious confection he'd been frightened to let himself be drawn into the path of temptation again. Rather, it amused her. At the moment she had fresh fields to conquer – her mornings of hymn singing at the orphanage impeded the freedom she craved. But it might be amusing to see how he fared with his battle with his conscience. 'You know how these women live with their minds as corseted as their bodies, they hide away when they are pregnant as if they are unclean. So how long would she go with him to see the little girls? And then there would be no fun for them at all. They are so small, all dressed in their ugly grey dresses. I take them humbugs so that while Marcos talks to them at least they have something sweet in their mouths. No, I cannot stop going.'

'Is it so arduous? Or have you something better to do with your time?'

She shrugged, palms to heaven.

'Anton's pony, he has a dull and lonely life with nothing to do but munch the grass of the paddock while poor Anton is a prisoner at school. It is time I rode again.'

Matthew said nothing, just watched her and waited, eyebrows raised in an unspoken question.

'And why not?' Yvette's eyes shone with silent laughter. 'Have you seen the new blacksmith, he has taken over the forge from the old man with the long white whiskers who I always feared would burn them off on his furnace. Now, the blacksmith, he is a man with such strength. He says very little. But his eyes are full of laughter.'

'Yes, I was called to see his daughter. Yvette, he has a wife and three children. They have moved to Brackleford full of hope—'

'Ach! You are just like all the others. So he has a wife. Good, I am glad. I do not want to marry him. There is no better companion than a man who has a wife.'

Sometimes she made Matthew laugh. Tonight wasn't one of those times.

Elsie had been in. Even though the little house was silent and empty when Ian came home, he could sense that she'd been there before he even came from the passage to the living room. Time and again, through the weeks he'd been alone, he had tried to persuade Elsie to move in with him, to defy convention and live as they would have done had he not messed everything up by getting ensnared with Jane. But, for all her loving warmth, for all her smiling face, Elsie had a will of iron.

The living-room table shone, she must have been 'giving it a bit of elbow grease' as she called it. The rugs had been shaken, the cushions plumped and, even though the grate was empty, the brass surround had been polished till it shone like gold. In the kitchen the fire had been banked up and kettles filled so that there would be plenty of hot water for him to wash before he went to the Queen Charlotte. After the first two or three weeks with Jane, Ian had taken pleasure in wearing his working shirt when he went out in the evening. He had known it offended her. Yet Elsie hadn't cared what he wore, she'd found the same pleasure in having him with her in his working clothes as she would have, had he changed into his Sunday suit. With Jane gone, he found a new pride. Each evening he stripped to the waist and washed, then put on the better shirt he had left hanging on the hook behind the door since the previous evening, leaving the working one on the back of the bedroom chair for morning. He did it as a gesture – mentally he was cocking a snook at Jane and her fancy ways.

And another good thing about having her gone, he no longer had to hand over most of his wages for her to waste on food that never compared with the suppers Elsie put before him. With the rent money left under a stone outside the front door, the rest of his earnings was his own.

It was Thursday and he still had a shilling or two in his pocket: no wonder, as he rubbed the macassar oil on to his unruly hair, he smiled with satisfaction. On the way to the Queen Charlotte he would stop at the barrow on the corner and buy a bunch of chrysanthemums. His own smile broadened as he imagined Elsie's pleasure. If the bar wasn't too busy and George wasn't going to need the barrel being changed, he'd persuade her to come back with him for an hour or two after he'd had his supper.

He sat down on the edge of his bed, a bed that she

always managed to find time to come in and make, even though very often it had to be when she did the afternoon shopping. When she bounced up the pillows and smoothed the sheets, where were her thoughts? Oh, he knew well enough where they were. And his too. Perhaps tonight would be the night she'd give in. He'd tell her what the chaps at the coopers had been talking about: the 'safe time', that's what they said. Jim Bowles had used it ever since his wife had her fifth more than six years ago, and never once had to feed her on gin and health salts to put her right.

But for him and Elsie it wasn't the real answer. If he couldn't marry her, that was too bad. But what was the point in marriage anyway – you make promises you can't keep, you get let down. Damn Jane, from the bottom of his heart he said it. But if Elsie cared for him as much as he thought she did, then surely she must see they were wasting their lives living like this. He could give up this rotten hovel (habit made him think of it as that, even though since Jane had gone it had shone as never before), he could go and live at the pub, be on hand when George wanted him. He and Elsie could live together just like husband and wife – and bugger the narrow-minded gossips. They ought to have children – my boy, poor little bastard. Elsie would give him sons, perhaps even daughters too, chubby and jolly like she was herself. Yes, tonight he'd persuade her back to the house . . .

The evening looked like going as he wanted.

'Go to your place?' she queried as he wiped his plate clean with the remainder of his crust of bread. 'But it's warmer here, love, Dad's downstairs, we can be cosy as anything.'

'But hark at them down there. Else, I want you to myself, somewhere where we can shut the door on the world. Tell you what, we'll put a match to the fire in the living room if you're cold. But you won't be. Else, Else please, come home with me. There's nothing of *her* there, if that's what stops you. Well, you know there isn't. That place is yours and mine.' No one but Ian had ever called her 'Else'; that and the thought of the little house being his and hers made it impossible for her to resist.

They didn't put a match to the living-room fire, neither did they stay in the warm but uncomfortable kitchen. Instead, walking behind her up the narrow stairs, he guided her to the bedroom. His pulses were racing. Tonight nothing would stop them. Willingly she let him take off her dress, willingly she unhooked her all-encasing corsets. Eagerly she helped him off with his tidy shirt and folded it over the rail at the foot of the bed; next came his trousers to be hung by its side. His underpants were those that a year ago Jane had touched with such excitement and reverence, the only difference being that now there were holes where then there had been thin patches. Elsie had a mind that could stretch two ways; naked in front of him, cradling his head to her more than ample breast, she was wondering whether he possessed any darning material. If he did, then she would mend his pants before she went home.

But what he was telling her took her mind off darning. Safe! He said it would be safe.

'You want us to,' he whispered, his hand caressing, his fingers exploring. 'You can't pretend you don't want to just like I do.'

She nodded. 'More than anything in all the world I want you. When you married *her*, I thought I'd die from being so miserable. No one knew. Every night I used to pretend, like you're doing to me now, I used to pretend it was you. Still do.'

'You're crying. Else, what you crying for? We're still here, you and me. We got the rest of our lives. Nothing stops us—'

'It's not your marriage vows, they don't stop me. Safe, you say. But Ian, suppose it wasn't. I want you to give me babies, but it's not fair to risk our babies being illegitimate, they're too precious. And I'm frightened. When you and

191

me come together – and every night I pray we will – then nothing must spoil it, not being frightened, not stealing moments like this would be.'

'Damn and blast Jane. She's run out on me, I could divorce her. But where the hell is the woman? I can't afford to put people on her trail. Elsie, she can't rule our lives for us. It's my fault, all this bloody mess is my own fault. I married her out of ambition, it's you I've always loved.'

'I know, Ian love. And we'll find out where she is, we'll get you free of her. Then nothing will stop us being together. But forget her, don't let's think about her, not now. She's spoilt enough for us already. This evening there's just you and me.' Forcing his knees apart she knelt heavily on the floor in front of him. She rested her head against his nakedness, she moved her face against the mat of dark hair on his chest. He saw the way she moved her tongue, moistening her parted lips, as she bent over him. His pulses raced.

All too soon he was lying back on the bed, breathless and exhausted, while she struggled back into her underwear. With her clothes once more on, she gently covered him with the eiderdown then, picking up the worn underpants from where he had dropped them, she went downstairs to search for darning material. All she could find was a brown paper bag where Jane had kept the things she'd used to alter her skirts. Cotton would take longer than wool, her stitches would have to be neatly woven, but it was better than leaving him with his seat out. Patiently and automatically she stitched, her mind going round in circles and bringing a solution no nearer. What hope had they of finding Jane? She'd left the district, perhaps she'd gone to some of her well-to-do acquaintances; perhaps she'd gone to London to lose herself in the crowd. And, even if they found out where she was, how could she and Ian find the money to pay for solicitors or judges or whoever it was had to arrange a divorce.

*

Twice Alice came to see Jane, each time on a Sunday, the only day she was free from the brewery.

'Tell me about everything,' Jane said eagerly. Then, fearing Alice would hear it simply as 'Have you seen Matthew?' she rushed on with, 'Are you getting regular news of your husband?'

'They let me see him last week,' Alice told her. 'Matthew was going on one of his visits, he drove me with him to Reading to the gaol.'

'How is he?'

'Matthew?'

'I meant your husband. He must have been so thankful to see you well and – and – strong. You've given strength to me, I'm sure you do to him.'

'Gerald never lacked strength, strength of character. That's been my greatest comfort. There is a doctor who visits the prisoners when they are sick, but Matthew is different. He goes to Reading specially, you know, just to see Gerald. Gerald and I have never had need of a doctor, but Matthew used to come if Terry wasn't well. To have him visiting is a link with the past.'

'How is he? Does he ever mention me? Does he understand why I left?'

'Oh yes, he mentions you. I hate lying to him, pretending I don't hear. And does he understand, you say. How can I tell? I believe he suspects I know more than I tell him. After all, it's not likely that in three months you wouldn't have written to me. But dear Matthew, he's a sensitive soul, he would be too careful of me to force me into a corner, I dare say. But why, Jane? Why can't you at least send him a message? How could that cause gossip or harm his reputation?'

'He was content before he met me. He'll be content again. But if I send messages, if I tell him – oh, never mind. No good can come from it, I've told you before, I'm nothing but bad news for him.'

'His wife isn't dependent on his adoration, if that's what you think.'

Jane's laugh was spontaneous. 'I never imagined she was. But he wasn't unhappy. That's what I want for him, that he can get back the sort of contentment he had before I came into the picture. No, that's a lie. What I *want* is just an impossible dream.'

'Now tell me how you're getting on with this job of yours,' Alice changed the subject. 'Mrs Phillpott seems to be a very kindly soul. Not every landlady would let a lodger have guests for tea – and make a special cake, too.'

'She's a dear, and so is he. As for my job. It's at the brewery, but it could be anywhere as far as the work goes. Not a bit like I remember.'

Going home in the train Alice relived their time together. This was the last train, half past seven from Addingford Halt; speeding through the November evening there was nothing beyond the window except darkness.

The following Thursday the fog hung cold and damp over the countryside all day. By the time Jane came out of the gate of the brewery soon after six o'clock it was already dark, the air dank and still.

She wasn't the only one to leave work at that time; other people were hurrying homeward. So when she heard footsteps behind her she gave them no thought.

Chapter Ten

Whoever the steps belonged to must have been in a hurry. She stood to one side, expecting someone to rush past her.

'Jane.' Frightened to believe her ears, frightened to answer in case it had been only in imagination that the voice was his, she stood stock still. 'I waited by the wrong gate.'

He was real. He was here, by her side, her gloved hand gripped in his.

'How did you know? Alice . . .'

'Don't blame Alice. Be as grateful to her as I am. Did you expect I could have let you walk away and picked up the pieces as if those months had never happened? I've imagined you in London, I've imagined – but what does any of that matter now? She *had* to tell me. She's too fond of us both not to.'

Jane only half listened. Leaning against him she felt his arms around her. Like a ship, tossed and battered by storm, coming at last to the calm safety of harbour, she looked no further than the moment.

'Why couldn't you have told me? It was not knowing—'

'If I'd told you I was going, I knew you'd try and stop me. And I couldn't stay—'

'With him? You thought I'd want you to do that?'

'Ian? No, he had nothing to do it. I'd already told him I was leaving him – that's why he did what he did—'

Matthew could only guess at what was left unsaid. But Ian was unimportant. He'd found Jane and, this time, nothing would come between them. He could feel the warmth of her breath; defused by fog, in the yellow lights from the brewery behind them he could see it in the cold, raw November air. His mouth covered hers. When the brim of his hat knocked the brim of hers, dislodging it to hang secured only by its long pin, they laughed. Whatever the future had in store for them, there was nothing to mar this moment.

'Mrs Phillpott!' she called a few minutes later as she led the way into the narrow passage of Haphill, 'I have a surprise visitor. Is it all right if I bring him in?'

Agnes Phillpott appeared from the kitchen, wiping her clean hands down her clean, afternoon overall. "Him", young Miss Bradley had said. Well, best she came out of her kitchen and gave him a looking over. The girl seemed moral enough, but it was up to her to make sure there were no shenanigans going on.

'You didn't say you were expecting anyone.' She kept the smile in her voice while she weighed up the stranger. A good enough looking young man, she had to give him credit for that. Yes, a serious face, yet when he smiled and held his hand towards hers the way it lit up was sudden and brief.

'That's because I didn't know,' Jane told her. 'Matthew was waiting for me outside the brewery. Matthew, this is Mrs Phillpott, she took me in when I was looking for some-where – and I've never lived better,' she ended with a laugh intended to dispel the landlady's suspicions. For, in the way that one woman can read another's mind, she knew she was skating on thin ice. 'Mrs Phillpott, this is my brother Matthew. He's been away for some time, and has only just arrived back in Brackleford.' Then, her story snowballing as untruths invariably do: 'He's been working in France. When he got back he went to see Alice, you remember Alice – Mrs Gregson. So she was able to tell him where I was.'

'Fancy that. France, you say? Working there, you say?'

'That's right,' Matthew answered, with that quick smile.

'He's a—' Jane interrupted. She was about to say he was an engineer but pulled herself up just in time. After all, the next question might be, what engineering company was he going to work for in Brackleford. 'He's a writer. A travel writer.' Yes, now wasn't that quick thinking? She was beginning to enjoy her fabrication, warming to the theme. Solemnly she and Matthew looked at each other, as solemn a glance as might be expected between brother and sister. Yet each recognized the suppressed laughter in the other's eyes. Their shared secret joke held them close and had to be enough to content them.

'Fancy that! A real writer.' Mrs Phillpott was impressed. 'Well, don't stand here in the passage, come along into the kitchen. I'll put another cup and saucer, and such, on the table. Can't ask you to stay for supper, Mr Bradley –' and, not surprisingly, at the name another quick glance passed between the two conspirators – 'we don't eat it until Mr Phillpott gets home from the station. In charge there, he is. Once the half past seven goes through he can lock the door. Nothing else stops at Addingford after that time of evening. Well, it wouldn't would it? Any last packages or pieces of mail to go that way he puts on the half past seven, mostly that's all it collects at the Halt. Would be no use people gallivanting off at that time of evening, for there'd be no way back for them. So it's no use asking you to keep Miss Bradley company for a bite of supper, it's the half past seven you'll have to be on. But a nice hot cup of tea will warm you and I'll cut you a good slice of my ginger cake. One for you too, Miss Bradley. I knocked it up this morning specially, you liked it so much last time.'

'Lovely,' Jane thanked her. Then to Matthew, 'You see? I've never eaten so well. It was my lucky day when I got off the train at Addingford and met Mr Phillpott.'

Agnes sat and watched them as they ate, Matthew even pleasing her by accepting a second slice. Nice young pair they were. Not every brother and sister were such friends, even though he must be a goodish few years older than her.

'You've never spoken about your family, Miss Bradley. Fancy, all these weeks and you never told me you had a brother in France. I suppose your parents have gone on to the better land?'

'Yes,' Jane answered. 'Mother died so long ago I can't even remember her.' And Father? She stopped short, even in this world of make-believe she was creating she couldn't form the words. So it was Matthew who answered.

'Father, about ten years ago.' And Jane knew that just as she'd told the truth about her mother, so had he about his own father.

'So you two will have been all in all to each other.' Agnes was apparently satisfied with the situation. She took the lid off the teapot and peered inside. That's how she missed the look that passed between Jane and Matthew. All in all to each other, silently it echoed her words. 'There's a drop more in the pot. How about you, Mr Bradley?'

To please her he passed her his cup.

'If you walk to the railway with your brother, Miss Bradley, you'll be able to introduce him to Mr Phillpott. But you don't need to go for twenty minutes or so. You two sit there by the fire while I clear away the cups and see to the veg for supper. Talk away, I shall be too busy to listen.' She laughed, well pleased with her own jollity. She supposed this brother had had to be parents and brother too to poor Miss Bradley. Fancy earning his living writing travel books; to one who'd never travelled further than Reading in one direction and, just once and an experience she had no ambition to repeat, to London in the other, it set him in a world apart. She must make sure to tell him he was always welcome to visit her here. And to be honest, it had brightened up the day no end having unexpected company for tea.

He accepted the invitation with alacrity, but it wasn't what either he or Jane wanted.

*

He came as often as he could but the visits became ever more frustrating. He was welcomed as if he were a family friend, the opportunities to be alone with Jane, even to speak to her out of earshot, were few as the year drew towards its close. He was tempted to come by motor car, but the journey was so much quicker by rail.

'You could motor to Ilkingham,' Jane suggested, remembering how her train had stopped there on the day she'd left Brackleford. 'On Sundays I could get off the train there and at least we'd have somewhere on our own.' The interior of a draughty motor car on a cold winter day might not be perfect, but the thought of talking freely was more than worth any discomfort.

She always bought her ticket to Brackleford, telling the Phillpotts that she was going to see both Matthew and Alice. It was hard to live a life of lies, but once having set out on it there was no other way. Alice had become so much part of her days in Brackleford; now they had nothing but letters. And even those Jane either hid or burnt once they'd been read. Not that she honestly suspected Agnes would pry through her things and read her letters, but it was all part of the web of deceit she'd woven.

When she'd run away from Brackleford she had believed that it was simply to protect Matthew's position there. Hadn't she told him that Ian had had nothing to do with it? Wherever she lived it certainly would never again be with *him*. Yet as the months of that winter went by, she was honest enough to face the complete truth. No one in Brackleford must know where she was or word might get back to Ian. More and more often in the night, sweating with terror, she'd wake from a dream that he was with her. Sometimes he'd be holding her down and forcing himself on her; sometimes beating her, his powerful hand made even larger and stronger in the way of nightmares; sometimes as she thrashed and twisted in her sleep it would be as he threw her to the ground. She would try to scream, the nightmare made worse because her mouth was stiff, no sound would come; she would try to push him off her but she had no strength. No wonder she woke with her heart pounding, her mouth dry with fear. Logic told her that she had deserted him, and that was enough for him to petition for his freedom. And surely he must want that as much as she did herself. But an even louder voice of logic reminded her that to end a marriage in the divorce court took money: something Ian didn't have.

Her freedom would have been more secure if, instead of following instinct and alighting from the train at the sight of a brewery, she'd gone straight on to London. But in London she wouldn't have had Sunday afternoons with Matthew, and sometimes an hour or so during the week in the welcoming warmth of the kitchen at Haphill too.

Her second Christmas away from Maybury House came and went.

'Dear Dad,' she wrote, 'I know now that you were right. I thought he was pure gold, I was too infatuated to see the truth – and too pigheaded to listen. I lost my baby. I don't want to tell you about it, I don't want to remember.' Her pen flew, her thoughts rushing ahead as she thought of her father; faster and faster she wrote. 'Why wouldn't you answer my letters? Surely you understood nothing could have changed me? We were angry – but all that is so unimportant. Dad, I have left Ian, I would have left him in any case, better to be alone than live with someone who – well, none of that matters now. My life is Matthew. That is the solemn truth, more solemn than the promises I made when I was married. He has a wife, but I am truly sure that even before he and I found each other he had no real marriage, not whole and complete like ours would be if only it were possible. It was because I care about him more than I do about myself that I left Brackleford. You see, he is a local doctor there. In the town he is respected. None of that must ever change because of me. So all I have of him is odd stolen hours at the weekends when we can drive into the country, walk, talk . . .'

Her thoughts had reached full stop, at least full stop as far as being poured out on to her writing paper. Reading through what she'd written she put down her pen. Turning the knife in the wound of their quarrel, she imagined her father opening her letter. Oh, he'd be glad she'd finished with Ian – or had he washed his hands of her so thoroughly that he wouldn't even be touched by that? Imagine the look of disgust on his face when he read that she'd fallen in love with a married man. She'd broken her own vows (albeit vows he hadn't approved of); now she was encouraging a married man to break his. What was the use of trying to make him understand? No use. If she sent this letter, it would end the same way as all the others. Why couldn't she learn not to care?

Going down to the kitchen, she lifted the lid on the kitchen range and dropped the firmly twisted pieces of notepaper on to the burning coals.

He was always waiting for her when she got off the train at Ilkingham and from there they'd drive the few miles into the country. They walked on the bridleway along the treed brow of Woodhampstead Ridges, they sat on the trunk of a fallen tree in Roundham Wood, they talked, they laughed, they both felt the joy of being thoroughly alive because they were together. But the hours were too few, dusk fell early and there was always the knowledge that Jane had to be on the train back to Addingford.

They were two weeks into the new year. In 1907 just as in every other year, New Year Resolutions had been made and were in the process of being broken. But Jane had made none: she lived each day as it came and didn't dig below the surface. It was a bitterly cold Sunday, the rain lashing against the windshields of his motor car and making walking out of the question. But she didn't even mind that. Enough just to sit here near each other, talking, relaxed and at ease.

'Jane, this won't do, you know. Not for me and not for you either.'

Matthew's sudden serious note was to her like a blow between the eyes. Please, I beg, don't let him stop coming. Is that what he means? What else can he mean? Frightened to trust her voice, frightened to look at him, she made an unnatural – at any rate, unnatural for her – gesture of rearranging her hat.

'Jane, say something.'

Wordlessly she shook her head.

'There's only one answer, and we both know it. We have to stop this pretence. Deceit doesn't agree with us. Look at me, Jane.'

With her chin high and fixing what she intended to be a smile on her face she turned towards him.

'I know you're right,' she forced the words, determined to hide her aching misery. 'We're neither of us cut out for leading double lives. Why do you think I left Brackleford? Why did you have to follow me here? Why couldn't you have seen then that what I did was the only way?'

Like a broken-hearted clown she kept her voice light, knowing that if she let her mouth lose that stiff smile a croak would escape her and she'd be lost. But she didn't fool Matthew.

'I came here because my life's empty without you. I told you once, we're two halves making one whole. Without each other we're not complete. Don't Jane, don't cry, darling.'

But in her relief she couldn't help it. When he pulled her into his arms, knocking her hat to be held just by its anchoring pin, nothing mattered except the moment. They weren't made for deceit, yet they had a plain choice: deceit or separation. Even Agnes Phillpott would close her door to him – probably to both of them – if she knew the truth.

'These few hours are a lifeline. But they can never be a life. Tell me, Jane, how much does your work at the brewery mean to you?'

'It means I can pay Mrs Phillpott my rent. As for it being at a brewery, it could just as easily be in the cash desk at the butcher's shop or in the accounts office of some factory.

If fate made me get off the train at Addingford it must have been because it was leading me to the Phillpotts, but certainly not to those dusty account books. If we can't go on, you mustn't worry about me, Matthew. I shall go on to London, like I'd intended. I'll find work. And I promise I'll write to Alice so that she can tell you what I'm doing so that you won't wor . . .' The end of her sentence was lost as his mouth covered hers.

'You think I'll lose you again?' he whispered. 'I'll give up my practice, we'll make a new life. We'll go where no one knows us. I've enough behind me for us to make a home together, I'd find work—'

'No! I won't let you do it. Doctoring is your life. Your patients love you—'

'And I love you.'

'But you wouldn't. You'd come to resent me.' She wouldn't listen to temptation. Someone must keep their feet firmly on the ground, and that someone must be her. 'Nothing will change my mind. Doesn't matter how much I wish it could be like that, I know it can't.'

'I shall find somewhere to rent where you can live and I can see you. Just you and me. I don't want to drag your name through the divorce court and, in any case, in the injustice of our laws, a wife has no grounds to divorce her husband because he has a mistress. Mistress! As if I could ever think of you as that.'

Her laugh was reaction to fear. 'Not as we are at the moment you couldn't. But with a place of our own – Matthew, call me mistress, call me lover, what's in a name. The world might prefer to call me a whore, at any rate some of the gossips with nothing better to think of might. Let them. I'd be proud.'

'I'll talk to Yvette. I'll find out what it takes for a woman to divorce her husband.'

Jane was letting herself be carried along by the images his words evoked. Only then did she consider the relevance.

'No, don't. I left Brackleford just so that something like this wouldn't happen. People trust you, people look up to you—'

'Then they shouldn't. Jane, we've made mistakes, both of us. But does that mean we have no right to finding our happiness now?'

'Of course we shall be happy. We'll have so much more than we have already. What does it matter if we tell one last lie to dear Mrs Phillpott, tell her that you are renting somewhere I can call my own? Is that such a rare thing for a successful writer to do for his sister.'

'Oh, I'm a *successful* writer now, am I?' His eyes laughed even though the smile only touched his mouth briefly, in that quick smile she loved.

'If I'm inventing a career for you, I certainly wouldn't be inventing one that was anything less.' She tried to move closer to him on the bench seat, but she was already as close as she could get. So she threw her hat to join his on the narrow back seat and snuggled her face against his neck. 'Let's make plans. I don't cook nearly as well as Mrs Phillpott, but for you I shall enjoy trying.'

Making plans the time melted. Soon she was alone on the train as it puffed and hissed its way back to Addingford.

On that same Sunday afternoon in the front bedroom of St Stephen's vicarage, Alayne gave birth to a daughter. Throughout her days of waiting, she had kept well. It was only the prudish code of the day that had kept her away from her parish visiting, and hadn't allowed her to relieve Yvette of the orphanage hymn sessions. Only her sewing parties had continued unaltered and what a joy it had been to her to sit amongst these dear, good ladies, conscious of their admiration for her that after eleven years of marriage and, already over thirty, she's had such obvious joy in the thought of a baby.

The birth was as uncomplicated as the preceding months had been. Tired and triumphant, Alayne lay back on her pillows and heard the infant's first lusty cry. Her heart was full of thankfulness. Her thoughts were a confusion of thanks, relief and humility, all of them a silent communion with the God she held above all else. You've blessed me, my soul doth magnify ... I won't fail You. You've blessed me with this sacred trust, I vow I won't fail. I'll do my part. In your love You've granted me what I wanted so much, so very much, to be given a baby. But I vow that I will never let my parish work suffer, I will always try to carry your message. Thank You, thank You ... Hark at him ... Him? Her? I don't even know that.

But she was too weary to ask. By the time the midwife had wrapped the unwashed newborn in a warm blanket, Alayne was asleep. It seemed a shame to wake her, but she had to be made ready for the vicar to be allowed in.

Half an hour later, mother and daughter both washed and put into clean nightgowns, the midwife went down to tell him his family would receive him.

If fate had drawn Jane's eyes to the brewery building, it must have been listening to the plans she and Matthew were making. They would find somewhere he could rent. Marriage was out of the question: there were no grounds for Yvette to divorce him and, as for Ian, he never had enough money to last from one pay day to the next, so he certainly wouldn't be seeking the services of a solicitor. But what did marriage matter? Both of them had made vows, both of them had intended to keep them. On that Sunday, with the rain beating against the weather-shield, with the leafless branches bending in the velocity of the January storm, for them the promises they made were binding and full of trust. They needed no man to raise his hand in blessing and no sacred building to hear their words. Here, in the cathedral of nature, they knew that what they were doing was right.

Perhaps, indeed, fate had been listening. Alayne, in her simple trust, would have said it was God.

At Ilkingham, Jane boarded the train which had come through Brackleford on its way to Waterloo. Soon there would be no need for this kind of deceit, soon they would have the freedom of a place of their own. In Ilkingham? That would mean she would have to find another job, but her work at Watford's was no more than a means to earn a wage. But was Ilkingham too near Brackleford? Steaming into Addingford Halt, she wasn't in the mood for imagining problems.

'Sight of you's enough to bring a bit of cheer,' Hugh Phillpott said, as he waved the train on its way towards Waterloo. 'Takes a bit of courage to smile on a wild old day like this, I'm jiggered if it doesn't. You don't look very wet, I wonder you could keep your gamp up in this wind.'

'There seemed a lull when I walked to the station.' But, this time, as she opened her umbrella it promptly blew inside out. She turned into the wind to straighten it, then put it down, telling him she would run home between the drops.

That evening when, the half past seven train gone on its way and the ticket office closed for the night, she and the Phillpotts sat round the kitchen table enjoying their Sunday roast, Agnes said something that must surely have meant fate was taking a hand.

'I caught Evie Hobbs as she went by this morning. You remember Evie, Hugh, old Mrs Hobbs's grand-daughter. I happened to be by the window and I saw her battling against the wind as she came along. Then, just like a cloud-burst, the rain started tipping it out of the sky. I called her in and she was pleased enough to come. She was on the way to the dairy to see if, sabbath or no, they'd let her have a jug of milk. The old lady is beyond looking after herself, that's the trouble. Evie said what food there was in the larder was going green with mould. Poor old soul. Anyway Evie has persuaded her it's time to stop arguing and go and live with her and her Bobby. You remember the boy she married, Bobby someone or other, a nice young fellow. To me she's still Evie Hobbs, but she must have been a married woman two years or more. No sign of a family, but perhaps that's as well until she gets poor old Mrs Hobbs settled and feeling at home.'

'Does the old lady rent her house? Where does she live?' Jane knew nothing of the people the Phillpotts were discussing, but what, if not fate, had made Agnes repeat the story at supper. She might just as easily have forgotten it until later when they were alone in their bedroom.

'Oh ay, she rents it. There's not many own their homes in Addingford. Nothing but a hamlet it must have been until the coming of the brewery. The present Mr Watford's father had a deal of building done, to house his workers you understand. Years ago when the old lady's husband was alive, that's where he worked. And Mr Watford's not the sort to turn a widow out.'

'Matthew says that if I found somewhere to rent he'd help with the payments. He has rooms in Brackleford, but he'd write more easily if we had a place of our own.'

'You mean he'd move out to Addingford? Well, now, that would be nice for you, duckie.' Hugh beamed his approval for such filial love.

'I don't know if he'd live here all the time, but he'd certainly find it quieter when he's actually working. Brackleford has a good reference library, I know he uses that a lot. I expect he'd still keep his rooms. But it would be like it used to be, to have a place together.' She might hate the need for deceit, but there was no doubt she was becoming an accomplished actress. 'Tomorrow I shall try and see Mr Watford.'

'For your sake we must hope the old gentleman lets you have Holly Cottage but there's no denying we shall miss having you here, Miss Bradley. And miss seeing your brother too. I hope you'll pay us a visit sometimes.'

'Oh, but we will. And I shall miss being with you too, both of you.' She was surprised just how true that was, although when she imagined how different things would be if she were able to rent the cottage, nothing else mattered.

Standing in the open doorway of Alayne's bedroom, Marcos looked at them unobserved. For Alayne had eyes for nothing but the tiny bundle she held in her arms. Gently she was cradling the dark head in her hand, her expression one of such joy that he felt he ought not to be watching.

'They said I could come in now.' His quiet voice brought her out of her silent communion with her daughter. He crossed to her side and stooped to kiss her forehead. 'Thank God you're all right.'

'Thank God for so much more than that, Marcos darling. Look at her. Our own little girl. Sit on the edge of the bed, then I'll pass her to you. I think she's going to look like you. I hope she is. But it doesn't matter what she looks like, she's perfect, she's – oh Marcos, I never knew there was such – sublime joy.' Her face was flushed, her eyes shone. 'Are you ready?' She passed the well-wrapped bundle into his arms. There was nothing self-conscious in his action as he touched the baby's forehead with the sign of the cross, then bent to kiss the spot. She didn't know what it was he muttered silently, only that it was a blessing. She closed her eyes as if that way she could lock the memory into her mind, always there to draw on when things were difficult.

'She'll need more than one name. We'd agreed that if the baby was a girl' (even before the baby was born and the sex known, Alayne had never said 'it') 'she should be Stephanie, but she ought to have more than one name.'

'What's wrong with Alayne, after you?'

'You know what I'd like? I'd like you to baptize her Stephanie Yvette. I know Mrs Bingley isn't of our church, but right from the first time I met her I have felt her to be my friend. I've never felt able to talk so freely to anyone – not even to you, Marcos. And you like her too, don't you? Think of all the months she has played the piano for you at the orphanage – wouldn't that be a way of showing her how much we appreciate her?'

'Rather a French name, isn't it?' Yvette ... his own daughter always to be a reminder of the consuming desire he had for Yvette, of the way she haunted his thoughts, a reminder of his resolutions, his prayers that he would find the strength to resist the temptation when it drove every-thing else from his mind. Worse were reminders of moments when he'd lost the power to withstand, when there had been nothing but the joy he found in her, and after that the shame, the self-hatred, the knowledge that again he had broken faith not only with Alayne but with his God.

'Marcos ...?' Alayne reached her pale hand towards him. 'Do you not want Yvette? What would you prefer?'

'Stephanie Yvette it shall be.' Yes, he must accept it, he must never let himself forget his shame and his weakness. Alayne had suggested the name to him, but Who had suggested it to her? Thy will be done. 'And one day, little girl, perhaps you'll be as beautiful as your mother.'

The baby gazed at him with that blank, unfocused look of the very young, while Alayne smiled contentedly.

'I'm in here.' Richard Foley called as he saw Jane pass his open doorway. 'That's Mr Watford's office at the end of the passage. What were you wanting me for?'

'It's Mr Watford I want, thank you.'

'Wait, wait, wait. In here a moment if you please.'

She did as he said, standing just inside his office.

'You can't just walk in and disturb Mr Watford like that. I'm sure I can handle any problem you may have.' Florid, pompous and unpleasant, that had been her first impression of the manager and, over the months, she'd had no cause to change her mind. As for Mr Watford, she'd never spoken to him and only seen him briefly, either arriving or being helped into his carriage to be driven away. The owner of a successful brewery, but he preferred life at yesterday's pace.

From his seat behind his large desk Richard Foley nodded his head in the direction of the chair opposite. Not a bad-looking filly, no, not bad at all, he made a mental assessment of Jane. Not nearly as pasty as he remembered her when she'd come looking for work. Pity she had such a grandiose opinion of her own importance. Not at all a bad-looking piece. He nodded appreciatively at her, giving what she was supposed to see as a smile but which she interpreted more accurately as a leer.

'I want to talk to Mr Watford about something quite apart from the brewery. I believe I heard him arrive?'

'I'll see if he'll speak to you. You'd better wait in here – and give me some idea of what you want with him.' Then, again with the smile that held neither warmth nor humour, 'I can't let the workers barge in on him willy nilly, you know.'

Hearing the voices – and, Jane suspected, hearing something of what they said too – Henry Watford came out into the corridor. A small man with stooping shoulders, his hair snowy white and his thick moustache drooping over his upper lip. The sort of moustache that would change colour according to the flavour of his soup, she thought, a smile twitching the corner of her mouth. His age was hard to guess, for just as he still travelled in the same carriage he'd used all his adult life, so he dressed in a black frock coat whose cut would have been fashionable before she was born.

'I heard voices,' he said. 'I believe I heard you say you wanted to speak with me, Miss . . .?'

'Miss Bradley, Jane Bradley. I help Mr Hopkins in the accounts office.'

'Ah yes, he told me. You'd better come into my room. We needn't disturb Mr Foley any longer.'

She ought not to let herself imagine from those last few words that Mr Watford thought no more highly of his manager than she did herself. After all, he wouldn't employ him if he didn't do his job well. One way or the other, she had no interest in Richard Foley; her mission was to be given permission to rent Holly Cottage.

Spinning her story, she told him about the brother who had returned from working in Paris and their wish to make a home together. She avoided carrying the fiction any further; there was no need to elaborate about the rooms in Brackleford.

'I'm in lodgings and he's always made welcome to call and see me—'

'What lodgings?' he interrupted, his question snapping through her story. When she told him he nodded with satisfaction. It seemed that if she was acceptable to the Phillpotts that was reference enough. So he agreed that when Mrs Hobbs vacated Holly Cottage Jane should take the tenancy for as long as she worked for the brewery.

'Where does my brother pay the rent?'

'The rent will be deducted from your wages. You can't expect me to take this brother of yours on trust. No, no, indeed. The rent is due weekly and that's the way it will be.'

'However it is paid, you will have it the day it is due.' She stood tall – and nature had given her the advantage over him.

'See Foley and tell him the arrangement. But remember, if you leave the brewery you lose the tenancy.'

With dignity that hinted at disdain she bowed her head.

'I'll bear the terms in mind. And thank you for agreeing to my renting it.' She turned to leave, her emotions confused. Thankful she was to be granted the tenancy and yet with each day she was at Watford's she disliked the atmosphere of the place more. How different an interview like this would have been at Bradley's. She pictured her father, always fair, always caring of his staff, genuinely interested in each man's name and circumstances. The men here never whistled as they worked, never called bawdy remarks to each other to bring the sound of laughter to echo in the great hall where they worked the mashing tuns.

On the way past Richard Foley's room she stopped to tell

211

him the outcome of her interview and, as unsmilingly as old Mr Watford had set out the renting arrangement to her, to pass on the instruction to the manager.

It was half way through February when Mrs Hobbs vacated the cottage, agreeing to sell some of her furniture to Jane and her brother.

While George Hamley was in the cellar, Elsie looked after the bar. On the bleak February morning there were only three regulars huddled by the fire. In her opinion they'd be better occupied helping their wives on their market stalls but, for them, market day was another name for a day off. One of them was Jim Slater who kept the fish shop at the end of Merchant Street. Most mornings he collected his boxes of fish from the train and manned his shop, but Thursday the routine changed. He piled his truck and pushed it to the market while Dolly, his wife, walked behind, carrying a basket with the weights and scales and a box for the money in one hand, a three-legged stool in the other, and with an umbrella tucked under her arm. Having got her stall set up, Jim considered he'd earned his freedom until he took over from her at teatime so that she could go home and prepare their supper, for, by the light of kerosene lamps, trading went on well into the evening. Each Thursday a sign on the door of the fish shop announced: 'Closed – fish for sale in Market'. It was much the same for Ernie Motts from the sweet shop, with the addition that on the sweet stall in the market his wife sold the local children's favourite toffee apples which she made fresh each Wednesday in readiness. The third man wasn't local, he brought his wife in on a cart from their smallholding and left her to sell eggs and any vegetables available.

Lazy devils, Elsie thought, as she rubbed the bar until it gleamed. You wouldn't get Ian behaving like it. No, he'd have too much pride. From morn till night he worked. Her bonny face broke into a smile of its own accord as she thought of him.

'. . . Always was a lass, that one, or so I've heard,' the smallholder whose name she didn't know was chuckling. 'True as I sit here though, she was a picture sitting astride that horse,' then with a guffaw, '. . . picture of mischief more like it. Leads the doctor a dance, make no mistake.'

'All the same, these people who think themselves above the rest of us.' Jim Slater settled nearer the fire. 'From what I've always heard about her she was nowt but a French tart he picked up on the street in Paris.'

'Hey, hey, Jim, that's a bit rich.' This from Ernie Motts of the sweet shop who was a staunch member of the choir at St Stephen's and recalled Yvette's contribution to the fund-raising concert – especially he recalled her contribution to the 'run through'. 'Professional singer, that's what she was. And, by gum, she knows how to get a man going – if you know what I mean.'

'I know what you mean right enough. So do a good many from round about. I've even heard a whisper – from Stan Hodge, he's a conductor on the trams, back and forth from Wemberton end to the terminus at Millsham – he tells me that vicar of yours is out there at her house pretty often.'

'Bugger me!' the smallholder chuckled and puffed contentedly at his pipe. 'Even after the vicar is she? Well, given the chance there's no difference between us, we'd none of us say no if it was handed to us on a plate, eh?'

'The vicar is as good a man as you'll find,' Ernie came to his defence like a loyal member of his flock. 'It would be my bet she needed a bit of help. Moral help, you understand. Spends his whole life on other people, does the vicar.'

'Like I was saying,' Jim Slater went on as if he'd not been interrupted, 'some of them think themselves a cut above the rest. But that doctor husband of hers, every day his car was down Mill Lane till you know who upped and offed. And I know that's the solemn truth.'

'Don't believe it.' Ernie seemed less inclined to think the

worst than the other two. 'Perhaps you two don't know the doctor like I do. He's been kindness itself to my old lady.'

While Elsie had continued to polish the gleaming counter she had strained her ears. Now she came closer.

'Give me an inch, chaps. I want to see to the fire.'

'An inch you say?' Jim nudged her chunky waist as she moved towards the grate. 'Say the word and I'll find more than an inch for you any day of the week.'

'Steady on, Jim.' Again Ernie tried to take control.

'Hark at him,' Jim laughed, winking at Elsie. 'Wouldn't know a joke if it hit him in the face. It's all that churchgoing you do, Ernie m'lad, takes all the fun out of you. Anyway, let the doctor and his Frenchie wife get their fun where then can, that's what I say. Gives us all something to chunter about.'

'Dr Bingley?' Elsie turned from where she was raking the dead ash. 'Oh, come off it, Jim – I say, I wish you wouldn't get so close to the heat, you don't half pong of fish.' Just as she intended, her remark was met with shouts of mirth. 'No, I don't believe a word you say about Dr Bingley. He was kind to Ian's wife, I know that.'

'And wasn't that what I said? There at the house being good to her every morning he was. You're too good for this world, young Elsie. Now that hoity-toity your Ian wed, she angled after him from what I've heard. Ought to have stayed where she belonged, not come here messing up people's lives.'

'Amen to that,' Elsie agreed. 'Still, she's gone now. Probably back where she came from.'

'Perhaps she has and perhaps she hasn't. Still, you can't believe everything you hear.'

'Enough gossiping over other people's affairs.' Elsie gave them her most friendly smile as she stood up from the hearthrug. 'Now, who wants me to get him another ale? If not, I'm off upstairs to see to that fire next.'

They watched her go with affection. A thoroughly good lass was Elsie. Deserved a husband and family. There was no justice in this world, having her nose put out of joint by a stuck-up young madam like Ian Harriman had got smitten with.

That evening while she sat and watched Ian eat the stew and dumplings she had kept back to warm up for him, Elsie told him what she'd heard.

'It's cruel the way people talk,' she said. 'I've got no time for Jane, but there was no call for stories like that to get about. And it's not fair on the doctor either.'

'True enough about his French wife. Must be true. I've seen her around – I've seen the way she looks at me. And she doesn't even know me.' He chuckled as he wiped his mouth with the back of his hand, then pushed his empty plate towards her. 'Got a bit more left in the saucepan? No, the Bingley woman, it's right enough what they say about her. A man can tell at a glance. If I'd liked to give her the look, I'd have been on my way to getting what I wanted from her.'

'And did you want it from her, love?' Emily teased.

'Tell you, I'm getting to the stage I want it from anyone who'll give it to me.'

She passed back the refilled plate then came to his side, drawing his head against her soft bosom.

'Tip that back in the stewpot,' he whispered as he nuzzled. 'You're the food I want.'

'Let's go to your place.'

Lately they were in the habit of going to Mill Lane. He may not get the food he yearned, but she was uninhibited and loving, she never left him hungry. It was she who ended her evenings knowing that life should be so much more than this.

That night, after he'd taken Elsie home and helped George 'put the bar to bed', he walked back to his solitary house feeling thoroughly disgrunted. What hope had they for the future? He had no idea where Jane had run off to – probably back to that bloody father to beg forgiveness. Slamming the front door shut behind him he went straight upstairs to bed. Elsie had already seen that the fire was banked for the night and the kettles filled and left to heat. Without lighting a candle he tore off his outer clothes then, still wearing his vest and those carefully darned underpants, tumbled into the rumpled bed. The sheets were cold. There was no comfort. Imagine going to sleep holding her soft, warm body. If only he had the money to get legal help, he'd track Jane down. She'd deserted him, refused to live with him. Yes, and she'd spited him even over the boy. If he had the money he'd drag her through a divorce court, he'd show her up for what she was, he'd knock her off her high perch, he'd . . . he was sinking into sleep.

Then suddenly his eyes were wide open. He knew just what he would do.

Chapter Eleven

Winter 1907

Whoever Yvette expected her visitor might be, it certainly wasn't the man who waited for her in the drawing room. She'd noticed him before, with his trimmed dark beard and his curly hair, his shoulders that told of his strength, his height that made him a giant amongst men. Oh yes, she'd noticed him – and left him in no doubt! But she hadn't anticipated he would call on her at home.

'You wanted to see me – or was it my husband, the doctor?' Her words, spoken in an accent that he found interesting and exciting, were as prim as he might have heard from any other woman he could have called upon. Only the light in her gingery brown eyes told another tale.

'It is you I need to talk to, Mrs Bingley. I've noticed you in town sometimes, I've often wanted to speak to you. I reckon you know that already. But that isn't why I'm here. Is this a good time? Can I be sure we shan't be disturbed?'

'My husband, he is busy with his surgery in the middle of the town. Here, there is no one except the servants. And they will not interrupt, unless I ring the bell and ask for you to be shown out.'

Ian smiled at her; nearer the truth, he grinned at her. 'I shan't give you cause to have me shown the door,' he said.

She laughed.

'Then, won't you sit down, Mr . . .?'

'Harriman. Ian Harriman. I wouldn't expect my name to mean anything to you – unless, of course, your husband talked to you about my wife. But I doubt if he would. Isn't it right that a doctor doesn't discuss his patient.' Then, raising his eyebrows, he added meaningfully, 'A doctor's private and professional lives never touch, isn't that so?'

'My husband, he never talks of his patients. Not that I want to hear. *You* cannot be a sick person? No, I can see you are not. To me you appear to be – to be – gloriously, yes gloriously healthy.'

'As healthy a man as ever was.' Yes, he was healthy, he was brimming with vitality and appreciation.

Sitting down opposite him. Yvette began to enjoy herself. Life could be so intolerably dull and never more so than in the dark winter evenings. Her fun had to come from the acquaintances she made to fill her idle hours. But not one of them – not even the wonderfully handsome vicar – could compete with the gift heaven had dropped so unexpectedly in her lap this evening. This Ian Harriman was surely every woman's dream. On the previous occasions she'd seen him he had been wearing the standard dress of a workman: a collarless shirt, baggy trousers for ease of movement, a well-worn jacket, hobnailed boots, a black felt hat. For his visit he had taken pains with his appearance, he was dressed in his only good suit of hounds' tooth check, a brown bowler hat placed on the side table as he took the chair she offered. No wonder she smiled and suddenly saw life in brighter colours.

'You and me, they must think we're stupid,' Ian said as he leant forward and, with the movement, seemed to link his situation with hers. 'Let me start at the beginning – at least, the beginning as far as your husband and Jane go. Whether he's acted the same with other patients, I don't know. It was when Jane – was expecting our son that she first had dealings with Dr Bingley. I didn't think anything of it. She'd been brought up soft, you understand. Most women have their babies without the need of a doctor,

218

what's more natural than a woman bearing a child – unless it's conceiving it. It's nature's way. But Jane had been brought up soft, like I said. She ran to the doctor right from the first. But I lived with her, I know for a fact there was nothing wrong with her to need a doctor. Yet, through those months a morning hardly went by when his motor car wasn't outside my house. You understand what I'm saying?'

'You think Matthew was – was – how do you say it? – having a liaison with this Jane of yours?' She laughed. 'Oh, but Mr Harriman—'

'Ian. Please call me by my name – Ian.'

'Ian. Yes, and you must call me Yvette, for if your wife Jane and my husband Matthew have been making love to each other, then surely that makes of us the good friends?'

'Yvette, that is a lovely name. It suits you.'

'Ian, I like to have you for my friend. I am happy that you have come to see me. But as for your Jane and my husband the doctor, what is your concern? Are you saying you think he has given her the child she carries?'

'God, no! The baby was mine. My son. Yvette, I wanted that boy more than I've ever wanted anything in this life. Jane could have been bedded with any Tom, Dick or Harry she chose and I wouldn't have cared, if I'd had my son. But could she give him to me? No. I told you, all the time she was pregnant she made an invalid of herself for doing what nature meant her for. And when the time came and I sent for your husband, expecting her to have the child at home in her own bed like every other woman, he took her to hospital. She hadn't the courage to stand a few hours of pain. It was her fault the boy didn't live. Now she's gone—'

'You mean your wife died too? Oh but I am sad for you. No wonder you sound bitter.'

'Jane didn't die. She left me. When she came out of hospital she came home while I was at work, collected her things and left me a note. I don't know where she is.' He leant even further forward, his voice intimate. 'I could divorce her for refusing to live with me. You know that, don't you?'

'And is that what you wish for?'

'A vain wish on a working man's wage. I made a dreadful mistake in marrying her. But not such a mistake as the doctor made in having a dalliance with a patient. That is about the worst thing a medical man can do, so I've heard. It could cost him his career.'

Yvette's quick frown didn't last; almost immediately it was overtaken by a laugh that lit the lamps behind her eyes.

'You do not know Matthew or you would not say these things. Falling in love is not of his interest. If he went to visit your wife each day, you may be sure it was to put his stethoscope on her belly. Just his cold stethoscope, nothing more exciting than that.'

Ian had known no woman make such suggestive remarks, he'd known no woman speak in that thrilling accent. It took all his willpower to keep his mind focused on his goal.

'They are the talk of the street. It's only since she's gone that people are outspoken to me about it. But neighbours watched, they knew the hours he spent there. And you say that's nothing. A pregnant woman bodes no risk to a man.'

Why couldn't she follow his train of thought? To look at her you'd think she saw the whole thing as a huge joke. Ian's temper was rising: he was angry with her for her light-hearted disregard for his story; he was angry with himself that the excitement she aroused in him was taking the interview a different way from the one he'd imagined. Trying to keep his thoughts in check, his only sign of emotion was the impatient way he tapped the fingers of his right hand against his knee. He made a supreme effort.

'You may see it as a joke, but if I took my story to the authorities they certainly wouldn't. There'd be no more doctoring for him if I chose to do that, you know.'

'But why should you? Your wife has left you, you say. Would it help you to win her back if you created a scandal? No, of course it would not.'

It was Ian's turn to laugh, seeing his hand of cards in a new light.

'Want her back? I may be a working man, Yvette, but I'm proud. I would not have her back if she came to me on bended knee. But look at me: I am still young. I have made one mistake, so is it supposed to be with me for the rest of my days? I want my freedom. Freedom from her, freedom from the memory that haunts me of what she did to my boy. Whether or not she and your husband spent their mornings in my bed I don't know and I don't care. But what I *do* know is that his daily visits were outside the call of duty – and if I chose to report it, it could bring him down.'

'I do not understand what it is you want of me. Do you want me to talk to Matthew? I will, of course, if you like. But, as for me, I cannot get too upset if he paid attention to some other woman, even if it had been one who wasn't already with child. But is it likely? No, no, no. He is too much like all these cold, dull people I meet here. I see it all around me, people who are afraid to show warmth, afraid of emotion, afraid of love. To me, that is a sin.' Reaching forward she covered his fidgeting hand with her own, pale, soft and beautifully manicured.

It was unusual for Ian to be less than sure of himself, but in that moment he avoided her eyes, he felt as though his Adam's apple filled his throat.

'If I had the money I could take her to court. I'd promise you not to mention the doctor, I'd just say that she refused to live with me . . .'

'Ah! So now I see. It is the money you want, that is why you came. I am disappointed. I have no money to give to you. I will have to think. I cannot just say to you, "Here is money," for where would I get such a sum as it would take to pay the court? Only from my husband. I will not mention your name, I will say to him that there is gossip. You must give me time. One word from me will not make him see the danger he is in. First I will say there is gossip, then there is a rumour that he is to be reported. We will work together, you and I. Yes? It is for me as well as for him that I ask you to be patient with me. For if he is no more to be a doctor, then I am no more to be a doctor's wife. You understand? Did I not know when I saw you in the town – oh, but you would not have noticed me—'

'I noticed you. You know I did.'

She laughed delightedly. Life was looking decidedly more interesting.

'Yes, I know you did.' She stood up, going to the small side table. 'Now let us have a glass of Madeira, we will drink to our plotting and planning and to our enjoyment of it.'

As she raised her glass to his, there was no doubting that she intended them to find enjoyment in plenty. And while he sipped his Madeira, poor Elsie waited for him, his dinner kept warm on a steaming saucepan.

The tramcar was waiting at the terminus, but Ian was in no mood to be jostled along the track, probably expected to make cheerful conversation with the conductor. This evening he wanted no company but his own as he strode back towards the centre of town. Even when he'd no more than exchanged glances in the street with the vivacious French woman, he had been aware of her attraction – and of her interest too. Plot and plan together, she'd tempted him with her bait, and get enjoyment in doing it. And so they would.

There were few motor cars on the road in Brackleford at any time of day, but in the evening the sound of an engine was enough to attract his attention. The doctor was going home. And what a difference between the home that awaited *him* in Millsham and his own cool reception that used to await him from Jane in Mill Lane. Life wasn't fair. Yet, if what he heard was true and the doctor had been getting his oats from Jane, what the hell was the matter with the man? The motor car came nearer, he recognized the driver and, with elaborate courtesy, even though his only contact with Matthew had been the night Jane had been taken to hospital, he raised his bowler hat and inclined his head in a mocking bow. Just wait till you get home, my fine fellow. Hear what the gorgeous Yvette has to tell you.

Why should she agree to help him get good money out of her husband? The doctor's loss would be her own loss. Plot and plan – and get enjoyment from doing it. Catching a glimpse of his reflection in the plate-glass window of Hindley's Emporium he smiled, his confidence growing with every step.

'Aye-aye there, you're done up smart this evening,' one of the locals called to him when he walked into the four-ale bar of the Queen Charlotte.

'I had a call to make. Something important.'

'Oh ah. Hope she was worth it, lad,' one old man chortled, then spat into the fire as if to give his opinion of womankind, one and all.

'The one waiting upstairs is worth it right enough,' George put in. 'She's keeping something warm for you, she said, but late as this it's likely got dried up.'

More guffaws from the beer swillers. Ian scowled. Any other evening he would have laughed as loudly as any, but tonight all he saw was the unfairness of life. There was that pansy doctor driving in style to his smart house – and with that mam'selle to warm his bed. Without removing the bowler hat he wore set at a jaunty angle, he mounted the familiar stairs.

'How did it go, love?' Elsie came out of the kitchen and held her rosy face for his kiss. 'Is she going to play ball?'

'She would if she had the money, that's for sure. I could see she was frightened when I reminded her what it would do to his career to have it known he'd been carrying on with a patient. She's going to talk to him – then I must see her again.'

'No wonder she made you welcome, Ian m'lad. Let me take a good look at you. My word, but you look posh in your best turn-out.'

His acknowledgement of her admiration was to give her bottom a friendly pat. It didn't take a lot to keep Elsie happy.

'Your food's all ready. Here, love, you'd better tuck this cloth into your collar to make sure you keep clean. Can't meet her next time with spots on your necktie,' she chuckled.

He laid his hat on the dresser then sat at the table and did as she said. But already the excitement of being with Yvette was giving way to darker thoughts. He drummed his fingers on the table, an outward sign of the way his heart had started to pound. Elsie knew nothing of the warning signs, she imagined he was impatient for his food so what he said took her by surprise.

'For weeks, more likely for months, Jane wouldn't let me touch her. I used to tell you how she pushed me away. She wasn't well, she said, it might hurt the baby.' Now, instead of his fingers, it was his clenched fist that took up the tattoo. 'That sod, what was he doing there day after day? Why should I keep my mouth shut? Why should I let him have the chance to pay me to keep quiet?' Even with clenched fists he couldn't still the trembling any more than he could steady the way his breath caught in his throat. Jane would have recognized the signal, she'd seen it often enough; she would have known how near he was to losing control and been sickened by it. 'Don't do it, might hurt the baby – and all the time what was that bugger doing?' His voice broke on a sob. 'That's why he didn't live, that's why I lost him.'

'Oh, Ian love, hush love.' Elsie cradled his head to her breast, lovingly she wiped her hand across his wet cheek.

'Now I've got nothing.' It wasn't easy to understand his words, she'd never seen him like this.

While he'd been spending each evening at the Queen Charlotte had he really just been running away from the fact that Jane hadn't wanted him? Elsie was filled with hate for the woman who could have done this to her beloved Ian.

224

'You'll never have nothing, love. I may not be much, but you've always got me. If I could find Jane and bring her back that's what I'd do if it's her you want. We'll find her, Ian love—'

'Jane? Bugger Jane. I've told you enough times, I never want to see the bitch again. She was no wife to me,' he gulped. 'But the boy – Else, if that sod of a doctor was poking her when she was carrying the boy –' he fought to find the breath to finish the sentence '– can't you understand what I'm saying? It's as if the baby that was growing in her belly didn't belong to me. What comfort would she give me? Eh? Eh? Nothing warmer than her hand, that's what. Now I've nothing.'

More than anything Elsie wanted Ian's happiness, she hated to see him brought so low. Strangely, through all the years she'd known him, this was the first time she'd been faced with a scene like this. Perhaps that was because she had never disappointed him. Now she went to the stone sink and took the face flannel that hung on a string fixed to the wall by the side of it. It was still damp from when she'd washed her face and combed her hair in readiness for him.

'Here love, have a wipe on this. Then when you've eaten your food we'll go along to your place. I'll help you get out of your best clothes. How'd that be?'

'Oh, Else. Don't know what happened to me. Couldn't help it. Just seems the whole world is against me. I ought never to have gone down to Deremouth, that's the real truth. My old lady had lived without me long enough, she could have got on and died without me. But I felt a duty, packing up her things and paying off her debts.' At that moment he chose to forget the outstanding rent he'd never paid, leaving the few sticks of furniture and no forwarding address. 'Jane tempted me with her money and fine clothes. Go on, tell me what you think of me! It's what I deserve. But she cheated me even over that, when it came to it she had bugger all.'

'Never mind, sweetheart, it's all over now. Things will

225

soon get sorted out. If Dr Bingley pays you to keep quiet you'll be able to afford to drag Jane through the divorce court. And serve her right after the way she treated you. And Ian, we'll make up for the bad times you had. We'll have babies, yours and mine. And no other man will do to me what that doctor did to your high and mighty Jane. I've got no money to tempt you with, but everything I've got is yours. Always has been, always will be.'

Like an elastic band that had been stretched and stretched until it finally snapped, so his pent-up emotions had given way to the hysterical weeping that brought him release. Already he was gaining control as he rose shakily from his chair and went to the sink. A glimpse in the mirror did nothing for his confidence; and yet a glance at Elsie reassured him.

'Fancy if you'd gone home with your heart so full of misery.' She slipped her arm around his waist. 'But you didn't. Instead, you told me. Sounds daft to say I'm thankful for what you said, but it's the truth. You and me, we don't want secrets. Now you give your face a good splash while I put your plate on the table. You'll have to take care, it's so hot it's sizzling.' Back to practicalities, she seemed to have drawn down the curtain on the scene. And after the man-size dinner she'd saved for him he was ready to face the world. There was even a swagger in his walk as, wearing his 'high day and holiday' garb as if to the manner born and with plump and adoring Elsie on his arm, he took her home with him.

Just as she'd promised, she helped him out of his suit and hung it away in the cupboard; she lay with him on the bed, excited by his need, frightened by her own. The echo of what he'd said earlier mocked her. 'What comfort was there for me? Eh? Nothing warmer than her hand!'

As he lay breathless by her side she turned towards him, one plump leg over him, her heavy breasts and rounded stomach warm against his nakedness.

'Won't always have to be like that,' she whispered. 'But when you put a baby in me, I want us to be husband and wife, wouldn't be right for our baby to be a bastard. Get rid of Jane, then, oh Ian love, I feel all full up with such a sort of aching longing, I just can't tell you. I'll soon be twenty-four and I'm still a virgin, but I bet the very first time you and me make love together like we ought to be able to, you'll give me a baby. We're so right for each other, it's just waiting to happen.'

'Waiting to happen right enough,' he muttered, but without the energy to pose a threat.

She laughed, wriggling closer, suddenly content. There was light at the end of the tunnel: soon Jane would be no more than a miserable memory.

On the way home Matthew called to see Alice, something that he often did. Although they seldom talked about Jane, for both of them the thought of her was always there, a bond that held them together.

'I'm glad you've come,' Alice greeted him. 'I've had such a strange letter from Gerald. He seems confused . . .'

The next day would be Saturday, when Jane left work at half past one, with a free afternoon in front of her. Matthew had promised himself he'd go to Addingford, but one look at Alice and he knew it wasn't to be.

'Why don't we drive into Reading tomorrow. It's time I visited and perhaps they would let you have a few minutes with him.'

She stooped to put another lump of coal on the small fire that burnt in the grate, but not before he'd seen the quick tears that sprang into her eyes.

'You are so kind,' she muttered, her jaw stiff.

'I'm no such thing. You say he's confused. It could be he isn't well. Perhaps I can help him. Do me a favour, will you? Have you a piece of paper and an envelope you can give me? I just want to write a note I forgot at the surgery.'

'Of course I have. And I have an idea I know what you want it for. Tomorrow is Saturday. Jane will be expecting you. Am I not right?'

'Come along now, woman, don't waste time arguing,' he laughed. 'Give Jane credit for understanding. You know and I know just what she would say.'

'You're both so good to me. You're like family.' Tonight Alice was worried and vulnerable; it wasn't like her to be on the edge of tears.

'That's about it, Alice. All three of us are like family. And one of these days your Gerald will be home to make a fourth.'

He wrote his note and addressed the envelope to Miss J. Bradley, Holly Cottage, Addingford. It would be in the bundle of post Hugh Phillpott collected off the first train in the morning. Even before he dropped it into the box at the post office a plan was forming.

'You're late,' Yvette said when he arrived home. 'I wonder any staff stay here, they must be tired of keeping meals back.'

'I had a call to make on the way home.'

With raised brows she looked at him, her expression hard to read. In fact he made no effort to try. Her moods were volatile, he'd long given up trying to keep up with them.

'Incidentally, I have an important meeting tomorrow evening out of town. First, I have to go to Reading but after that I shall drive straight on. If it gets late, I shall stay overnight.'

'What a day this one!' Did her eyes mock him? Accuse him? 'I was not intending to talk of it, you know these things do not bother me. But perhaps I should tell you. This evening I had a visit from the husband of – of – should I call her your lover? He tells me that that is what the gossiping neighbours are saying of your visits to her. Where she is now I do not know. I expect you could tell me if I asked. But do not worry, I have not the urge to enquire. These tiny-minded people, so corseted and blinkered, they have not the wisdom of the animals in the fields, or the dogs on the streets. If there is some woman who welcomes your loving, then enjoy it.'

228

'Yvette, you don't begin to understand. It's not as you think.'

'Oh, hush, do. I do not want to be your confessional. I am only telling you about the handsome visitor I had so that you will take care. These small-minded people talk, that is the only pleasure they have in their petty, narrow lives. We should pity them. They see you as wealthy and successful I expect.' She shrugged. 'Compared with them, perhaps you are. Then that devil jealousy creeps in. There are those who would like to bring you down. If you want a dalliance, then you should not become lover to a patient. Is that not the rule?'

'Never mind what people are saying. Yvette, we must talk.'

'How could you be so stupid? Yes, stupid. Not only to feed their empty minds with rumours that you are having a romantic affair with a patient, but a pregnant one! To some, perhaps that might be exciting. But to the boring little drabs in – was it Mill Lane? – it would be disgraceful. Why else, though, were you there on such long visits every morning if not to—'

'That's enough! Yvette, there is truth in the gossip you say you've heard. But it isn't as you imagine it. I have never been Jane's lover – not as you mean it. And, incidentally, she has never been my patient.'

'But the so handsome giant said it was you who took her away to the hospital—'

He ignored the interruption.

'As for the gossip, let them say what they will. None of it is true. Even if it were, unfortunately it wouldn't give you grounds for divorce. And that's what I want, Yvette.'

'Divorce! But you cannot even think of it. You brought me here from my own country, you have made of yourself a father to my son.'

'And so I shall continue, at least as far as the financial arrangements are concerned. Don't pretend you'd be heart-broken if I weren't here.'

'I never pretend! If you were not here I would hardly notice. How often do you come to me as a husband? If I did not find my pleasure in other places, then what a miserable life I would have. And would you notice? No. Would you care? No. You have taken from me the years of my young time. Now you want to throw me away on to the scrap heap, on to the heap where Biggs makes his compost.'

Matthew suspected that the performer in her was enjoying herself.

'We have lived together amicably enough,' he said. 'I've no doubt you think my life boring – and honestly I used to worry that your search for pleasure must be fruitless in a town such as this. But we've accepted. No doubt, if I followed you around on your escapades I would find evidence enough to take to a solicitor. You know that, after all these years, I won't do that simply because the timing suits me. You find living here irksome, often enough you've told me so. But if you prefer, you needn't even leave the home. Simply refuse to behave as a wife . . . that would be grounds enough. I'll go on bearing the expenses, you can keep the house. Won't you do your part to give Jane and me a chance? That great brute of a man can cite me—'

'Divorce! You are asking me to turn you from my bedroom and lock the door so that you can break the vows of our marriage as if they meant nothing. I tell you, husband, I would hardly notice the difference if we parted. But, divorce! Never! My faith is not your faith, so I should not be surprised that you can so lightly talk of breaking your vows.'

'My dear girl, don't pretend. Vows of faithfulness mean nothing to you.' But the vows he and Jane had made alone in the rain-battered motor car were part of his very being.

'I am not a saint.' That sudden light shone in her eyes, and the sight of it filled him with shame. He recalled how, when first he'd known her, it had been the telltale expression in those eyes that had captured him. So who had first

230

broken faith with their vows? Yvette and her procession of romantic encounters, or he with his absorption in his work, in his own way of life – until now, finally and abidingly, in Jane? 'There are plenty of people in this so dull town who pretend they are good like the saints simply because they never look at a person to whom they are not wife – or husband. We were not given the gift of life to half use it. If I had no liking of you, if you did not give me pleasure, then, Matthew, on those not very often times you come to my bed, I would not welcome you. Being wife to one man does not mean you find no joy in the love you share with another.' Then again that impish twinkle. 'Just ask your Jane.'

'Leave Jane out of it. This is no real marriage.'

'Bah!' With a flourish of her hand she swept his words away. 'So you think marriage is just what happens in the bed? Men! You think everything can be dragged down to sex, and sex can be dragged down to routine, habit – as joyless as cleaning your teeth or bathing your body. You know nothing!'

'I know we can't go on living like this. You talk of vows . . . what we have makes a mockery of them.'

And again 'Bah!' and an angry sweep of her hand. 'I am your wife. I shall be your wife until I get put in my coffin and buried beneath the ground. Even if I wanted to be free of our marriage, my church would not permit.'

The next morning Elsie looked after the bar while her father 'worked' in the cellar. That was the routine most mornings and, indulging him, she never enquired what he found there to keep him so busy. For she knew that, if she opened the cellar door and looked down the stone steps, she'd see him sitting on a barrel puffing at his pipe and reading the paper. Looking after the bar suited her very well; she enjoyed the men's friendly bantering.

On that particular morning her mind was on other things. Reason and women's instinct told her that the doctor's wife would find some very good reason why her husband's patient needed his attention so regularly during what had been a difficult pregnancy. As Ian said, Jane had been brought up soft. Add to that she had no family, no friends of her own age, so it was quite believable that Dr Bingley would have had a feeling of responsibility towards her. And that would be the attitude his wife would take. Any woman would defend her husband in those circumstances, even if behind closed doors she gave him the sharp edge of her tongue. She wouldn't be party to risking his career and neither would she be blackmailed into parting with good money. When they had first thought of the scheme, it had seemed a heaven-sent opportunity to find the money Ian would need if he were to get a solicitor's help. But was any of it more than a pipe dream? Jane had gone. Even if they had the money, how were they going to find her? Bill Saunders had recognized her when he'd sold her her railway ticket to London, so what chance had they of tracing her in a place like that? And who would take any notice of the gossip there had been about the doctor and her, with her gone and the doctor still in Brackleford just as he always had been? All he'd have to do would be to tell some yarn about why his visits had been necessary and none of them would have enough learning to prove him wrong.

'Where's your smile this morning, lassie?' her solitary regular prepared himself for a chat.

'Reckon I forgot to bring it down with me,' but she forced a laugh as she said it.

'Some days that's the way it goes. How's that Ian of yours? Silly devil he was, rushing off after a bit of skirt like he brought here. One look at her was all it took to know she'd never fit in. Pity. Ah, that's what it was, a rotten pity for the both of you, getting himself lumbered like he did.'

'Maybe she wasn't all bad, Mr Giles. Maybe she was just a square peg in a round hole?'

'Too good-hearted, that's your weakness, my dear. And

you listen to this tit-bit ...' Although he was the only customer he spoke in a whisper and beckoned her closer.

'What juicy morsel have you got for me today, then?' she teased for, old and toothless he may be, but Arthur Giles had ears that missed nothing.

'About that doctor chappie. It must have been out of respect for your Ian that the neighbours kept their own counsel until she'd upped and left. But now, of course, there's nothing to keep their lips stitched. After all, it's plain as the nose of your face that you're the lass your Ian wants. But listen here. My ol' woman told me this last night, she'd heard it from Evie Saunders, Bill's wife from the ticket office you know. That doctor chappie, him with a smart motor car to drive, yet time and again – whenever he has no surgery would be my guess – he catches the five something train to Addingford. Can't hardly be worth his going if you ask me, he has to be back here before eight when the last stopping train gets in. Now then, just you add two and two together and tell me what you make the answer. He used to go on Sundays, had longer there then, so Evie told me, but now it's just the weekdays when he doesn't have a roomful of people to see at the surgery.'

'Perhaps he has a patient there—'

'Perhaps my arse! Mind you, you can't blame the man if he kicks over the traces, not with a flighty bit like that mam'selle he's wed to. There's a word for women like that—'

'Now then, Mr Giles, keep the party clean,' Elsie laughed, wiping the table where he sat with her cloth. He mustn't guess at the excitement that was coursing through her veins. Addingford was only about twenty minutes away. If they could track her down ... then if they could get the money ... the pipe dream began to gain substance.

'Nympho something or other, that's the word I was after. It means she can't leave the men alone. With a wench like that at home, I wonder he strays. Shouldn't wonder he'd had others before your Ian's woman. And now, you see, he's off sniffing after someone else. I said to my missus, "You count your blessings, m'gal, all these years I've stayed the course and now I s'pose I'm too old to catch anything worth taking even if I cast my net".' He laughed delightedly at his own humour.

'You know when you're on to a good thing, that's the truth,' Elsie answered, just as he'd hoped she would.

'Pour me another half, m'dear, then I'd better be getting home to see what my old treasure's been making for m'dinner.'

Alone in the bar Elsie polished the already shining tables and made up the fire, but her thoughts were miles away – about fifteen miles. She wished she could have told Ian what she'd heard, but she didn't want to raise his hopes for nothing. So she made her own plans.

She told herself it would have been more sensible to wait until after the weekend, for Arthur Giles had told her that it was during the week the doctor visited his mysterious friend. But dusk still fell early and, after that, who would be likely to be on the street in Addingford? In the afternoon it was possible she might catch a glimpse of her prey, see where she was living. On Saturdays Ian finished work at five o'clock, earlier than the other days of the working week. Imagine, when he came in the evening being able to tell him she knew where Jane was – and, even better, about Dr Bingley's regular visits there.

'Lovely afternoon, m'am. Let me just have a look at your ticket,' Hugh Phillpott greeted her as he waved the train on its way towards Waterloo. 'Not left anything on board, I hope?' It seemed to him that the most likely reason for a stranger to alight at Addingford would be to bring shopping from Reading for one of the few residents.

'No, I wasn't carrying anything.'

'Visiting someone, I dare say.'

'I think so. I hope so. I believe Mrs Jane Harriman is

living in Addingford. There can't be many people here, so perhaps you know her.'

'No, afraid I can't help you there. Not many round here I can't give a name to. But Harriman, no. You've got me foxed there.'

'Oh, dear, then it seems I've come for nothing. She left Brackleford about six months ago. I thought she'd gone to London, then someone said they'd been told she was here. It looks as though I shall just have to get the next train back.'

'Jane, you say. No, it couldn't be the same one. The back end of summer me and the missus took a real nice young lady to live with us, Jane Bradley. When her brother turned up – a writer, would you believe, been living in Paris – well, like I say, often he used to come visiting. We were sorry when, a few weeks back, they got the chance of renting Holly Cottage up the top end of the street. Said it would be somewhere nice and quiet for him to write, better than his rooms in Brackleford. That was the scheme. But I reckon he just said that so that she wouldn't feel bad about him being the one with the money for the rent. Always struck me as an independent young lady, but they get along good as gold. He comes out two or three times a week to see she's managing all right on her own. Always short visits though, her being at work all day and the last train back to Brackleford going out at half past seven. It just reassures him that she's managing, I dare say. Nice to see it between brother and sister. Your train doesn't go for an hour, an hour and ten minutes to be on the dot accurate, miss. But as for this Mrs Harriman you're after, I'm afraid you've drawn a blank there.'

'Never mind. It's a nice afternoon, it really feels like spring. Perhaps I'll take a walk until it's time to go back.'

And walk she did. She stopped at the one and only shop to buy herself a bar of chocolate and two ounces of toffee, then munching happily she strolled on. When Jane came out of Holly Cottage and hurried towards the dairy, Elsie

235

showed not a flicker of interest. And, as for Jane, whether or not she noticed her could make no difference for she'd never seen her before. In any case on that Saturday afternoon, with Matthew's note in her pocket, she wouldn't have noticed if King Edward himself had walked past her.

At the time that Ian had brought his bride to Brackleford, Elsie had watched out for her, often shadowing her, driven by a compulsion to feel the pain of Ian's change of heart. It hadn't lasted long for, as soon as Ian had woken up to his folly, she had been there for him and Jane had counted for nothing. On that Saturday afternoon she immediately recognized the tall, well-dressed woman she used to see as her rival.

It was the sound of a train that reminded her of the time. She mustn't risk missing the quarter past five train; she wanted to be home before Ian arrived. Elsie was a plump plodder, running didn't come easily to her, but run she did in the direction of the railway halt. The train at the platform was already huffing and snorting ready to move off and her first reaction was thankfulness that it was travelling towards London.

Then she heard another sound – a motor car. Some inner voice seemed to tell who she would see as it rounded the bend past the buildings of the brewery and came towards the little village. Probably Matthew didn't even notice the woman by the gate to the platform and, if he had, it's unlikely he would have connected her with Brackleford. She wasn't one of his patients, or indeed anyone else's, and he never frequented the Queen Charlotte.

Even if she hadn't recognized him, the friendly ticket collector had heard the motor and looked out too.

'Well, fancy that!' He was always ready for a chat in his lonely job. 'You remember I told you about Jane Bradley, her who lodged with the missus and me, you remember I said she had a brother who took good care of her. That's him, in that smart motor car would you believe! No use me looking out for him on the last train this evening, he'll go when he's ready. I dare say he'll give her the whole of his weekend. Like I said, it's good to see a brother and sister so fond of each other.'

Elsie's heart was hammering. Tomorrow was Ian's day off work, he could come here, he could catch them. Not that he had the money to get his freedom ... not yet. No, but just think what a trump card to play against the doctor. Imagine if he could catch them in bed together ... her mind raced ahead of her reason, it jumped from Ian walking in on a scene of lurid love-making to another, even more glorious, a scene not with Jane and the doctor but with herself and Ian. No wonder her heart hammered.

'I noticed the motor of course,' she answered. 'What a treat for her, perhaps he'll take her out for a spin. I thought, coming, the countryside looks lovely at this time of year.' Words, just words. But they seemed to keep him happy.

'Never mind showing me your ticket, I saw it when you came. You've timed it just right, I can just see the smoke. Had a nice walk, did you? What did you think of our little village, eh?'

'Yes, I've had a lovely afternoon. I'm glad there wasn't an earlier train or I wouldn't have had my walk.'

Well satisfied that his corner of the world had put that smile on her rosy face, he opened a Ladies Only compartment and saw her safely inside.

Chapter Twelve

Only half awake Jane felt a sense of inexplicable joy.

'Good morning.' Matthew's words were no more than a whisper; he'd sensed rather than seen that she was waking.

Her eyes opened to the pale grey of morning so early that even the birds, eager for spring, hadn't yet filled the air with the sound of their dawn chorus, and to the realization of her happiness.

'Yes, a good morning. A perfect morning.' And in the precious intimacy of the moment her voice was as hushed as his. 'A perfect end to yesterday, a perfect start to today.'

He drew her closer. His unshaven cheek was rough against hers and she was glad. Beneath the sheet and blankets the nearness of their naked bodies was natural – two halves of one whole. Wordlessly she drew him closer as she changed her position so that as, in those waking moments, he moved on to her she wrapped her legs about him as her hand guided him. Neither of them spoke, it was as if they were living a dream. In that dawn light they weren't driven by wild passion, they needed no pleasure or excitement of adventurous foreplay to their love-making. Slowly, deeply, he penetrated her; did he even know what he said as barely audibly he murmured. 'My love . . . like this for ever . . . blessed . . . beloved . . .' Her joy was almost too much to contain, her own murmurs formed no words, nothing but a half-moan, half-cry in her throat. Then, like a starburst, passion gripped them. They'd wanted it to last for ever, but by then they were hurtling out of control onwards and upwards. In that second Jane believed there could be no greater bliss. Yet seconds later, fulfilled, drained of passion, Matthew breathless and exhausted, she still held him in that same embrace, loving the warm weight of him.

'Too heavy for you,' he breathed, making as if to move off her.

'No. Stay like that.'

With one hand he felt her wet cheek. 'Tears? Jane, why tears?'

'So thankful,' she whispered back to him. 'Feel so loved.'

This time he raised himself on his elbows and, even if he'd not spoken, his expression said it all.

'I think it's more than love. No, there's nothing more than love. You are my heart and soul, I feel as if I only half lived until you came.' In the barely perceptible light of that early dawn emotion was heightened.

She nodded. 'And for me too. Just never knew . . .' Then she pulled him back once more to lie against her. They were wrapped in a peace that was beyond all words. Whether they stayed like that for seconds or minutes didn't matter, or how it was that instead of being on her he was lying at her side. Perhaps they sank into a contented sleep.

When next she opened her eyes it was still not light but night was truly over and the birds were proclaiming that dawn had broken. Her brief euphoria was held firmly in her memory; later when she was alone she would relive those moments. Now, though, the practicalities of the situation loomed large. Adultery! That's what the world would say. Well, let it say what it would. How could it be adultery for Matthew and her to be together? Forcing herself, she thought of the vows she'd made when she and Ian had married. In her memory she tried to rekindle her early certainty that theirs was a love that would last for ever. Think of it . . . don't shirk from facing it . . . you really expected nothing would change how you felt. So when did it happen? Was it the way he watched for a letter from Dad? Watched, not as I did, wanting it for the thankfulness of knowing the breach was healed, but with something in his expression that made a stranger of him. Was it even before you conceived the baby? Were you just not woman enough to face the sort of life he could give you? No, that wasn't the cause, not the whole cause. None of that would have mattered if only he'd tried to understand how different your life had become? No, it was more even than that. But surely it couldn't all have been his fault, he must have been as disenchanted as you. If he'd been gentle, if he'd sometimes laughed, if he'd been a companion, then would you have gone on loving him – or at least believing you loved him? Remember – yes, make yourself remember – how you used to thrill to the sight of him, a giant amongst men you thought him. Remember lying in bed watching him, remember your eagerness, your excited anticipation, knowing at a glance as he walked towards you that he was ready to take you. Don't run away from the memory, face it. Was none of the fault yours that your feelings changed? When was it that the sight of him like that started to repel you, made you compare him to a stag at rutting time, made you feel no more precious than a mare being served by a champion stallion? 'You can't do that, you'll hurt the baby.' But did I ever really believe that? If I were expecting Matthew's child how different it would be. I would want him to make love to me, his nearness would bind us together, him, me and the child.

Thoughts of the baby filled her mind. Her baby . . . Had it been taken from her to punish her for not keeping faith? Trying to rekindle that aching longing she'd felt for the unborn child, she pressed her hands against her flat stomach, then against her hips. Her bones seemed barely covered. Her hands moved up to her ribs, each so pronounced that she could count them and, finally, to breasts that were once again as small as before nature had

240

prepared them for the child they were to nurture. As small, yet there was a difference. That had been the figure of a young girl. What would have happened if her baby had lived? The child that had been part of *her*, yet Ian would have seen him simply as his own. My son ... how often he'd said it. It was impossible to imagine how their future would have been. Think of those silly, childish dreams of a cottage in the country, somewhere in clear fresh air, where Ian would build up his own business. Supposing he'd agreed, supposing it were Ian by her side and the crib standing in the corner. But the image was as removed as the man in the moon. It was as if that part of her which had longed for her baby had died with it. She felt her angular body, and for the second time in such a short while, she felt a tear roll down the side of her face as she turned her head into the pillow. Why are you crying, Matthew had asked, and she'd said her tears were because she was thankful.

'Take care of my baby,' she pleaded silently. 'He had so much life, I used to feel him. All gone. Take care of him, let him know how much I loved him.'

She reached out to touch Matthew. In his sleep he turned towards her, drawing her close. Looking at him, she sent another silent message to that unknown deity. Thank You, You've made him love me. Don't let it be wrong just because he's married to Yvette. She doesn't love him – she doesn't love him like I do. Surely, if she had, he could never have wanted me. Yvette, so full of life, so talented, smart ... and remember how I was, pale, sick, fat, plain – no, don't think back, not to that. Think of the vows we made to each other – and think of how it was for us last night.

Until last night they had never made love, not in a physical sense. How different even the act of love-making had been. Again she made herself recall with honesty. There had been times with Ian when her body had responded – yes, but nothing, nothing, had been as it was with Matthew. She felt that her whole soul had reached out to his – 'with

241

my body I thee worship' came the echo of those vows and the echo of her own untried understanding of the words. Her body had responded, she had believed that that was enough to build a life on. She hadn't known, she hadn't understood the union of body and soul.

Ghosts still haunted her as she watched Matthew standing stripped to the waist at the kitchen sink, taking off his stubble with the cut-throat razor he had brought with him – and intended to leave. Not that Ian ever stripped except when the weather was hot; his winter ablutions had been carried out with his collarless shirt opened at the neck and his sleeves rolled to the elbows. Yet in the beginning the daily sight of him inspecting his face in the hanging mirror, sometimes clipping his dark beard, rubbing macassar oil into his curly hair, had thrilled her.

'Better?' Matthew held the palm of her hand to his face.

'Either way I love it,' she laughed, rubbing her cheek against his. 'Go and get dressed before I decide to come and help you.'

'Our first weekend ... if only ... But I can't let her down.'

Jane had known just how concerned he was about Gerald Gregson as soon as he'd arrived after his trip to Reading.

'Perhaps things will look brighter for her today.' She tried to instil hope into her words.

Matthew shook his head.

'His fever was high. He didn't even know Alice. As you say – perhaps. But Jane, he has no strength to fight. He's a shadow of himself, this life is killing him as surely as the illness. And now, even though he's been taken from his cell and put into the medical wing, there's no comfort. He rambles, he has hallucinations, he calls out to Terry, he curses and rants as if he has those two youths in his vision. In my profession we have to be used to seeing suffering – but it breaks my heart to see Alice.'

'I know you've been worried about him, even before all

this happened to him. What do you honestly think, Matthew?'

'If he is to pull through, it will need a miracle. And how can we wish it for him? He will never stand another seven years of what his life has become. But Alice? She has no one. All her hope is pinned on some sort of a hazy future when he is back with her.'

'She has *us*.'

He nodded, gently rubbing his newly shaved face against her temple.

'She said something of the kind when I was with her on Friday. She misses you badly. Not that she says so. But I've come to know her too well for her to be able to hide it. Perhaps because of Terry, they had no close friends. As a family they were close knit, probably people looked on them as aloof. When the troubles came she was left with no one.'

'Once she can see Gerald is getting better, perhaps she could come here to stay for a while. We have no secrets from Alice.'

'Soon we'll have no secrets from anyone. And why should we? If we obeyed the conventions demanded by society you would look to a lifetime with Harriman; I would have to be content with a marriage that at best gave tolerant friendship.'

'What's happened couldn't have been completely their fault, not Ian's or Yvette's either. Somewhere all of us failed.'

'But we have been given another chance. Darling, we'll face all the malicious gossip. We'll find a house to rent in Brackleford. Let the world say what it will. You know and I know what we've done is right. That's why we have been brought together.'

'Go and dress,' she whispered, frightened that to let herself imagine how life could be if they did as he said might be tempting an unkind fate.

When, a few minutes later, he came downstairs the

kitchen table was laid for breakfast, a small vase of prim-
roses she'd gathered the previous afternoon in pride of
place. The sun streamed through the window of the little
cottage, tempting them with thoughts of how the day might
have been.

'I wish I could come with you,' Jane said, 'but Alice
won't want anyone. At least no one except Gerald. And
you, of course. She'll be hanging on to faith and hope in
what you can do for him.'

Matthew shook his head.

'He's not my patient, Jane. But the prison doctor has
done all that's possible. What a waste. They've faced so
much trouble – their boy being as he was. But trouble only
seemed to make them stronger. She deserves better than
this. They both do. She pretended to believe he knew her
yesterday, but in her heart she must have known he didn't.
If only there were something I could do . . .'

Jane reached her hand across the kitchen table and
touched his, rewarded by the grip of his fingers.

'You do more than you give yourself credit for. Just
being there with her. It's because of *you* that she is able to
be with him.'

'Yes, but what's the future? She has no one, you know.'

'She has us. Oh, I know at the moment we can't count,
but we'll never let her feel she has no one. She taught me to
understand so much. What was it she said, way back when
I first knew her? There's no emotion as strong as love. She
was talking about her Gerald and his obsession to revenge
what had been done to Terry. That love will still be with
her, whether he recovers or not. I think she may even get
some sort of comfort in the end from knowing that he has
joined Terry. No. Pretend I didn't say that. If we accept
that that could happen, it's as if we've not kept faith with
her. It's just that grief might be easier to bear than helpless
anxiety.'

He nodded. He'd listened, following the truth of what
she said. But when he spoke, it wasn't about the Gregsons.

'Jane, being here is a gift, a glimpse of what our lives could be. But being here like this is leading us nowhere. Going back to what I said earlier – we have to make our own lives. For Yvette there has been a long series of escapades. I'm sure you know that. Everyone must know it, she's made no secret of it and none of it has touched me. Perhaps it did in the beginning, it's too long ago for me to know whether it ever hurt more than my pride. I suppose I could have petitioned for a divorce when I first knew how she behaved; if I had, she couldn't have done anything about it. But I didn't. I think my main reason for ignoring how she was, was the boy. He was three years old when I brought them from France. Nothing will ever make an Englishman of him,' he laughed, 'even years at my old school can't do that. But I am truly fond of him and would never have done anything to hurt him.'

'It doesn't matter. Yvette doesn't matter, Ian doesn't matter.'

'No. Not as far as we two are concerned. But there's a big, cruel world out there.'

'I know *that*. You know I left Brackleford so that there would be no gossip about you. You shouldn't have fol—'

'No?' His smile teased. 'Anyway, it's too late to worry about gossip. Not that I do. Another of Alice's truisms is that the only people who gossip about others are those whose own lives are empty. We shouldn't grudge them their pleasure, my Jane.'

'For myself I don't care, not a jot, not a damn. But it could ruin your career.'

'To love one woman and be married to another? Why should it? It's not *that* we have to think of. It's how we are going to organize our future. For come what may, Jane, we are each other's future. Yvette won't consider making a case against me; in her faith there is no acceptance of divorce. Ian Harriman is still your husband and, even though I'd be proud to be cited, he makes no move to find you. Perhaps it suits him better to have a missing wife and a generous welcome at the Queen Charlotte.'

'Don't! I used to wake from nightmares that he was here. Why do you think I'm known as Jane Bradley?'

'We weren't cut out for lies, Jane. What if the good folk of Addingford knew the night you spent with your "brother"?'

This time she laughed. Suddenly nothing else mattered but that, come what may, they would face the future together. Convention presented high hurdles, but somehow they would surmount them. On that sunny Sunday morning, they cared nothing for those who stood in their way; gossip couldn't touch them; they were conscious only of the rightness of their being together.

Soon after ten o'clock – an hour before the train was due to stop at Addingford on its way to Brackleford – he drove away and not many minutes later Jane had a visit from Agnes Phillpott.

'Fancy, Miss Bradley, your brother driving in a motor car to see you. I heard the sound of it and looked out. Not often anyone in the village gets a visit from anyone with a motor. Fancy! But what a pity he's gone off again. With a day off from the brewery, you would have enjoyed a nice ride out with him. Perhaps he'd only borrowed it, would that be it?'

'Yes, that's right,' Jane lied, thinking quickly. 'He'd promised to get it back this morning. At least it gave him a chance to stay overnight and that was nice.' Why couldn't she have answered honestly and said the motor car was his own? Because, if she had, questions would have snowballed: 'Why doesn't he drive here more often instead of using the train? He could stay longer, he wouldn't always be tied to getting to the railway halt on time.' What chance was there of his staying longer, with a practice to run and a wife at home? 'If he has a motor car why does he never take you out?' Oh but he does. On Sunday afternoons he meets me from the train at Ilkingham when you all believe I've gone to Brackleford to see him and Alice. 'He rented somewhere for you so that you could be together – and even if he needs to use Brackleford library for his work, with a motor car to let him come and go as he pleases, he could easily work from here.' If only it could be that simple!

So just as she had when she'd introduced him as her brother, Jane said the first thing that came into her head. For a moment she imagined Mrs Phillpott's reaction if she'd been told the truth. She knew well enough the attention his arrival and departure had attracted in Mill Lane.

'Well, if he's gone off and you're all by yourself, perhaps I'll stay and chat for a while. Except for locking the ticket office and slipping home for a plate of my nice home-made soup between the five to one Waterloo and the ten past two the other way, Mr Phillpott will be down at the halt. Not always there so long on a Sunday, but he had a few odd jobs he wanted to see to. Time to tidy up the bit of garden and spruce it up for the better days that'll soon be on us. I'll be glad of a bit of company, and I'm sure you will, with your brother gone.'

'Lovely,' Jane smiled. Another lie. She wanted to be by herself, to relive the hours, to dream of a future beyond the mists of uncertainty.

And so the morning went, her thoughts returning time and again to Alice, to Gerald whom she felt she knew even though she'd never met him and occasionally to Yvette.

Elsie looked on admiringly as Ian brushed his curly hair then ran his hand over his trimmed beard.

'Better by far than just leaving that French wife of his to carry messages. How's he to know that she isn't making them up to suit some purpose of her own? Anyway, Ian love, if you catch them red-handed like you probably will on Sunday afternoon he won't have a foot to stand on. Turn around, let me put the clothes-brush on the back of your shoulders. My! But you look fit for a king. You know what I wish? I wish I could be a fly on the wall and see it when you come face to face with them.'

But, of course, it was important Ian should go alone, the forsaken husband his wife had run out on; for, if the doctor agreed to buy his silence, that was the evidence Ian would use to get his freedom.

'I'll see you after,' he told Elsie, 'but don't come right to the station. Ten to eight my train will be in. My train, did I say? *Our* train more like it. From what we hear, that's the way he always travels. Damned if I would if I had a smart motor car to use. Still, I dare say he attracts less attention to sneak in by train and there's not another after the seven-thirty from Addingford. After they've listened to my tale of neglect, it wouldn't do to let him see I'm met by a lady. Come on back here to my place and wait for me.' Putting his brown bowler on his head at a rakish angle, he smiled at his reflection. 'Let the bugger see me setting off back home to an empty house,' his grin broadened. 'Enough to tear your heart strings, eh?'

'I bet you'll be the only two to get off the train at Brackleford on a Sunday evening.'

'Ah, very likely – and a good thing if we are. That way he can't be off seeing what a lonely life the bitch has left me. Have a bite of something ready, won't you, Else.'

'Something on a plate, you mean?'

'You hussy, you,' he chuckled, tipping her face up so that he could cover her mouth with his. 'It's no joke, Else. Going on like we are, it's more than a man can stand. This man, anyway.' She thrilled at the hint of his sexual prowess and rubbed her plump leg against his to let him know she understood. 'Had a dream last night – you and me – I gave you such a—'

'Me? It wasn't *her*?'

'Oh it was *you*. I woke up as weak as a kitten. It's what I want, Else – you, every warm inch of you. I was such a bloody fool. I'll get free, Else. Soon it'll be right for us.'

Her heart was hammering with excitement. Today was more than a step, it was a huge stride, towards the only future she'd ever wanted.

At Addingford Halt Ian showed his ticket to Hugh Phillpott and moved towards the gate to the road.

'Lovely afternoon, sir,' the friendly station keeper welcomed him. 'Nice to see someone getting off here, it doesn't often happen on a Sunday afternoon. I dare say you'll be paying a call on someone. You won't forget the time of the last train back, will you? Miss the seven-thirty and you'll find yourself stranded.'

'I shan't miss it. I just have a bit of business to do with my wife.'

'Your wife? In Addingford?' Mentally Hugh was picturing the local residents, not disguising his curiosity.

'Jane Harriman.'

'Well I'm damned. You're the second in two days come here looking for her. The first went home empty-handed and I reckon it's going to be the same for you. Precious few I can't put a name to around here, but I've never heard of a Mrs Harriman.'

'When a woman runs out on her husband she covers her tracks. But she's here right enough. I've heard it from a good source. Before she married me she was Jane Bradley.'

'God bless my soul. Our Miss Bradley. A married woman. There's no ring on her finger . . . well, I go to sea. Just wait till I tell my missus.'

Ian grinned broadly, well pleased with the way things were going.

'I'll be in good time for the train. I've come to persuade her to come back to me. Tomorrow when I finish a hard day's graft I shall find her there, the house will be a home again, there'll be a fire burning in the range and a bite of something to eat. All these months, can you imagine what it's like for a man, a house as silent as the tomb, empty grates, never a hot meal except what I can get from the pie shop. I heard a rumour she's found herself a man friend . . . well, I'll soon find out. I try to keep myself respectable, but I tell you it's bloody hard going for a man alone.'

'But Miss Bradley . . . Seemed a decent enough young

lady. Lodged with us, you know till she and her brother heard of Holly Cottage. Turn right out of the gate and it's at the far end of the village street on the left. Well, I'm jiggered. Got real fond of her we did, the missus and me. And her a runaway wife. Well, I'm jiggered.'

'Brother? Jane has no brother.'

Taking off his cap, Hugh scratched his balding head.

'I go to sea,' he muttered, for the second time.

Agnes Phillpott stayed for most of the morning, then Jane went for a walk. By the time Matthew had driven to Brackleford, collected Alice and taken her to Reading the morning would have gone. After that everything would depend on how long they were able to stay with Gerald. Silly to let herself hope that he might come back to Addingford – but that didn't stop her imagining that when she got back to the cottage his car would be outside.

She walked for more than three hours, in the solitude of the country her thoughts taking her where they willed. The house she conjured up in her imagination was like none she knew in Brackleford; but Brackleford was where it would have to be, for he ran a busy practice there. Of course there would be criticism for both of them to face, but it would be short-lived. For herself she cared nothing for what people said and, as for Matthew, he was a good doctor, well liked. What he did with his private life couldn't change any of that.

Having seen them established in their new situation her mind jumped ahead. She pictured herself opening the front door and finding her father standing there. If she wrote to him again, told him everything, surely, surely he would understand. Married to one man, living with another ... without knowing Matthew, how could he possibly know how right it was for them to be together? On she strode, a solitary, tall figure, aware of the glorious spring day and yet hardly seeing anything of it so deep was she in thought. The one person who played no part in her imaginings was

Ian. It was as if last night had cleansed her of all that part of her life.

When, at nearly five o'clock, she climbed over the last stile into the lane that would lead her home, childishly she crossed her fingers and kept her head down, not looking up until she was within sight of Holly Cottage. Was the car outside? Nothing. The narrow street was empty. She closed the gate of Holly Cottage with a click, the sound of it seeming to shut out the rest of the world and leave her isolated. It was too late for him to come now. She told herself it had been stupid even to hope. But her afternoon had been full of hope; every dream had become a certainty.

In Addingford, indeed in most places, no one bothered to lock the front door, so she lifted the latch and went inside. The little house was just as she'd left it. She was ashamed of her feeling of disappointment: if the automobile had been outside then it would have meant that Gerald had been too sick for Alice to stay with him, it would have meant that Matthew had driven her straight home, then left her by herself. Ashamed or not, disappointment couldn't be lifted so easily. She took off her coat and hung it on a hook in the passage, then unpinned her hat and took it upstairs to put away. It was as she reached the tiny landing that she heard him moving about in the bedroom. He'd come! He must have taken the afternoon train back for quickness! Flinging open the door she rushed into the bedroom.

'You came back,' she cried unnecessarily.

'My! My! But what a welcome.'

At the sound of Ian's voice she seemed to freeze. Every nightmare of the past months crowded back, depriving her even of the power of speech.

'You're disappointed, my dear.' The endearment held spite, even sarcasm, but certainly no warmth. 'You were expecting a visit from the doctor?'

'What do you want?' she rasped, making a huge effort to control herself. 'You and I have finished. You don't want

251

me any more than I want you. Why have you followed me here?'

He crossed the room to stand only inches from her, forcing her to back away until she stood against the wall. But still he came close, not touching her but, with his hands on the surface just beyond each of her shoulders, making a prisoner of her.

'Think a lot of the good doctor, do you? Cosy little place you've got here – you and "your brother". I've been having a rest on the bed while I waited.' His soft laugh was filled with innuendo. 'Pretty little love nest. Brought back memories. Pleasures you well, does he? Humph?' He pushed his face nearer; she could feel his beard brush against her temple.

'Why have you come here?' She could hear the fear in her voice; she was sure he must hear it too.

'I'll tell you why. Your precious lover has broken the oaths of his profession. Did you ever think of that while you were lying there with him?'

'That's a lie.'

'A lie? You mean each time he comes here it's to give you professional care? Oh no, those days finished when you killed my boy.'

'Stop it! Stop it! I won't listen to you.' She covered her ears with her hands, she shut her eyes. In a minute she must wake, just as she had so often after he'd haunted her dreams.

But there was no waking. She felt her shoulders taken in his strong hands, she felt his force as he shook her, she felt her head knock against the wall behind her. She daren't look at him, for she knew by the choking sound of his breathing just what she would see.

'Whose fault was it the poor little bastard didn't have a life?' The pitch of his voice rose unnaturally. She dreaded the uncontrolled weeping she'd faced so often. 'Every day that bugger was there. Don't deny it. You were the talk of the street, no wonder the women wouldn't mix with you.

252

Thought yourself better than the rest, but you're a fraud. A fraud and an immoral bitch!' She ought to have been prepared for the force of his hand on her face; her eyes watered with pain as it landed on her left eye and the bridge of her nose. 'Examining you, was that what he was doing? By Christ, I bet he was. "Don't touch me,"' he mimicked on a high squeak, '"you'll hurt the baby." You turned me aside because he'd been there first and satisfied you. Was that it? *My* boy – but what was it to you, opening your legs to your bloody doctor.'

'That's not true. And Matthew was never my doctor.'

'What about when you fell over and knocked your head? Left alone, nature would have healed it. But, no. He bound you up as though you'd come out of the infirmary, came every day to change the dressing. Wasn't that what you used to tell me?'

'I didn't fall. I knocked my head when you pushed me down – but you were too drunk to remember it! Matthew knew we had no money for doctors, he treated me as a friend.'

A minute ago Ian had made no effort to stem his flow of abuse; rather, caught up in the momentum he'd grown more full of anger and self-pity. But, at her words, his cunning took over. The doctor had never been paid for his regular visits, at least not in shillings and pence. But there were other ways. And what would the authorities make of his behaviour if it were reported?

Still gripping her shoulders, Ian stood further from her, spite and triumph in his expression.

'Paid him in kind, did you? Isn't that what I've been saying? Isn't it what the street is saying? Isn't it the gossip of every alehouse in the area? Well, my dear, he's burnt his boats this time. Only you can save him.'

'Let go of me. I don't understand what you're talking about. But as for the alehouse gossip, who better to hear it than you?'

'I could report him to the authorities.' He sounded more

confident than he was, for in truth he had no idea who these nameless 'authorities' were, or how he had to make his report. 'He wouldn't be the first doctor to be struck off their list for having an affair with a patient.'

'You can't do that! I tell you he is a friend, of mine and of Alice's.'

'That gaol bird's woman? Man enough to satisfy the pair of you is he?'

'You sicken me. Why was I ever such a fool as to think I cared about you? I ought to have listened—'

'To dear Daddy? Ah, but running away to marry me is nothing to what he'll hear now. You were generous enough with your favours before we were married, but I had the decency to make an honest woman of you, even though you hadn't two farthings to your name. But wait till I tell him about how you've behaved, wait till he hears that because of you the doctor has been struck off? Eh? Eh?' He bent so that his face was inches from hers. 'Serves the old bugger right. If he'd treated me right none of this would have happened. We could have been settled comfortably, yes and the boy would have lived. The boy . . . You couldn't even do that right. You and your bloody friend, driving off to the Infirmary, leaving me. If you'd been like any other woman you would have had the boy in your own bed, put up with a bit of pain. But you had to make an exhibition, get the neighbours in, have your precious doctor called for – and then you hadn't the courage to push the poor little devil into the world.'

'We ought to say thank God. What sort of life could he have had with us for parents?'

'I'll tell you one thing. If you lay there on that bed and begged me, I wouldn't touch you.'

In misery they looked at each other, misery rooted not in their failed expectations but in what their life together had become.

'Why have you come here?' Jane asked in an attempt to escape the memories his visit was re-awakening.

'I can divorce you and drag his name through the court, expose that he's had an affair with a patient – and because you didn't pay him in money for attending you doesn't make you any less his patient. He was the only doctor you saw right up to when he carried you to the hospital. But, listen, how's this for a deal?' She lowered her gaze rather than recognize the expression she knew she'd see. Expectancy? Cunning? Greed? Perhaps something of each. Into her mind sprang the memory of the day he'd come home from work to find her dressed in her favourite tawny-brown gown and he'd believed she'd heard from her father. 'You get me the money I shall need to take you to the divorce court and I'll not bring his name into it. Tell him that. He can't be short of a few bob. Don't you let him beat you down, you see he pays well for my silence. It's either that – and I'll say that you have deserted me, refused to live with me – or I'll tell the whole sordid truth and that'll be the end of him. And of you, too; I'll put my shirt on it. He'll change his mind about you when he sees what a mess his philandering has put him in.'

'Go away and leave me alone. If you tell lies like that I'll fight you all the way. Take me to court, there's nothing I'd like more than to be free of our marriage. But freedom must be based on truth and I'll swear on the Bible that I have never gone to Matthew Bingley as a patient.'

'I'll go when I'm ready. Unlike your moneyed friend, I have no motor car. I'm stuck in this one-eyed hole until half past seven. Just you bear in mind what I've said and talk to him about it. I'll come next Sunday. Oh, yes, and one thing more. This won't come as a surprise to him, his wife knows how the town is gossiping, she will have talked to him.'

'Just go. Wait for the train somewhere else.'

Still he stood close in front of her; his hands had loosened their tight grip on her shoulders but not let go. Now, with no warning, he stooped closer and covered her mouth with his. She tried to pull away, her fists pounded his shoulders but her resistance did nothing to curb him. Whether it was bitter hatred or frustrated passion that drove him she couldn't tell, neither did she care. As he pushed her back against the wall and anchored her with one hand she knew why his other was busy unbuttoning his trousers while his tongue probed deep into her mouth. All too well she knew his strength. She closed her teeth as hard and as suddenly as she could, and in the same instant raised her knee high. As momentarily he reeled in pain and shock, she made her escape from the room. If she could get down the stairs and through the front door, surely she would be free of him. But he was fast behind her and as she reached the top of the stairs he pulled her round to face him.

Her knee had crushed his physical desire, his passion had turned to blinding rage, and blinding rage to despair. He'd never felt such hatred for anyone as he did for Jane at that moment. She'd cheated him, she'd used him then she'd discarded him when her fine doctor came along. The choking sobs rose in his throat, beads of sweat broke on his forehead, his hands shook.

'Bitch! Why couldn't you have died with the boy?'

It couldn't be happening to her! She was living a nightmare, watching his contorted face, hearing his high-pitched, uncontrolled sobs, feeling the vice-like grip as his huge hands once again gripped her. On the small landing table was a candle in its brass holder, just near enough for her to reach. He hadn't noticed it, but he knew she had something in her hand. As she raised her arm ready to bring the candleholder down on the back of his head he moved his hands from her shoulders to her throat. With all her might she struck him, but fighting for breath as she was she hadn't enough power to do him much damage. In that second, as he caught his breath and stumbled, she saw herself standing accused of murder.

After spending some minutes with the assistant governor, Matthew waited alone while Alice said her final farewell to

Gerald. When they'd arrived at the prison they'd been told that he had died in the night. Peacefully? Mercifully unaware? Or had his mind cleared in his final minutes? No one knew, for his body hadn't been discovered until morning.

Closing the door quietly but firmly behind her, Alice came along the corridor towards Matthew. She held herself very erect, her hands clasped in front of her as if she found strength in the grip of her own fingers.

'We'll leave when you like,' she told him.

'You must stay as long as you wish, you know that.'

'There's nothing of him in this place. His spirit is free of it.' So why was it she couldn't bring herself to meet his gaze as she answered him?

Putting an arm around her shoulder he led her away. Each door had to be opened, then once they were through, the key turned again. At last they came out of the main gate. It had been the part of her visits she'd dreaded. Looking across the road towards the Forbury Gardens, the spring sunshine seemed to mock them.

In silence they started the drive home, over the narrow Holy Brook which centuries ago had been part of the abbey.

'So much history . . . so many lives.' Was she looking for comfort in the thought of all those countless thousands before them? 'Nothing lasts . . . there's no certainty.'

'I've arranged that he is to be brought back to Brackleford. He'll be laid with Terry. I thought that's what you'd want.'

Whether her stoicism had come from bravery or fear of facing what had to be faced, hearing his words, it was lost. Watching the road ahead as he drove, he knew she was crying and he was thankful. She'd been brave too long over these last years.

'They'll let him be brought away from that dreadful place. Matthew, I don't know what I'd do without you.'

'I'll take you home to collect some things, then what about a few days with Jane? She suggested it to me.'

'You knew he was dying?'

'I thought so, yes. I was fearful of his future if he'd struggled on. For him, surely today must mean release. It's *you* Jane and I care about now.'

'Keep crying – so sorry.'

He covered her hand with his, saying nothing. They drove along King's Road in its Sunday afternoon quietness, passing just one or two families dressed in their best and out for a walk in the sunshine. At the junction they took the Wokingham Road then, a few miles on, turned towards Brackleford. Neither talked until, suddenly, as they went through the Market Square, another devil of doubt gripped Alice.

'Suppose Reverend Warborough won't take the service – or won't have him put to rest in his churchyard? You know the wicked things people said about him – not true – he was a *good* man. There was no hate in Gerald, only love. Love that couldn't accept what had been done to Terry.'

'I know. The trouble with people, Alice, is that they get pleasure out of anything unusual, anything that adds colour to their days. Not a lot happens in Brackleford. But malice, wickedness? Insensitivity more often.'

'Forgive them, they know not what they do? Is that what you're saying?'

'I've dealt with so many of these chattering busy-bodies. But, you know, taken individually, there's no real spite in them.' Turning to her with that quick smile that seemed to light his eyes then vanish: 'Some of it comes from lack of confidence. It's easier to whisper together than to offer friendship to someone they don't know.'

'Well, they can't touch my Gerald now. Can you understand what I mean when I say I'm thankful for this day? I wanted him home, I wanted him to be as he was before all the trouble. But the three years he's endured have been worse for him than death.'

'I've watched it. He could never have taken another seven like the last three. He was too gentle a man.'

Arriving at her small villa, they went inside together and he waited while she collected the things she would need for the next two or three days. Then they set out for Addingford. The shadows were already lengthening and before they arrived he had to light the lamps on the front of the motor car. Driving past the railway halt he could see there was no sign of life, the last train had gone through and Hugh Phillpott had gone home. The village street was deserted and from behind closed curtains came the warm glow of lamps.

'She must be out,' he said when he saw that Holly Cottage was in darkness. 'I'll see you safely indoors, then I'll go down to Phillpotts' place, that's bound to be where she is.'

'Do you have a key?' Alice was only speaking for the sake of speaking, wanting him to feel that she was interested in the plans he was making for her.

'No one here ever locks a door until they go to bed at night. But, yes Alice, I do have a key.'

'My dear, I'm sorry. I wasn't prying. I just don't know what I'm saying.'

'Sit where you are while I come round to help you out. The brick path to the front door is uneven, I'll take your arm in the dark.'

So they went the few steps to the door and he lifted the latch to usher her in. But there was something inside preventing it from opening. He pushed harder, then telling Alice to stay where she was, he wriggled through the narrow aperture. He had no idea what he expected to find blocking their entry. With darkness coming upon him slowly as he'd driven, his eyes were already attuned. Alice was forgotten as he dropped to his knees beside Jane's still form.

Chapter Thirteen

Much too early for his train, Ian walked in the opposite direction, crossing the stile just as Jane had a few hours before, his solitude shared only with a few disinterested cows. Unlike Jane, he didn't follow the track round the edge of the field and beyond; instead, he sat on the step of the stile, his head bent, the haunted expression on his face out of character with the rakish angle of his best brown bowler. What had he done? But it hadn't been *his* fault, it had been *hers*; hitting him with that bloody candleholder had made him stumble. He must think. He must decide on his story and get it so firmly in his mind that he could tell it as if it were true.

His mouth was working, his clenched fists hammered his knees. She'd lain there so still . . . suppose she was dead. Dead. What if he'd killed her? They'd accuse him of murder! But they couldn't call it 'murder'! It had been an accident. So why hadn't he called for help? The cards would be stacked against him. He'd got to make them see that it had been an accident. Yes, and more than that, it had been Jane who'd caused it. If she hadn't given him that crack on his head he wouldn't have grabbed her, trying to get his balance. That was it, that was how the two of them had crashed down the narrow stairway.

The stillness of dusk was broken by the sound of his blubbering.

'Never meant to do it – not *that*.' He heard the echo of his own words telling her he wished she'd died with the boy. Taking off his hat he felt the lump on the back of his head. From head to foot he ached, he felt as though he'd been kicked and trampled. So what of her? It had happened in a moment: when the knock on his head had made him reel, instinct had tightened his grip on her throat, then they'd both toppled. She'd tried to grab the hand rail but hadn't been able to, his weight falling on top of her had pushed her headlong forward. He still seemed to hear the sound as they bumped down the stairs; he felt dizzy at the memory of that moment of helplessness as he'd been flung forward. In seconds they'd been lying in the passage just inside the front door, Jane underneath him. She hadn't moved. Supposing she never moved! Think, man, think. That fool of a chap at the railway station will be watching, expecting you'll be taking her home with you. He'll be waiting to say goodbye to Miss Bradley. Goodbye. Was that what it was? For him? For everyone?

Ian's clenched fist beat a wild tattoo on his knees as he rocked backwards and forwards, sitting cramped on the low bar of the stile. The sun had gone down, the evening air was chill, the day had forgotten its promise of spring. He shivered even though he was sweating, his clothes clammy against his skin.

'Never meant to do that. Must think. Must think.'

Perhaps when he walked past the cottage on the way to the railway, he would see the lamps lit. Yes, that's how it would be. She'd probably been conscious all the time, just trying to frighten him. In the isolation of the cow field he voiced his thoughts aloud, needing the comfort of hearing his own voice even though his tongue seemed to cleave to the roof of his mouth.

'Must get to the station. God, but I must be black and blue. She will be too. If I've left marks on her neck they won't even show with all the other bruising. I'm a hefty weight to fall on her. It's all gone wrong, everything's gone wrong. Got to get home to Else. Everything in my life is a mess – and all because of that stuck-up bitch. What's that old fool at the station going to think when he sees me in this state? Can't stop shaking.' Dragging himself to his feet he gripped the stile, forcing himself to stand erect, then he took off his hat once more so that he could settle it back at the right angle. A brisk walk through the village would do him good – and more good than anything would be to see a light from her window.

But Holly Cottage was in darkness.

'I've been watching out for you. Train'll be along in about four minutes. She's not with you, then?' Hugh looked at the big man who was so clearly upset, his eyes full of sympathy. 'Now that she knows you want her enough to find out where she's been hiding herself and come chasing after her, give her a night to sleep on it, son, and she might well change her mind.' Dear me, the poor young man's properly knocked for six, eyes red as if he's been crying. Wouldn't you think that seeing how he'd sunk his pride to come begging would have reminded her of the vows she'd taken. Hugh put a kindly hand on Ian's arm. He and Aggie had been taken in by Miss Bradley right enough, thinking her such a fine young lady! Didn't it just show, give a person nice quiet speech, a gentle manner, and there was no way of guessing what went on in her mind. Young hussy, that's what she was, breaking her vows of faith and treating her poor hard-working husband like that. Perhaps she'd found out that he'd been kicking over the traces, perhaps that was what had driven her away. But, if he had, he wouldn't be the first man and he wouldn't be the last. The ladies, they were satisfied with a home to look after; and that's how nature designed things. It had always been different for the male of the species: look at the animal world. For himself he'd lived contentedly enough with Aggie, but there would always be men who needed more sex than they found with their one partner. It stood to reason. The ladies had to accept – a bit outside didn't mean that he couldn't keep her happy too, if that was what she wanted. But a woman leaving the home her husband provided, earning her own living – ah, and being friendlier than she ought to be with that young chap they pretended was her brother, quite upset him. And this poor chap, all got up in his Sunday best, came here full of hope, now look at him! His wife's place was back home looking after him; that was the job she'd taken on when she wed. Whatever the trouble had been, it was up to her to forgive and forget. Well, of one thing he was certain: as far as he was concerned – he and Aggie too – they'd done with the young minx. The sooner she took herself off from Addingford the better.

'Let her sleep on it, man. If she's been romancing with someone else, she'll want to make sure she finishes it off, make him understand she's done with him – or you'll have him following her. You'd not want that. Give her a bit of time to think about the way she's behaved and she'll come to heel right enough.'

'Please God she will,' Ian croaked, this time making no attempt to hold back his tears. 'She's got this other chap, you see. None of the things we shared seem to matter to her. What can I do? I tell you, I'd give my right arm to bring her back to me. She was out when I got there, so I went inside and waited.' He didn't try to control his emotion, instead he looked Hugh full in the face, his own contorted as his words tumbled out in a distraught squeak. Despite his sympathy, Hugh found the scene embarrassing. 'When she came home she heard me moving about and you should have heard how she cried out: "You've come back," she cried. You'd think she'd found a crock of gold. Didn't expect it to be me – thought it was her fancy man. Wouldn't listen to a word I tried to say to her. Begged her, I did.' Then, from his pocket he pulled a handkerchief that Elsie had boiled back to something like its original white. 'Can't bear it there without her. If she doesn't come back, I don't think I can go on.'

263

There was no need for him to worry about making a plausible story; anger, terror, horror at what might be the outcome of his afternoon, had built up into a display of hysterical weeping it was beyond his power to prevent.

'Here she comes,' Hugh muttered – referring to the train. 'You give your face a wipe and I'll find a compartment for you by yourself. Never many people aboard on this one. And, Mr Harriman, if I see Miss Bradley – your wife I mean – I'll put in a word for you. She never meant to get you upset like this. Silly wicked girl. And that man you say isn't her brother – well, he might as well be. They never gave the wife and me a hint of any goings on. No, brother or not, you've got nothing to worry about between those two.' He hoped he sounded more certain than he felt, for only that mid-day while he'd been eating his soup, Agnes had been telling him how nice it had been for Miss Bradley, her brother had been able to stay the night at the cottage.

'I'm coming again next Sunday.' Ian tried to steady his voice to make sure there was no mistaking what he said. 'I told her I would. I begged her to think, to remember all the good times, to let us start again.'

'That'll be it then, man. She won't want to seem too eager. Funny creatures, women. Now don't you spend the week worrying. I'll look out for you next Sunday.'

'Wait where you are, I'll light the lamp,' Matthew told Alice.

'What is it? Why doesn't the door open?'

'It's Jane. She must have fallen down the stairs.'

'But, my dear, there are no lamps lit. She must have fallen while it was still light, she must have been lying there for hours.'

He didn't answer. With a hand that was far from steady he held his lucifer to the wick of the lamp, then carried it into the passage and put it on the bottom stair.

'Jane . . . Jane can you hear me?' He took her wrist, his

264

fingers on her pulse. 'Thank God . . . thank God.'

Alice was forgotten, but it wasn't in her nature to stand idly. There was a brass candleholder lying by Jane's side and, a few stairs from the bottom flight, a candle that must have fallen out when she fell. Why had she been walking about with an unlit candle? The question didn't stay in Alice's mind long enough to demand an answer. She felt for where Matthew had left his lucifers on the table of the little sitting room, lit the candle, then busied herself lighting lamps. While she did that, Matthew was gently feeling Jane's arms and legs, making sure there were no fractures. One ankle was badly swollen, the blood from a gash on her head had soaked into the mat just inside the front door. But nothing was broken. Getting to his feet he bent to lift her.

'I'll help you,' Alice told him. 'You won't get her up these narrow stairs on your own.'

He nodded, his thoughts just on Jane. How long had she been unconscious? Probably for hours. If she were in a deep coma, what damage – no, he shied away from letting himself imagine. He went first, walking backwards, taking the weight with Jane leaning back against him, as though she were in a chair and Alice following holding her legs.

'Suppose we hadn't come . . . suppose you hadn't suggested bringing me here,' Alice panted, not expecting a reply. Suppose they'd found Gerald as they had yesterday, then Matthew would have taken her back to her own home and probably not come here again tonight. Fate. Had it been ordained that her Gerald should be taken from her when he was, so that they were all here together when Jane needed them? She wanted so much to be brave, to make herself a rock Jane could depend on. Yet each time she believed she'd strengthened her resolve, a wave of despair would swamp her. She was being selfish; with all her willpower she resolved to think just of others. But her heart ached with misery, her future held no hope, no shape.

'I'm going down to get my bag,' Matthew told her. 'Watch her, Alice, see if there's the slightest change.'

Carrying one of the lamps he went downstairs, leaving Alice in the shadowy light thrown from the one that hung from a bracket on the wall.

'Jane . . . Jane . . . wherever you are, come back to us. Don't leave him without you, Jane. All alone. That's what's happened to me now, Jane. Gerald's gone. Do you think Terry knows?' If Jane had been conscious she couldn't have talked so freely, but what a relief it was to speak from her heart. 'Do you think they're together, my two dear loves? That's my only comfort. But Jane, what's to become of me? Oh, dear Lord forgive me, self, self, what sort of devil is eating into me that I can just think of self. Jane, open your eyes. When he comes back upstairs give him a sign, anything, just open your eyes and see him.'

Jane lay like a waxen image.

Matthew tried all he knew to bring some sign of life. Her pulse was stronger, but her face was a pale, expressionless mask. It was an hour or so later when, one on either side of the bed, he and Alice both heard a sound, a whimper full of terror in a voice unlike her own.

'Darling, Jane my love, tell me.'

'No . . .' she cried. It was barely audible, but it was life. 'Go 'way . . .'

'*He's* been here. That's what it is.' It was Alice who understood the torment Jane was fighting to escape. She leant nearer. 'Ian was here, Jane.' It was a statement, not a question, the words piercing Jane's consciousness.

'No . . . no . . .' Jane's head thrashed from side to side. Matthew took hold of her hands, but it only made her struggle harder. Then, without warning, she pulled her hands free of him and forced herself to sit up, her eyes wide open and full of fear. 'No . . . no . . .' she sobbed. 'Don't let him come back.' Her hands flew to her neck.

'He won't come back. He'll never come back.' Matthew pulled her into his arms, rocking her as if she were a frightened child. 'It's all over, darling.'

Neither of them noticed Alice go quietly out of the room

266

and along the little landing to the tiny second bedroom, the room she knew would be hers. She'd been thankful to come here, dreading the hours, weeks, months, years – oh please God not years, how was she going to bear it? – of loneliness ahead of her. They were still there waiting for her, but for the next day or two she would have Jane to look after. She went downstairs and found her bag so that she could unpack her few things. From Jane's room she could hear the occasional sound of voices and she knew that Matthew would be making sure Jane hung on to consciousness and stayed awake. Please don't let her memory be damaged. No bones broken, Matthew had been able to make sure of that. But how badly had she hit her head? Wasn't it said that if a person went into a deep coma there could be brain damage? Not that, please not that for Jane. A broken leg, oh that would have been nothing, she would soon have overcome that. But her head . . .

Catching sight of her reflection in the mirror fixed to the cupboard door, Alice pulled herself straight as she sat on the edge of the bed, then stood up. Life's given you a chance to be useful; be grateful. Can you see me, Gerald? Again she slumped on the bed, determination forgotten. Three years you were in that hell-hole, all you knew was what I told you – and Gerald, love, I didn't tell you the half of it, you must know that now. Did you guess it was all an act when I tried to be cheerful, full of hope for that future we shall never have? Three long years, separated by more than that great high brick wall; separated by the false picture I painted of how I was living. Well, now it's all done. You can see for yourself, you can look into my heart and know my hopelessness. Can't help it . . . She felt the hot tears roll down her cheeks. Ought to be down on my knees thanking God for taking you. Just wish He'd take me too. With you gone – there's nothing.

The lamp flickered. When had Jane last filled it? Or did the wick need trimming? Everyday practicalities had to be her strength. She wiped her face and once again stood up.

Food would be needed – she'd go downstairs and see what she could find in the cupboard. Keep watching me, Gerald, don't leave me alone, let me always feel that you're close.

'Alice, is that you?' Matthew called as he heard her step on the landing. 'Come and see her. She's awake.'

'My dear,' her voice giving away nothing of her recent weak moment. 'What a fright you gave us. You must have tripped. But it was a mercy you didn't break your neck.'

'Matthew's told me – about your Gerald.' Jane held out her hand. 'Don't know what to say.'

'Say what I'm trying to say, Jane. He is with Terry in paradise. Fate – call it what name you like – has given me a chance to be useful for a few days. You'll let me stay and help you until you're on your feet again?'

'I wish you would.' What Jane wanted to say was: 'Didn't you say we were like family? Stay with me as long as you like.' But she knew Alice couldn't accept pity, she wanted to be needed for her usefulness.

The train arrived at Brackleford precisely on time at seven-fifty-three. The journey had distanced Ian from the nightmare of his afternoon and by the time he stepped down on to the platform, except for bloodshot eyes which were more obvious to him than to a stranger, he was the same handsome man who had set out. Elsie would be waiting for him with something warm for his supper, but it wouldn't take above five minutes to stop off at the Railway Arms for a pint of ale; his mouth felt dry as dust.

His first pint slipped down his throat in one long draught. Putting the tankard back on the bar, he had every intention of leaving until the man standing next to him spoke.

'You downed that as though you needed it.'

'That I did, too. Been dreaming of it all the way back from Addingford.'

'Addingford, you say? There's a coincidence. That's where I come from.' Then with a laugh, 'And not many people can say that. One-eyed hole of a place if ever I saw one.'

'Certainly pretty quiet on a Sunday afternoon. I had to go there to pay a call.' Now here was a stroke of luck, a chance for him to tell his tale and spread the word. 'Fill my jar, landlord, the same again.'

'Let me.' His new acquaintance pulled a handful of money out of the pocket of his checked trousers. 'If you're not in a rush we could sit and chat while you drink it. Not every day I meet a man who's had cause to visit God-forsaken Addingford for pleasure.'

'That's decent of you. No, I've nothing to hurry for. An empty house now my wife's run off. That's what took me to your village. She's walked out on me and taken a cottage there. Got herself work, so I've heard.'

'I thought you looked a bit down. That's why I spoke. Not prying, mind you.' But the pregnant pause after he said it hinted otherwise. 'Landlord, the same for me if you will – and a couple of double Scotch to chase them.'

'I say, that's good of you. I tell you I could do with a shot of something after hearing what she told me. Let's sit over here where it's quiet, shall we. Truth to tell, it'll be a relief to have someone to talk to, to get if off my chest.'

He had no idea who the stranger was, but what did it matter as long as he could spread the gossip around the local community. It did occur to him that Addingford was hardly the place he would have expected to find a man of that sort, red-faced, flamboyant, drinking his beer and whisky as though it were a routine beverage.

'So you went to see her? I take it she wasn't co-opera-tive, sent you home to your lonely life. Well, man, there are plenty of others. Not one of them worth breaking your heart over.'

'You say that, but I doubt if you're married.'

Richard Foley laughed. 'Not likely, I'm not. What do you want to buy a book for when there's a good lending library. Eh? Eh?' He dug his finger into Ian's ribs as he spoke, laughing at his own joke.

'Begged her, I did. But she's stubborn. I blame employers

taking on women. Give them the chance to earn a few bob and they think they're as good as the men. Not that I'm belittling her, no, I was always proud as a peacock of her. Better background than me, you know. Used to more or less run the show for her old man at his brewery down in the West Country. But she and I, we held the world in our hands. Money? As if that mattered. That's how it was in the beginning. How it always was, as far as I'm concerned. I've tried, I've worked all the hours God sends to try to give her a few comforts. Then, one day I came home from work and there was her note saying she was off. I thought she must have gone back to her father. But no, when I told him he was as worried as I was.' He was warming to his tale, almost believing the image of the close attachment between himself and Amos Bradley. 'Then, by chance I heard that she was in Addingford.'

'Brewery? Her father has a brewery you say?'

'That's it. Bradley's Beer. Well known down in that part of the world.' But, once in full spate, Ian didn't welcome interruptions, he wanted to get on with his story. 'So I went there today, I begged her, I pleaded. I'm not a man to take kindly to begging favours, but I just want her home again. Can't tell you ... every time I open the front door I seem to hear her voice. Then today she told me. She left me because of another man. Her brother, that's what she's letting people think he is. Well, nothing odd about having a brother spending nights there.'

'Gone back to her maiden name, has she? Jane Bradley? Well, I'm buggered.'

'That's what I found out today. She even spurns my name.'

'Let her go, that's my advice, friend. You saw the brewery there at Addingford? That's why I'm there, I manage it. She came to me for a job. I shouldn't have listened but that's the worst part of my sort of work. It's not easy to turn people away, I suppose I'm not hard-hearted enough. Tell you the truth, I wasn't easy about her.

270

Well, now I know what she is, you may be sure of one thing, my friend, she's come to the end of the track as far as I'm concerned. Lying young bitch.'

'Hey, steady on.' Ian remembered his role of the adoring husband. 'I know how you feel, of course. No man likes to be tricked – and I should know. But I've pleaded with her to give up this man she seems so besotted with. I've *begged* her. Well, you noticed for yourself the state I was in. If she won't come back to me, I swear I don't want to go on.' Ian took a gulp of neat whisky, belched quietly, muttering, 'Beg pardon. Drinking on an empty stomach. Couldn't eat a thing at mid-day – too keyed up even for my usual bread and cheese. Hoping, hoping, hoping . . .' Another draught of ale before took up what Richard Foley had just told him. 'I told her I'd come back next Sunday.' Another belch. 'Next Sunday . . . sounds as though I'm confident doesn't it, but it wasn't like that. Can't believe I could have grovelled as I did. Beseeched her to think about all the good times, to give me another chance. A week for her to think about it, to remember the hope we used to have, then I'm coming back to Holly Cottage – that's where she lives.'

'I know where she lives right enough. The cottage belongs to the brewery. She was in lodgings then she came to me with some yarn that she wanted a proper home so that her brother could be with her. I tell you, friend, I'm too soft-hearted for my own good. Too gullible. Landlord, bring us the same again, will you. But tomorrow I'll give her her marching orders and as soon as she loses her job, out she goes from that cottage.'

'No! No, don't kick her out his week. Give her notice by all means, that might tip the scales my way, but tell her you give her a week or so to be out of her home.' He tipped the second Scotch into the remains of the first. 'This is damned good of you. It's my turn really, I know that. Haven't the cash. It's rotten, you know, always counting the coppers. Manager of a thriving brewery, you can't ever be hard pushed for a tanner. She used to sneer at me for not having

271

money like she'd been used to.' His mouth worked, self-pity promised to envelop him. 'All I can give her is love, devotion.'

'More than she deserves, my friend. By the way, you must have a name?'

'Harriman. Ian Harriman. By trade I'm a cooper, and a better cooper you'll never find.'

'A cooper, eh? Well, now, what about this for an idea? What if I take you on at my place – Watford's. Can't you just see her face when you turned in for work?' Sitting back in his chair Richard laughed, imagining the scene, his podgy freckled hands drumming a tattoo on his rounded stomach. 'I could kick her out of that cottage and put you into it. Would that suit your plans?'

'No. No. I couldn't do that. I want my wife back in our own bed – not *there*, knowing her fancy man has got his pleasure from her before me. But listen – sir—'

'Foley's the name. Richard Foley.'

'Hang on to her for another week. She may not deserve it, and I understand how you feel about being cheated by the way she lied, but I've told her I'll see her next Sunday. If you sack her before then God knows where she'll disappear to, I'll lose track of her again. Don't do that to me . . .' His already bloodshot eyes filled.

So a bargain was struck and half an hour or so later Richard Foley drove Ian to the corner of Mill Lane before setting off back to Addingford. He supposed he hadn't been invited right home with his new acquaintance because the poor chap was ashamed of the uncomfortable state of the place. And all for that haughty dame!

Despite spending each evening in the Queen Charlotte, Ian was quickly affected by alcohol as Jane had had plenty of reason to know. His walk was less than steady as he made his way the sort distance home. The lamps were lit and as he opened the front door his nose was assailed with an appetizing smell of supper.

Over the last hour or so, he had almost made himself

believe the story he intended should be put around Addingford. Now, the reason for it hit him. He'd been covering his tracks in case Jane was still lying as he'd left her. Supposing she never regained consciousness, when news was brought to him that her body had been found he must be surprised. So the lie wasn't over yet. Above all else he wanted to tell Elsie every single thing that had happened, he wanted to find comfort in her love and understanding. But he daren't.

'There you are!' She came into the passage to meet him, her rosy face filled with concern. 'I was just going to get my hat and coat on and walk to the railway station. I thought there must have been an accident.'

He held out his arms and was rewarded by the familiar warmth of her embrace. He'd come home. This was real.

'My Elsie . . . my anchor.'

'Run up and take off your tidy suit while I dish up. I hope it's not got dried.'

'It'll be perfect. Everything you give me is always perfect.'

She nuzzled her face against his neck, feeling the stiffness of his white 'worn for the occasion' collar, a face that was flushed with pleasure at his words.

'Chump,' she said, and he knew she was smiling.

'We'll eat first. Then you can help me take off my good things. How's that?'

'All right, love. I expect you're starved. And I want to hear all about it.'

He tipped her chin so that in the shadowy light from the lamp in the sitting room he could look at her.

'Did it go well, love? Did she agree? We're going to be all right, are we?'

He didn't answer, indeed he was gripped by such a longing to tell her every terrifying detail that he couldn't find his voice. Ushering her back to the kitchen, he laid his bowler on the dresser then sat down in his accustomed place at the table.

'So empty, I wonder you can't hear my stomach rolling.'

She served his mutton stew in a soup bowl; she knew he liked plenty of room so that he could soak his bread in the gravy and mashed potatoes ('No one mashes potatoes like you do, Else.'), then she opened the dresser drawer to find a serviette.

'Here, love, tuck this into your collar. You don't want greasy spots on your tidy clothes.'

He made no attempt to take it, instead he held up his head and waited, letting her fix it for him. Practical, caring, sensible Elsie, she was more sensitive to his moods than he realized. No wonder she could smell ale and whisky on his breath, she could see how upset he'd been.

'However it went, don't you let her rattle you. Eat up your supper while you tell me about it. We'll work it out together.'

So he told her, if not the whole story, at least some of it.

'Do you believe in fate?' she asked. 'I never thought I did, but doesn't it make you think it must have been planned for you to meet this man you say she works for. Told him a good tale, did you? Even if the doctor plays ball and pays you to keep his name out of it, the more people who know the way she's treated you, the better.'

With something akin to a smile Ian nodded.

'I told him I begged her to come back, laid my soul bare to her, beseeched her.' The warm food was giving him back his confidence, lifting the memory of Jane lying still and silent. 'He was going to give her the sack, as soon as she turns up for work in the morning he was going to send for her. Her cottage belongs to the brewery she works for, so that would put her out on the street. But – oh, Else, you'd have been proud if you could have heard me, I reckon the theatre lost the chance of a fine actor when I took up making barrels – I made him agree to give her another week before he let her know her game was up. I told him that I'd begged her not to turn me down like that,

274

to give herself time to think about things. I'd threatened to come again next Sunday—'

'Threatened? That's a funny way to describe it, when you're supposed to be there to tell her you can't live without her and all that sort of thing.'

'Ah yes, well, threatened wasn't the word I used to him. That's what I'm saying to *you*. I threatened Jane that she'd not seen the last of me as easy as that, I should be back next Sunday and that would give her time to talk things over with Bingley and come to their senses. She's keen enough to be free, doesn't even deny that he gets his oats from her. Just keeps repeating that she's not his patient. I don't give a bugger how they decide to sort it out, but if he wants to keep his nose clean, then best he pays up front. As I said to her, get his name in the Court and likely it would put an end to his doctoring, for it would only be *her* word against all the others who used to watch how often he was here. What I can't understand is, how any man – least of all one with a wife at home like he's got – would want to hang his trousers over the end of the bed for a woman like she was while she was making such a song about being pregnant.'

'Oh, Ian love, she couldn't help it that she was so poorly.'

'Not saying she could. All I'm saying is that no man could have fancied it.'

'You used to come home to her. You used to get in a state because she didn't want to make love, you used to tell me.'

'It wasn't her that got me so pitched up, Else. It was *you*, *you* know that. But *you* I couldn't have. I'm not a man who can go without. Having a woman is like meat and drink to me.' Still holding his knife and fork he looked directly at her, forcing her to meet his gaze. 'And that's the truth. You're a good lass, you don't get me all pitched up and leave me, I'm not saying you do. But the way we have to do things isn't the same, isn't like it could be. You're not a cold woman, you must want to do it as much as I do. Just talking about it . . .'

'I do, I do. More than anything in all the world I want us to really be *one*. And soon we will be. Now that you know where she is, she'll persuade Dr Bingley. Or even write to her father. He might pay up willingly enough if he thinks it'll end her marriage.'

'No justice in this unfair world. No money . . . no wife. There are limits to how long a man can go without a woman—'

'Oh Ian love, you make me feel awful talking like that. You're not without a woman. You know I love you, you're all the world to me . . .' Her rosy face was even pinker, her blue eyes entreating him.

'Love goes further than cooking meals and sewing on buttons.' Getting up from the table he came to her side, pulling her hand to press against him. Holding him around the waist she pressed her face against him. Then she, too, stood up, reached to turn the lamp low, then pulled off his serviette, untied his tie and unfastened his stud. His pulses wee racing as he fumbled with the buttons on her skirt.

There was nothing new in these preliminaries, they occurred almost nightly. This evening would be different. In front of the kitchen range, a warm hearthrug and a hard floor would be their bed, the unwashed dishes forgotten on the table.

That Sunday night Matthew stayed at Holly Cottage, leaving before it was light as he had to be in Brackleford when his morning surgery started at eight o'clock. On the way past Watford's Brewery he put a note through the letterbox saying that Miss Bradley would be absent from work for the next few days as she had had a fall and sustained a sprained ankle. He wrote it on headed paper he carried in his medical bag showing his qualifications and the address of his surgery. No doubt it would be thought strange that she'd been seen by a doctor from so far away, but that couldn't be helped.

Ahead of him was a busy day. Monday was usually a long surgery, then he had a list of calls to make. Even so, foremost in his mind were the visits he must make to the undertaker and the vicar. So much had happened in the last few hours that, for him if not for Alice, Gerald's death had been pushed to the background.

Nearing the town he took his watch out of his waistcoat pocket and glanced at it. Half past seven: he had time to call at the house and see if he had any messages before going to the surgery.

From the breakfast room he could hear sounds of yesterday evening's fire being cleared and this morning's lit. Yvette usually stayed in bed until the house was warm for, as she often said, there was nothing to tempt her to get up. There was nothing new in her morning grumbles. He'd always listened to them with tolerance, knowing that once she was dressed, her hair arranged to her satisfaction, perfume behind her ears, on her handkerchief and, with a final optimistic flourish, tipped into her cleavage, she would be ready to wrestle what fun she could out of the day ahead.

'Good morning, oosbond,' she greeted him from her bed. 'And was your meeting the 'appy one you 'oped?'

'Did any messages come for me?' He ignored her question just as he ignored the teasing light in her eyes.

'No one was in need of you. And me? What did I do with my weekend? I will tell you. I played my piano, I walked by myself, I wrote to my poor Anton imprisoned in that so 'orrible place. Oh, but yes, I did one thing more. I went to church. To your church – well, it would be if you went to it. I am what is called a godmother. We 'ad the service yesterday afternoon and I made all the promises so that the vicar and his so pretty wife could make their new baby a member of their church. And you? No, do not tell me. I do not want to 'ear. But if you enjoyed it and if your lady

277

friend found you to her liking then I am 'appy for you. It is time, more than time, you gave yourself some fun and 'ad some games.' He saw her expression as teasing; he heard her words as meaning just what she said. If there was any underlying fear that the even tenor of their life together was beginning to go awry, he wasn't interested enough to look for it.

'I've a busy day ahead, I must go if there are no messages. Don't hold your meal back for me this evening. It's unlikely I shall be home.'

When he'd gone she stretched, her arms in the air, her feet reaching to the foot of the bed. She knew Matthew too well honestly to believe he was having what she liked to call fun and games. So how seriously did he care about the wife of the handsome cooper? And how much did the thought disturb her? She was his wife and that's what she intended to remain.

Soon after she heard the front door close behind him, she rang the bell to let them know in the kitchen that she was ready for someone to bring hot water. It was time to start the day. Matthew and his uncharacteristic interest in another woman slipped into the shadows of her mind; if she thought of the affair at all it was only as far as her own association with Jane Harriman's husband was concerned. Now how would she fill her day? Her interest in the black-smith had been short-lived. He was a good-looking young man, flattered by her attention, but presented no sport at all. Now the gorgeous vicar, he was much more complex. Sometimes she believed he was frightened of her – or more likely frightened of his own sensuality and plagued by a conscience that made being with him a challenge. She was baby Stephanie Yvette's godmother, so what more natural than she should want to see her namesake? A smile started in her eyes, then tugged at the corners of her mouth, as the thought of her morning took shape.

On the breakfast table she found a letter from Anton. Just to see the envelope was enough to destroy any cheer she'd found in her plans for the morning. She knew what she would read. He never complained, sometimes she wished he would; for then, at least she would feel he was writing from his heart. But these short, bald statements, they were as dry and dull as she knew he found his life to be. No matter how many years he lived in this sober, strait-laced country of Matthew's, nothing would turn him into an English boy. He had been here since he was three years old; only twice in the intervening time had Matthew taken them back to their homeland; but just being there had seemed to light a spark in Anton. At this so stuffy school Matthew thought was so important for his training, it was only in French lessons that he spoke his own language. Talking together he and she always used their native tongue, just as they did when they wrote. She was thankful she had brought him up to speak it with the same ease as he did English. One day he would go back there. Neither of them ever admitted it to the other, but she knew he was as stifled here as she was.

Natural optimism came to the fore and by the time she was ready to sully forth into the bright, breezy morning she looked forward to the pleasure of spending an hour or so with Alayne and the baby. No one would have expected the two women to be friends: in outlook they were poles apart. But the early foundations had been proved strong, unalike as they were in thought and deed, yet companionship flourished. So when, as Yvette crossed Market Square towards the path that led beyond the church to the vicarage, she met Alayne going on her hurried way to keep some appointment, she was naturally disappointed.

'It was to see you that I have come. And now you are to be gone. Is my god-daughter in the care of that girl you call Martha? But what difference to me? I shall not call to see you if you are not at home.'

Alayne laughed affectionately. Since she'd come to know Yvette so much better, the accent she'd first heard as an affectation no longer irritated her.

'Martha is in the house in case he runs into trouble,' she said. 'But Marcos has Stephanie with him in his study. I am on my way to the infirmary, it's such a joy to be doing all my own little tasks again after being housebound for all those months. Not that a few months was anything of a sacrifice, compared with the miracle of having her.' She seemed to radiate happiness. 'Go and talk to Marcos, he will be delighted.' Then, with a chuckle, 'Delighted and probably relieved too. It's the first time I've gone away from the house and left him with her. She was asleep, he was very sure of himself.'

Two minutes later, long-serving Edith knocked on the study door, then immediately opened it a few inches.

'Caller for you, Vicar. That foreign lady, Mrs Bingley. I'd better tell her you're engaged I expect, hadn't I? Looking after our little miss won't leave you much talking time.' Clearly she wasn't impressed by what she'd seen and heard of the doctor's wife who had been unceremoniously left to wait on the doorstep.

'No, bring her in, Edith. It'll be Stephanie she's come to see rather than me.' His voice was full of bonhomie, he gave no hint of anything but friendly pleasure at the interruption. 'I think she's about to wake,' he added, ashamed of the lie as he peered into the Moses basket.

'Perhaps it's as well she's come then. One thing keeping an eye on her while she sleeps, another when she cries and you don't know what to do. If you need young Martha to take her off your hands, just you pull the bell. I've only put the girl on to giving the cutlery a shine to keep idle hands out of mischief. Turn my back for two minutes and she's off out in the churchyard chattering to Bill Hodge's boy, hindering him when he's supposed to be cutting the verges. So, if you say so, I'd best tell her to come in.' Edith never said two words when twenty-two would do and, on this particular occasion, Marcos had been glad of the extra time to prepare himself for his unexpected visitor.

'I have spoken with Alayne,' Yvette greeted him, aware

that Edith still hovered by the half closed door. 'When I saw that she was going out, I did not expect to visit Stephanie Yvette. But she said I was to come, she even thought you might like a little support.'

'Edith has just been hinting much the same thing. Come in, Yvette, and close the door. Despite the sunshine, there is a sharp easterly, and the draught cuts into this room. See, she's getting restless, I believe her eyes will open any second.'

Assured there was no need for her vigilance, Edith went back to the kitchen.

'Waking?' Looking first at the sleeping baby, then at him, Yvette raised her brows. Her expression teased him, tempted him to remember what he fought to forget. From the Moses basket came the sucking sound as, in her sleep, Stephanie tried to fit her fist into her rosebud mouth.

'No, she seems to be settling again. I expect it was the door being opened disturbed her. Alayne said she would probably sleep for two or three hours.'

'So, may I take off my coat? Feel my hands. Indeed my gloves could not keep my hands from the cold.' Without waiting for his reply, she threw her coat on to a chair then knelt on the hearthrug, holding her hands to the warmth. 'I was not born for this cold place, for sunshine that cheats. Just look at it, a sky so blue. But there is no warmth, Marcos. I am chilled, not just my hands – feel them, cold as if I have already died – but my body.' From where she knelt she looked up at him, her expression changed now. 'Perhaps I am cold because I am so alone. Sometimes I believe I belong nowhere, not here, and after so long not in my own country. Like your bright dragonflies that skim over the water, my life is no more than a series of days, one to follow the last, none mattering more that the one before or the one after. Do you find me lacking, Marcos?'

When was it he'd fallen to his knees too? Now he put his hands on her shoulders.

'I find you like a miracle,' he whispered. 'You know I do. I dream of you, I ache for you.'

'Do not be so solemn, Marcos. Loving is not some sinful thing to make one ashamed, to make one miserable. It is nature's gift. Why do you think God made man and woman? Just to dutifully fill the world with babies? The gift of music touches your soul, but it is your ears that carry it. The gift of the scent of springtime touches your soul, but your God gave you a nose so that you could breathe in the beauty. Are those things a sin, to make you ashamed of the joy your body brings? The gift of love, oh yes, it is a miracle, a miracle that two people together can find. So we were given bodies, not just hands to work and brains to learn, but bodies that are a wonder of eroticism. Is it a sin to use the gifts that have been bestowed?'

'Yes. Yes, for us it's a sin. Unfaithfulness scars your spirit. Yvette, I want to make love to you with every fibre of my being. If you knew the battles I've fought—'

'But I do know, Marcos. And I know, when you lose your battle, the joy we give to each other. Is that not so?'

'No!' he rasped, struggling to his feet.

She knew she was losing the battle and decided it was time to withdraw. She stood up, and when he reached to pull her towards him, she stepped back.

'I did not come here meaning to disturb your thoughts.' Her voice lacked its teasing laughter; she might have been one of Alayne's sewing party come to collect another skein of wool for the hassock she was embroidering. 'I am sad that Stephanie has not woken to greet me, but when she does you may tell her that I visited her. Yes?' Their whispered conversation before the flickering flames might never have happened. 'I shall see you at the orphanage at ten o'clock tomorrow. You will teach the small girls how to live godly lives and accept each dull day without complaint, we will sing a hymn saying how happy we all are. What a fraud it all is, Marcos.'

'No. If any of it is a fraud, that is because we don't play by the rules. Those children have the gift of innocence. Please God they will grow up with the courage to keep it.'

'Like Alayne?'

'Yes. Like Alayne.'

'I should not have spoken of her. She is a *truly* good woman, not like so many good women who are dull and prim and plumped up with their own – their own—' it was seldom she couldn't think of the word she wanted, 'their own righteousness.'

Despite himself, Marcos laughed. With her, laughter came naturally. She awakened a primitive joy in him, just as she awakened emotions he battled to repress. Sometimes his dreams of her were no more than the sensual desire that in the daylight hours he tried to keep at bay, but sometimes as he slept he was aware of a sense of freedom, of light and laughter, and always he knew she was there.

He held her coat as she put it on, then walked with her to the door.

'I've been grateful for your help on Tuesdays, and I know the children look forward to your being there. But Alayne says she is able to leave Stephanie with the nurse-maid and she has reorganized her time for visiting the workhouse, so she is keen to come back to the orphanage.'

'You mean you do not want me tomorrow? Are you giving me what in your so silly tongue you say is a sack?'

She watched his so beautiful mouth twitch into a hint of a smile, even though his eyes were solemn. He answered so softly that, even if Edith were not too far away and with an ear cocked, she would be thwarted.

'I am saying, Yvette my very dear, that I am not man enough always to win my battles. So I am taking the coward's way out.'

'Hark, I hear Stephanie. You must go to her. And me, I must find myself some other use for my time.' Then, her face lighting into a smile, 'See that Alayne has some humbugs in her purse for those poor small girls in their ugly grey dresses. They will not miss me, but we both know why they so enjoy their Tuesday mornings.'

He watched her walk away down the path. He ought to

feel relief, but all he felt was a great sense of loss. By then Stephanie had settled to a steady and demanding cry, something he'd not anticipated for Alayne had assured him that she could be relied on to sleep well in the mornings.

The familiar musty smell of the church enveloped him as, holding the wrapped bundle close, he quietly closed the heavy door and walked up the aisle to the chancel and then to his seat in the choir stalls. For years this place had been his sanctuary, in good moments and bad he had come here alone.

Not for the first time he'd come seeking absolution, for mentally he had broken his vows of faith even this morning. He longed for the relief of confession. There was no reason for him to have had to bring the baby, he could easily have left her with the nursemaid. But it was right that she was here. These moments were important. Looking down at the tiny child who stared at him in such innocent trust, he was overcome by an emotion that knew no words: complete and utter love, selfless love, tender love, all these things and more. Cradling her close in the crook of his left arm, he rested her head in the palm of his right hand. She gazed towards the stained-glass window, the colours bright in the morning sunshine then, as he stooped to touch her forehead with his lips, she looked back at him and opened her mouth in a wide smile as if to say, 'This is our secret, being here like this belongs just to you and me.'

Chapter Fourteen

On that same day, late in the afternoon, Edith once again knocked on Marcos's study door. He'd heard the front-door bell jangle – apparently it was he the visitor had called to see. An indication that it must be someone meeting with Edith's approval, she waited for his call for her to 'Come in' before she burst in on him.

'Dr Bingley to see you, Vicar. I've shown him into the drawing room to wait. The mistress is up in the nursery. Will you see him in there?'

Yvette's husband! Marcos didn't look up as he answered; instead he busied himself stacking a sheaf of papers and putting them away in the desk drawer. Yvette's husband! Was this to be his punishment? This morning he'd made the final break; he'd believed he'd found forgiveness. In the confusion of his contrite mind, he'd seen that smile of recognition from the babe's pure innocence as a sign; he'd felt weak with tenderness for her and thankfulness that he was purged of his sin. Now here was her husband! There could be no other reason for the doctor to call on him: Alayne was well, the baby thriving.

'Bring him in here, Edith,' he answered, his voice giving no hint of his sudden panic. If they talked in the drawing room Alayne might come in. Alayne mustn't guess . . . What could he say? He'd made love to another man's wife. How much did Bingley know? Was it possible that, to spite him, Yvette had gone home and confessed?

Again Marcos remembered the peace, the certainty, he'd known in those minutes holding Stephanie, through the stained-glass window the sun sending a shaft of coloured light with all the promise of a rainbow after a storm. Where now was his trust? What sort of faith had he that he could forget so soon?

'Good of you to see me,' Matthew greeted him.

'Not a bit. Have you come to tell me how pleased you are with my family? To be honest, I was worried for Alayne; a first child after so many years seemed a risky business to a layman.'

Matthew sat in the seat Marcos indicated. Surely that wasn't the act of a man who had come to do battle?

'It's certainly easier for a twenty-year-old than a thirty-year-old, but I've never had a patient look forward to her confinement with more confidence than Mrs Warburton. And with good effect. You have a beautiful, healthy child. No, it's not about them I've come.'

Marcos gripped his teeth firmly together; his palms were sweating and it took all his courage to look Matthew in the eye as he waited.

'You'll remember Gerald Gregson, the father of the poor young man who was killed when he fell from an upper window at Blundell's.'

'I remember the case. In fact I called on the Gregsons many times during the weeks after the poor lad's death.' He smiled ruefully. 'From my point of view, it's been easier not to try to recall it. They were locked in their own pain, I've never failed so utterly. It was the same after he was locked up; she built a barrier around herself. You say do I remember them – why do you ask?'

Matthew told him about Gerald's death.

'I must visit her, I'm grateful to you for telling me.'

'She's with a friend, she's not in Brackleford. I want to spare her the funeral arrangements. That's why I'm here. Terry, their son, is buried in the churchyard. I've had permission from the prison authorities to arrange for the undertaker to bring Gerald's body to Brackleford. In view of his conviction, are you prepared to give him a Christian burial so that he can be laid to rest in the family grave?' If Marcos proved difficult Matthew was ready to argue his cause.

Instead Marcos was ashamed of the relief he felt. In that moment he believed he would have promised anything.

'We so often condemn each other out of lack of understanding,' he heard himself say. 'And how can we even begin to understand what the Gregsons suffered. Vengeance is mine, said the Lord.'

'So you will carry out the service?'

'Dr Bingley, there isn't one of us without sin, any more than there is any among us completely evil. The battle is constant.'

So, with a lighter heart than the occasion merited, Marcos agreed the date and time for the funeral on the following Friday afternoon.

The fall had left Jane feeling even more bruised and trampled than it had Ian, for it had been the force of his weight that had hurled her down the stairs. In terror, as she tumbled, her teeth had clamped on her bottom lip and it was that which had left the bloodstain on the mat. Five days on, it was still swollen and painful, making talking difficult and eating worse. But at least her teeth were intact. That wasn't the only swelling; her eye looked as though she had been in a fight. All in all, she was not a pretty sight. Most of her other bruises were covered with clothing. Even her swollen ankle was hidden by the folds of her skirt as she lay on the none too comfortable sofa making a less than half-hearted attempt to read a book which wouldn't have appealed to her even with two good eyes.

She had wanted to go with Alice and Matthew to the funeral. What was a damaged face compared to Alice's suffering? However, she'd had to give in and agree to stay at home when she found how impossible it was to get into even her most comfortable pair of shoes.

'I feel like one of the Ugly Sisters,' she'd tried to joke even though her face hurt when she laughed.

So she was alone. Giving up all attempt to read, she lay back with her eyes closed, happily letting her thoughts carry her where they would. That people would condemn the way she intended to live didn't enter her head and, even if she had considered it, the knowledge wouldn't have diminished her certainty; she felt loved as she had never dreamed possible. Two halves of one whole, he'd called them. And so they were. Whether they were talking or silent, whether they were together or apart, nothing could alter their sense of the rightness of belonging. Perhaps Ian would take her to court to get his freedom, perhaps he wouldn't. Either way would make no difference, for marriage to Matthew would never be possible; Yvette wouldn't be persuaded to seek a divorce. But none of that mattered. If people wanted to look on her as a scarlet woman, then let them.

The medicine Matthew gave her to dull the pain made her drowsy; sitting there alone she drifted into a state somewhere between sleeping and waking, wanting to dream about that golden future that lay before them. Yet even that was darkened by the shadow that time made no lighter: it was as if all the happiness of her childhood, all the pleasure of learning to work with her father and of the easy companionship they'd known, was tarnished by what had come after.

In Addingford heads usually turned at the sound of a motor car, but the clip-clop of a horse or the rattle of a cart aroused no interest. She didn't even notice it until it stopped outside the house and, even then, she supposed it was Frank Hobbs from the dairy coming to fill the jug she knew Alice had left on the doorstep. When she heard the rap on the front door she opened her eyes and reached for the stick that had been left on the floor nearby.

'Just coming,' she yelled, 'I'll get my purse.' Hopping

on her good foot, leaning on the stick, she started across the room. That's when she glanced out of the window and saw, not Frank Hobbs's cart carrying its urns, but a carriage. He'd come! Her brain didn't stop to wonder how her father could have traced her. 'Coming . . . coming.' He must have come all the way from Brackleford in the station carriage, for he'd not have found one waiting at Addingford. 'Dad, I'm coming.' Oh, the joy of hearing herself call his name.

Forgetting the shock her swollen face and mouth would give him, she flung open the door. Just as her spirit had soared, so it dipped. Standing before her was the small, Victorian-looking figure of George Watford. If her first reaction was disappointment, her second was surprise, quickly followed by appreciation that he could concern himself for so lowly a member of his staff. The Phillpotts had told her he was a fair man, but surely this was beyond fairness.

'How thoughtful of you to call. Do come in,' she welcomed him with an easy grace that only served to irritate him further. That he didn't return her smile should have prepared her, but it didn't.

'Yes, I'll step inside the door. I have no wish to broadcast what I have to say even further than it's probably gone already.'

'Because I'm off work, you mean? You can see for yourself what my fall did to me.' There was nothing defensive in her reply, she simply stated a fact that she assumed he hadn't properly understood. 'Naturally I don't expect a wage packet for this week, so I imagine next week two weeks' rent will be deducted.' Was her non-payment for this week the reason behind his visit? Surely not.

The little man glowered at her; his drooping moustache added to the hostility of his expression.

'You will be paid for this week, I'll not have it said that Watfords' don't stand by the rules.'

'I'd not expected it for absence. But I appreci—'

'I'll thank you not to interrupt me, young madam. You note what I say. "Madam" not "Miss" as you would have us believe. Mrs Harriman. How do I know? My own affair, I believe. A nice little nest you inveigled me into letting you have, somewhere for your brother to visit. Madam, you disgust me! And what sort of a fancyman you've found for yourself, prepared to go along with your lies, I dread to think. However, I wash my hands of you and your immoral behaviour. Yes, yes indeed.' When his face twitched with anger, his drooping whiskers seemed to get the message and bristle. Jane had a wild desire to giggle.

'If you're telling me that I am to leave Watford's, then it is the best solution from my point of view. I've been wasting my knowing of the trade on a job that any young man with a quarter of a brain could do. I assume you mean this week to be in lieu of notice?'

'You have a very inflated opinion of yourself, young madam. Yes, this is your notice – and you have Mr Foley to thank for persuading me to let you stay in the house until the end of Sunday. I understand that to be when your husband is coming to fetch you home. Such loyalty from a man who has been used as he has deserves my co-opera-tion. But by Sunday night you are to be out, lock, stock and barrel. You hear me? You're to go home to your husband and take up the duties of a wife. And be grateful. There are few men – yes, indeed, few men – who would be prepared to wipe the slate clean.'

'I'll show you out,' Jane said, speaking with the same gracious politeness, patently unmoved by his tirade.

'Disgraceful. I'll not have Watford's name linked with such behaviour. The Phillpotts are a good-living, God-fearing couple. You took their hospitality knowing you were lying and cheating. I like to think of the workers at the brewery as like one family – and a family can do without a member behaving in such a dishonourable way. Addingford will be the purer without you, Mrs Harriman, and you ought to be down on your knees giving thanks that you have a husband prepared to take you back.'

'I'll see you out,' she repeated, her manner almost regal despite her hop and hobble movement to the front door to open it for him. When it was closed behind him she stayed in the gloomy passage until she heard his carriage move away, only then, and not for the first time in moments of crisis, dropping to sit on the second stair. Ian had threatened to come here again on Sunday, but how did anyone except she herself know? Did it mean that since last Sunday he'd come back again to Addingford and talked to the hateful Richard Foley? Not that she cared how the truth had come out. Truth? Truth that Ian wanted her back?

She had been sacked from her miserable job, she had been exposed as a liar, yet her overriding feeling was of relief. So much of these last months had made no impact; even the heady smell of the brewery had lost its evocative appeal for there was little resemblance between Watford's and Bradley's. But there had been other times during those months, moments that would stay with her always.

It was much later that evening when she told the others about her visitor, for their return from the funeral belonged to Alice. So, after a supper prepared by Alice and cleared up by her too, with Matthew's help, Jane said, 'I had a visitor this afternoon. Mr Watford. It seems I've got the sack! That'll knock me from my perch, won't it,' she laughed. 'The only snag is I have to be out of Holly Cottage by Sunday.'

'It's time we moved on,' Matthew answered. 'If I'm to carry on practising in Brackleford, then Jane, that's where we must find a home. I have no intention of asking Yvette to move out even if I could; that's her home and Anton's.'

Alice felt she ought not to be listening to their plans, their future together was private. But the thought of Jane having to give up the cottage so soon gave her a heaven-sent opportunity to be useful.

'Tomorrow I shall go back to my own place, I can't run away any longer. There's a future to be faced,' she told them. 'I shall go by the early train, there's one just before ten o'clock I believe. And when you're ready, Matthew my dear, you must bring Jane and leave her to share with me until the two of you can find somewhere together.'

Planning the next stage, grasping the chance to be needed, Alice took a stride into that new life that she had to find the courage to build.

'Nothing wrong is there, Elsie child?' Shrivelled and stooping George Hamley looked at his plump and rosy daughter, his face creased with anxiety. She may look a picture of health, but it was her expression when he caught her off her guard that worried him.

'Now what could be wrong, Dad?' Her smile was genuine enough, even her eyes carried the message as she looked at him with affection.

'Ian? Is that the problem? Not easy for you, not for either of you. Sometimes I have thoughts about what I'd like seen done to that wife. Ah, that I do. Puts the wind up me that there's that much evil in me, makes me ask to be forgiven. But if there's any justice in this world, why doesn't the Lord see fit to carry her off?' Carried away with his imaginings, he took his eyes off his daughter so he was surprised to hear the gulp as she tried to swallow her tears. 'Come on, love, it's not like you to take on like that. Main thing is, it's *you* he really cares about; getting mixed up with her was a mistake, he knew it almost from the first. If only a knot could be undone as easy as being tied.'

'I don't know what to do, Dad. So hard to talk about what I mean.' She chewed her quivering lip helplessly. It was only her love and understanding for Ian that made her able to blurt out what was on her mind. 'He's the same as any other man, any man without a wife I mean. If he can't – well, you know what I'm trying to say – with me, then I can't expect him not to go to some woman – well, you know the kind of woman I'm meaning—'

'I don't know about how to undo a marriage.' George

couldn't bear to see her so upset, there was nothing he wouldn't have done to help – if only he knew how. 'There is divorce, but I've never known anyone have dealing with it. Don't know how he could set about it.'

'It takes a long time. Anyway, it takes the sort of money that he hasn't got. He's been talking to people, trying to find out. He thought the doctor might pay up to have his name kept out of it, then Ian could get rid of her on the grounds of her refusing to live with him.' All attempt to fight her tears was lost. Her plump, round face was a picture of misery, even her nose produced a dewdrop in sympathy. 'But a mate at work told him, he can't do that until she's been gone for three years. Three years! We can't go on like this for three years. Especially now – not after . . .' George understood the unfinished sentence. 'Don't know what to do, Dad.' She looked at poor, troubled George, her eyelids already so puffed she could scarcely open them.

'Have to wait three years, you say? Where's the justice. It's *your* life that's being messed up by the silly bitch. But you say after three years he could get rid of her for refusing to live with him, without making any mention of how she's behaving with the doctor? But what's going on is common knowledge, I've heard it talked about in the bar often enough. What if Ian went to the solicitor and told him about her goings-on. No woman is allowed to give her favours to some man outside wedlock.'

'Don't say it like that, Dad. Me and Ian aren't wed. But I feel we are, we belong together. Such a mess . . .'

'Now then, duckie, we'll see to finding a way. What I was just saying, about getting rid of Madam High and Mighty on account of the doctor, would that take three years just the same?'

'No, but it might as well for all the chance there is of it. It takes the sort of money we've no hope of.'

The seed was sown in George's mind, but he said nothing of it to Elsie. By evening when he was ready to go down to open the bar, he told her to send Ian down as soon as he arrived.

'I want a word with him before the place gets full of sharp ears.'

'Oh, Dad, not about what I told you about me and Ian – belonging – you know what I mean.' Her tear-stained face flushed as she groped for words. 'He didn't do anything I didn't want him to. You can't get at him—'

'No one's getting at him, girl. You just see to having a plate of warm food ready to feed him on, I won't keep him down there above five minutes.'

In fact it was less than five minutes between Ian going down the steep, straight flight from the kitchen to the bar, remembering Sunday and having noticed Elsie's still-swollen eyelids, and his bounding back up again taking the stairs two at a time.

'Why didn't you tell me what he wanted?' He hugged her with more excitement than tenderness.

''Cos I didn't know, silly. Go on, tell me. I made a proper fool of myself today, that miserable I was that I couldn't help it. I thought it was something to do with that.' She could say it now, for clearly she'd been wrong.

'I suppose it was, in a way. He says he's always tried to put a bit away, never able to manage much, but each week he's added something even if it's been no more than a bob or two. Always thinking of the time when he can't run the pub, see. But we've struck a deal, him and me: he's going to give me his savings so that I can get a solicitor, then when he's past working he'll make his home with us. How's that?'

'But of course he would have made his home with us anyway. He didn't need to pay us. But Ian, just think what it means. It'll rub *her* nose in the scandal – and the "what a good chap I am" doctor's too. But serves them right.'

They clung to each other, laughing not from the humour of the situation but from relief that not far ahead of them was light and hope.

*

Yvette looked disconsolately out of the window. She found no cheer in the sight of the colours of spring, forget-me-nots, grape hyacinths, the first hint of tulips coming into flower. Beyond the neat beds, the garden boy was giving the despised privet hedge its first trim of the year. How she hated this joyless place; it sapped the spirit from her.

Idly she wondered what sort of a woman the handsome cooper's wife could be. She'd met her after the church concert, but hadn't taken much interest in her. Tall, nothing wonderful to look at surely or she would have made more impression, pregnant too at that time. Yvette frowned. She never had understood Matthew. Except for one brief visit, he'd not been to the house for a week. Well, she wished him joy of his new paramour. In her present mood, she even envied him.

The cooper had said he would come and see her again, but he hadn't been. As for the priest, did he imagine she hadn't realized why he made excuses for them not to be alone together? She smiled as she thought of him, but there was more scorn than affection in her expression. If she wanted, she could put herself out to win him back. But did she want to? His love-making had held very little skill or finesse; what had excited her had been his animal passion. But on each occasion it had been she who had set the scene. Could one say that a man was raped, she wondered, and this time there was a twinkle of fun in her smile. Certainly she'd brought him to a pitch where he had only one way to go. How thrilling it had been to be the receptacle for such repressed passion. Yes, if she decided that's what she wanted, then the poor idiot wouldn't stand a chance; neither his conscience nor his saintliness would be strong enough to defy nature. But she'd played that game and it had lost its appeal. She yearned for new fields. The cooper had understood her message, he had showed promise of putting a spark of fun into her boring life.

But what was the point of any of it? The house was more prison to her than home. The promise of colour in the garden mocked her. Eleven years of her life had passed while she'd lived here. She was thirty-four, but her heart was still that of the young woman who had come here, excited at the prospect of change.

In her hand she held Anton's weekly letter that had arrived that morning. She'd let Matthew organize his education, but that had been *wrong*. There was too much of *her* in her son to let him fit into the scene of the oh-so-English school, to fit as snug as a well-cut piece of jigsaw.

Turning her back on the window she went to the bureau intending to answer his letter. Then, her expression changing, her eyes lit in the expression of – of what? Hope? Determination? Mischief? The garden was forgotten, dingy privet hedge and all; Matthew and his love life was yesterday's story. With the excitement of a girl invited to her first party Yvette hurried out of the room and ran up the stairs. She knew just what she meant to do.

'Beautiful morning, Mr Phillpott,' Matthew said as he ushered Alice through the gate on to the platform.

Hugh Phillpott managed a nod in agreement, then took the easy escape route back to his ticket office. If he were half a man he would face 'Jane Bradley's brother' with what he knew. Not that it was any business of his the way people ran their lives. But it was hard to forget how upset that husband of hers had been that she'd refused to go home with him. Handsome great man he was, too, and all dressed in his best. Hugh's mouth set in a tight line as he thought of Jane. Disgusting way for a woman to carry on. Add to that the wicked 'brother and sister' lies they'd told so convincingly, pulling the wool over Aggie's eyes and his own too, then the sooner they took themselves off from Addingford the better. Tomorrow Mr Harriman was coming back for her. Oh dear, oh Lord, one can but hope she'll have come to her senses. If she turned the poor fellow away again, then Hugh didn't look forward to the state he'd be in.

Hearing the train he came out, whistle in one hand, flag

296

in the other, watching as, shrouded in a haze of smoke, it snaked towards them. Never once did he let his glance move from it; Matthew and Alice might not have been there at all.

Back again at Holly Cottage Matthew found Jane in the bedroom, most of her clothes already in the trunk, despite his having told her to keep her weight off her foot.

'I obeyed doctor's orders,' she laughed, seeing his expression. 'I've become quite adept at negotiating the stairs on my bottom. Anyway, my ankle is almost back to normal.'

'It wouldn't have been if you'd taken liberties with it.' Sitting on the edge of the bed he held out his hand and drew her down to his side. 'Jane, I shan't stay with you at Alice's, although she would agree if that's the way we wanted. The accommodation over the surgery isn't splendid, but it'll only be until we find somewhere.'

She nodded.

'You won't go back to Millsham?'

'A week living with you, then home, as if that week counted for nothing? My boats are thoroughly burnt, I couldn't go back – and neither would Yvette want me to. But of course I shall continue to keep the home going, for her and for Anton. I must go and see her, perhaps tomorrow evening, and try to work out some sort of arrangement.'

'Oh, Matthew, what have I done?' She turned to him with eyes full of uncertainty; even the one that wasn't fully recovered from last weekend's fall, carried its message of anxious love.

'What have you done? You have given me such happiness as I didn't know existed. Just being with you, talking to you, sharing our thoughts . . . loving you with everything that I am. That, my darling, is what you've done.'

She leant against him, her forehead rubbing against his chin.

'Even with a foot I can't walk on and a face I'm ashamed

to look at, this week has been like a miracle.' For a minute or so they sat silently, savouring the miracle as they looked back and remembered, then forward in certain confidence. Or so Matthew imagined until Jane broke his reverie, speaking so quietly that she might have been thinking aloud.

'Perhaps nothing is ever completely perfect, perhaps it's not supposed to be. We get what we deserve. I must have hurt him just as much as he hurt me.'

'Ian?'

'What? No, Dad. I wouldn't listen to him. I knew best. Both of us were angry. But, Matthew, why couldn't he have sunk his pride and answered my letters? When I told him he was going to be a grandfather, even then he didn't write. The other day while I was resting my foot like you told me to, I wrote to him again, I told him about *you*, about *us*. Then I tore it up. I couldn't bear it if he knew about us and still wouldn't speak to me. We were such friends, Dad and me. Acting like he has makes me frightened to remember how happy I used to be, it's as if he never really loved me, as if I took him for granted.' She was ashamed to hear herself, her outburst seemed childish and emotional.

'Perhaps jealousy came into it, too, darling. He wouldn't be the first father to be possessive of his daughter's affection. Don't be frightened to remember the good times before any of that happened; surely, it's because they meant so much to him that he finds it hard to accept you chose someone else against his will. So you've not told him you've left Ian?'

She shook her head.

'I can't write again. Watching and waiting each day, hoping for the postman, getting nothing. I can't. Not any more. Anyway, our future will be so good, I'll not even think about the past.' She pulled herself a little away from him, sitting upright and looking at him seriously. 'Ought we to feel guilty about what we are doing? Both of us married, both of us casting off our vows as if we never made them, and yet I have never felt so right, so – so – so *pure*. The world would say we are sinners.'

'Worldliness and understanding can be poles apart. I've made mistakes – we both have – but I feel no guilt, only thankfulness that the past is over and the future is ours. Now, Jane my sweet,' he said, standing up and hauling the trunk towards him, 'if we are to be out of our little love nest this afternoon, I'd better fasten your trunk and get it strapped on to the luggage grid. Anything else to go in first?'

Back to practicalities their moment of emotion was gone. What remained was the easy friendship, the sense of rightness for what they were doing.

By early evening she had unpacked that same trunk, while downstairs Alice had cooked supper for the three of them – a supper of lamb chops they'd stopped to buy as they'd driven through Brackleford, feeding grist to the mill of local supposition. Matthew had been to the surgery to make sure were no messages put through the letter-box and to get his makeshift accommodation ready.

When they sat at table they all had a feeling of 'moving on'. For Matthew and Jane this was the first step towards the rest of their lives; for Alice it was a lifeline to clutch as she was swept along on a tide of hopelessness.

'You mustn't feel you have to rush at the first letting you find. It's got to be just what you want,' she told them. 'I dare say it's selfish of me, but the longer Jane stays the better I shall like it. Both of you know that.'

They heard the message behind her words and knew she was only holding at bay the loneliness and emptiness she dreaded.

'I'm not that well house-trained, Alice.' Jane knew her too well to let her sympathy show. 'Domesticity and me have never been soul mates. You may come to regret your generosity.'

Alice laughed too. It was all a charade. Her heart ached with misery: *she* knew it; *they* knew it; and she knew they knew it. Yet her help had to come from forcing her face to smile.

After the meal Matthew said he was leaving early. The sooner he talked to Yvette the better, he'd rather not wait until the next day.

'Will you come back to tell me?' Jane asked.

'Not tonight. It may be late. I don't know how long it will take to sort things out with her. And there's the boy to consider. I try to pretend he's happy at my old school, but I know it's not the truth. He mustn't be upset even further for something that's not his fault. I'll come in the morning. If the weather stays fair, the three of us might have a drive out somewhere.'

Alice busied herself carrying the dishes to the kitchen, hiding from them how near tears she was. They were both so good to her, but in her present vulnerable state sympathy was more than she could bear. Tomorrow she would make an excuse, pretend she had letters to write.

After the early spring daytime sunshine, the evening was chill and she lit the fire she'd already laid in the sitting-room grate.

'You've walked about more than enough for one day, Jane. The more you rest, the quicker that ankle will be ready for the rushing about you like to do. And it will need to be, too, for there are plenty of letting houses to be had if you know where to look. Another week or so and the two of you will be running your own home and you'll need two good ankles. I'll not be five minutes finishing off in the kitchen.'

'I can help, I'm almost as practised as a stork at standing on one leg.'

But Alice would have none of it. And true to her word, by the time the flames were licking around the coals she was back. The evening stretched ahead of them. Always they were at ease in each other's company but, on that evening, even though their conversation gave no hint of it, their thoughts were somewhere else. Was he having a hard time? Jane imagined him talking to Yvette, carving out their future. There in the home they had made together .. 'I'm leaving you . . . I love someone else . . . you can still live in our home, but you will be alone . . .' What have I done? If I hadn't come into his life, his marriage would still be intact. Remember how I used to listen for the sound of his motor, remember how those hours with him became my life. Could I have prevented it? Ought I to have prevented it? No! 'I'm not whole without you,' wasn't that what he'd said?

Alice's thoughts took wing too, but she was adept at keeping them hidden; she'd had years of practice.

'Hark, there's Matthew's car!' Jane held up her head, listening to the familiar sound. Alice had locked the front door for the night when he left, so now she hurried to open it for him while Jane swung her legs off the sofa and waited expectantly.

'I've just got to put some washing away upstairs,' Alice lied. 'Jane's in there by the fire.'

'You don't need to run away, Alice. You can both of you hear what I have to tell you.'

But Alice muttered something about being only a few minutes and disappeared up the steep, narrow flight of stairs.

'You came back after all.' Jane held out her hand to him. 'Was it hard? Is she all right?'

'She's not there, Jane. I found this.' He passed her an envelope. 'Apparently she'd left two letters, this one to me and another to the maids. They showed me theirs. But I'll tell you about that later. Read what she says.'

Matthew,
    I know you do not want me for wife, but I have already given you my answer. We are married, we made our promises that have to last for all the time we are

301

living. I cannot live in this so dull and lonely place with no one. For you this grey, miserable town is home – but for me it never can be. But I kept my promises as long as I was wife to the so good doctor. Now I am no more than nothing, like a worn out garment I am thrown away. So I shall return to my own beloved country, I shall find people who know how to make jolly, I shall be like the person I was, I shall have friends who are persons like myself, loving to sing and to dance, to laugh and to live. If the cooper's wife makes you a happy person, then I must be glad for you. It was something that I could not do after we left my beloved Paris. Or is it that in this grey land you find joy in being solemn? You spend your life with people who are sick and miserable, it is sad for you. I hope this Jane will find being the sober doctor's woman – for wife she cannot be – is what she wants and not become so wretched as

Your wife, Yvette.

'To France? Has she a family to go to?' Whatever Jane had expected, it wasn't this.

'Her only family is Anton. She doesn't even mention him. Can she have gone without even telling him? I can't believe it.'

'She didn't say anything more to the maids?'

'Nothing, except that she was going away, she'd never be coming back. They're weeping and wailing, they were both fond of her. And of course, they realize the house will be sold if Yvette has gone.'

'How will Anton feel about what's happened? His mother gone ... you with someone else ... You don't suppose she's taken him with her?'

'The thought hadn't occurred to me. He's been here pretty well all his life. I can do nothing tonight, but in the morning I'll have a telephone call put through to the school and speak to the headmaster. If necessary I shall have to take a train up to see Anton and explain things. But I'll call here first whatever I decide.' Then, with that fleeting smile she knew so well: 'At least I can sleep in a decent bed instead of over the surgery.'

From the telephone call made to the school he found that Yvette had called there on that Saturday teatime (probably just about as he was arriving in Brackleford with Jane) and had collected Anton.

'It was a situation I had never encountered, but it would not have been in order for me to forbid her taking him. I understood from her that you were both unhappy about him – and I must say, the boy made no secret of his relief. She'd come to rescue him, she said. And, from the look on his face, that's precisely as he saw it.'

Alice insisted that she had writing to see to and encouraged the other two to leave her by herself for a few hours. For sentiment's sake Jane suggested they should drive to Ilkingham. Once there, they parked the motor car in the shade of the trees where, with the rain pounding on the roof and pouring down the weather-shields, they had acknowledged their love and sworn eternal faith.

'Our special place,' Jane said, as he opened the door for her to climb out. 'It seems a lifetime ago. Then, a few hours at Ilkingham was all we had.'

They walked for a while in silence and a quick glance at him told her his thoughts were somewhere else. Yvette? Anton?

'She ought to have talked to me first.' His words told her that she'd been right. 'At home she's never been short of anything she needed, but as for actual money – Jane, I don't know how she's going to manage. And there's the boy to think of . . .'

'She's not a stupid woman, she probably has people there to go to. As soon as she has an address, she'll write to you, Matthew. She couldn't take Anton away from you as though he were some sort of a parcel with no feelings.'

'Let's sit on this log.'

That cheered her, it was where they'd sat on previous stolen Sunday afternoons.

'If Yvette went all the way up to the school to collect Anton,' she said, 'she must know just what she's doing. I don't feel sorry for *her*, she's an adult, she has made her own life. But he must be feeling so confused. It's important that you find out where he is quickly, so that you keep in touch with him. Matthew, never, never let him feel that you didn't care about his going away. You're the only father he's known. If he doesn't know you care, it will be far harder for him than being in a school where he doesn't fit. All that was unimportant – but to feel you hadn't really loved him – it would take away all his happy memories—'

Matthew pulled her nearer; she buried her face against his neck.

'One day, darling,' he told her, 'when everything is settled and you are saddled with the so boring doctor in our grey and cheerless home, you must write again.' And she knew he was thinking of her father, just as she was. 'Tell him everything, don't hide how hurt you've been. It's probably been just the same for him—'

'Can't have been,' she rasped. 'I've written – that first Christmas, I wrote. Thought he'd be sure to answer. The first Christmas we'd not been together. We always had a tree and he had the staff in, even the garden boy, they all had presents from the tree. I used to buy them and wrap them up, even when I was quite small. We always did it together. But he didn't answer. I'd always thought it was all so important, but he'd probably only done it out of sort of duty – to me and to the others.'

'I don't believe it. Sit up, Jane.' He took his handkerchief out of his breast pocket and very gently wiped her face. 'That eye won't get better if you treat it like that.' He smiled and was rewarded by a watery laugh.

'Don't know why I cried when I'm so happy.'

It was as they drove back through Brackleford that he referred to what she'd said about Anton.

304

'You're right, Jane. I'm sure Yvette won't blacken my name to him, she's much too fair-minded for that. But he mustn't be left in doubt. Somehow I must make him realize that I am still his father.'

His words came back to her when, as he prepared to leave that evening, he told them that he planned to be away for a day or two, but would see them as soon as he returned. On the way home that evening he would call on Dr Rutter, a retired physician, and ask him to stand in for him.

'But you don't know where she's taken him. How can you hope to find him?'

'I believe I know exactly where to find him. I shall leave tomorrow, I should be back on Tuesday or Wednesday. After that we'll start looking for that house, but I want to make this journey first.'

She told herself it was the right thing for him to do, so why did she feel so frightened? He'd been married to Yvette for eleven years, he called her fair-minded, he'd always talked of her with affection. She'd been his responsibility for eleven years, now he was worried that she wouldn't have money enough. Was that the real reason for his chasing after them, was Yvette his reason?

In the lonely night her imagination knew no bounds. From the home he and Yvette had shared it jumped to a cross-channel steamer taking him to find her; and from there to the streets of Paris, as unknown to Jane as any desert or jungle but familiar to Yvette and Matthew. What was it she'd written? The words escaped Jane, but she remembered the implication that in Paris they had been happy. The three of them together, Matthew, Yvette and, binding them, their affection for Anton. And if that was the way it happened, then she ought to rejoice for them. But she couldn't. Bring him home to me soon. Please, don't take him away from me. '. . . not whole without you,' he'd said. And neither was she whole if she couldn't be with him . . . she was *nothing* . . . Then she thought of Alice, a son and a husband both gone and life stretching ahead of her.

'Marcos!' It was out of character for Alayne to interrupt him, and his brows pulled into a quick frown as he looked up from the notes he was preparing for the evening's confirmation class. 'Marcos, Yvette's gone! I just met Ada Watson coming out of work at the pickle factory – what a nasty smelly place to have to work, I really do feel so sorry for her.'

'Yvette – you say she's gone. Gone where?'

'I don't know. Marcos, I am frightened to think. Ada has a sister who works in the doctor's house and she came to see her last night. Terribly upset about it all. It seems Yvette left a note – well, two notes, one for the maids and one for the doctor. She said she was tired of her grey life, there was no joy, people were always so solemn. She said that she had tried, but she could never learn to be an Englishwoman. She did not know whether the doctor would keep the house or sell it – oh yes, and she thanked them for helping make her life not so without cheer. Oh Marcos, I never guessed she was so miserable. Have we failed her?'

Marcos closed his eyes, but he couldn't rid himself of the image of their parting. What had he done to her? Had *he* driven her to this, pushed her beyond the limit of endurance? Dear Lord, if she still lives, guard and help her, make her know she is never without love. But does she still live? Has she thrown away the divine gift of life? Forgive her, in paradise give her the peace she couldn't find in life.

'I ought to go to see Bingley, he must be distraught.'

'Ada's sister says he is never at home. Ada says she pretended to be surprised, but she'd heard gossip that he had broken the marriage of that couple you asked me to witness, Harriman I think she called them. No wonder poor Yvette was driven to such depths. It's too dreadful to imagine. Hark! I hear Stephanie calling, I must go. Just had to come and talk to you.'

Getting up from his desk he came towards her, drawing her into his arms and kissing the top of her head. She was comforted just as he'd intended and she had no suspicion of the haunted misery in his dark eyes, or his thankfulness that Stephanie needed her.

By Tuesday evening there was no news of Matthew. He had been so certain he knew where he would find Anton; yet Yvette's note had given no hint except that she was going back to France. Did he know who her friends were? Would he have gone to wherever it was she used to live in those days when they were happy together in the city she so loved? Jane tried not to imagine.

'He won't get here as late as this.' Alice must have read her thoughts. 'The best thing we can do is get to bed and put the day behind us. You may be sure tomorrow will bring him. To my way of thinking, Yvette has much to answer for. A fast lot, we all know that. But, be that as it may, her main consideration should have been the boy. She ought to have stayed where she was, he would have had a good home. As for her, she could have gone on just as she always has. There never was a shortage of men – married or not – ready to be tempted by her. If you or I had kicked over the traces like it, no one would have found it interesting. But being the doctor's wife is different. Ask me how I heard these things when most of the town's gossips shun me: I have seen it for years, I have a brain between my ears and I use my two good eyes. How he stood it I could never understand.'

'She doesn't accept divorce. For her, marriage is for life.'

'A lot of tommy rot coming from a minx like that! Marriage is for life right enough, for life and beyond. But that was no proper marriage. But hark at me! I deplore gossip – and just hark at me! Let's put up the guard and go to bed, Jane my dear. Tomorrow is another day.' It was only just ten o'clock, earlier than usual, but there was no point in listening for him any longer.

Even so, sleep eluded Jane. She heard the sitting-room clock chime the quarter, then the half hour. With her eyes closed she tried to will herself to relax, yet when finally she drifted between waking and sleeping she saw a clear picture of a gas-lit Paris street, she heard laughter and knew it was Matthew's – or was it Yvette's? At last came welcome oblivion. Had her room been in the front of the house instead of the back, even the deepest of sleep might have been disturbed by the sound of that familiar engine. It was Alice who heard it and struggled out of bed and into her dressing gown. Nearly eleven o'clock, could something be wrong? It was out of character for Matthew to come so late, especially when he must have seen the little house was in darkness. Expecting his knock, she hurried down the stairs. Why was he taking so long? What could be wrong?

Chapter Fifteen

Spring 1907

'Jane wake up! Didn't you hear the motor?'

Immediately Jane was wide awake.

'He's here? What's the time?' Already she was out of bed, reaching for her dressing gown. As if time mattered!

'You go into the sitting room,' Alice told her. 'I'll come in in a little while, but first I'll make a warm drink, I'm sure he can do with one.'

Jane wanted to rush down the stairs, but her ankle wouldn't let her. Holding the candle high, Alice followed behind her, her own unhappiness forgotten in those minutes as she rejoiced with Jane. The sitting-room door was on the left at the foot of the narrow stairs and, opposite it, on the right was the way into the kitchen. The gas had been lit in both rooms so as Jane opened the one door, Alice went through the other, immediately closing it behind her. These next moments belonged to Jane – to Jane and to *him*.

'Mat—' Jane started, then stopped, standing as if rooted to the ground. The man standing in front of the fire moved a step towards her, leaning heavily on two sticks. It was a ghost from the past, the same and yet so different she was frightened to believe the truth of what she was seeing.

'Janie . . . found you . . .' His face was working in a way she'd never seen.

'Dad. Dad, what have you done?' His moustache was

quite white and his hair grey, his face deeply lined. Even his voice had changed, as if his tongue was too stiff to move to his will. She didn't wait for his answer, somehow she was across the room, her arms around him. As he held her one stick clattered to the ground, she felt his need for support and steered him into a chair. Then she knelt in front of him.

'You never wrote. Why, Dad? Why? And how did you find me now? Did Ian tell you? Did he write to you for money, was that it?'

'Slowly . . . not so fast . . .' He felt helpless in her rush of questions. 'Matthew came to the brewery. Janie, child, he told me everything.'

'Matthew brought you here? But where is he?'

'He and your friend are in the kitchen. They wanted us to have these moments.'

'Dad, you *do* like him? You *do* understand?'

'He is a good man, Jane.' Then with a smile that carried her back to those happy times she'd tried to school herself to forget, 'As a son, he'll suit me admirably.'

'You know I can't marry him?'

'Didn't I say he told me everything?'

Jane nodded. For a full minute they were silent, she moving to sit at his feet, he resting his hand on her bed-rumpled hair.

'You've been ill?' Jane was the first to break the silence. 'What happened? Tell me.'

He closed his eyes as if to shut out what he'd rather forget.

'We have to fill in the gaps, Dad. Was it an accident?'

'It happened the night you left home. A stroke, that's what they said. I can't remember any of it. And afterwards . . . days . . . weeks . . . can't remember. I was in bed for what seemed like months, my right arm wouldn't move, nor my leg. Couldn't even talk. Not easy even now. Can you understand me, Janie?'

In truth she had to concentrate hard on what he was

trying to say, but her only answer was to smile at him and nod her head.

'Knew you would.' He seemed satisfied.

'But why didn't Dulcie tell me? She must have read my letters.' Another long silence, but this time Jane had to have an answer. 'Did she think I wouldn't have cared?'

'Hard to understand,' he started, his words even less clear than before. 'Blamed you, you see. Didn't tell me you'd written – wouldn't have understood anyway. Was just a cabbage. Don't be hard on her, Janie. She'd good to me, Janie. So much she does for me. I'm no husband to her – no partner – no companion. Try not to blame her. She ought to have told me, think I might have got better sooner if I'd known you'd written. And the baby, she shouldn't have kept your letter from me about the baby. My poor child—'

'It was *wicked* of her.'

'We've all made mistakes. Poor Dulcie. If what she did was wrong, then she has been punished. What life is it for her now? She protects me, helps me,' he closed his eyes, 'sometimes she must think she's more nurse than wife. Don't be bitter, Jane. Let it all go. Just be grateful Matthew did what he did. Yesterday, my working day nearly over, he came to find me at the brewery.'

'I don't think I ever told him where we lived, he would have had to come to the brewery.' She thought of all those hours when she'd been punishing herself, imagining him with Yvette in Paris and she was ashamed.

'He told me all he knew. Took him home for the night. Faced poor Dulcie with it.'

'Poor Dulcie,' Jane moved back on to her knees and knelt up straight, her eyes level with his, 'you can call her *that*. Mean and selfish, that's what she was, frightened that you might want me to come home.'

'Yes, yes, child, I know. Jealous that we'd always been so close, I always knew that. But, Jane, she made me happy, you don't know how happy, before all this

311

happened. Things are different now. I told you, she's more like a nurse than a wife. But she's kind, never taunts me that I'm so useless. I'm glad she has friends outside. I ask no questions, she must grasp what pleasure she can. I'm grateful to her. I'm not the man she married.'

'Bosh! Of course you're the same, you're the same Dad anyway.'

'Oh Jane . . . so thankful.'

Another silence, broken this time by the clock on the mantelpiece chiming the half hour, half past eleven. An hour ago Jane had lain awake, frightened by images of Matthew in Paris. And all the time their train must have been arriving in Brackleford. She imagined Amos left to wait for him on the wooden bench at the station while he fetched his car from where he would have left it in the yard behind the surgery.

'We've made cocoa,' Matthew's voice cut into her thoughts as Alice opened the door and he followed her, bearing a laden tray. 'A celebratory drink.'

Jane sat back on her heels, her hand on Amos's knee, looking at Matthew with eyes that told him more than any words.

That was in the spring of 1907 and it marked the beginning of a new life for all four of them, although they weren't aware of it as they drank their cocoa. It stemmed from a chance remark of Amos's.

'Never had a day's illness until this,' he said as the minutes ticked away, carrying them into tomorrow. 'You remember Dr Burrows, Jane? He's giving up. Have to get used to someone new, I suppose.'

Two halves of one whole, was that why their thoughts moved in the same direction? A silent glance passed between Jane and Matthew, the shape of the future suddenly clear. 'Has he sold the practice yet?' Matthew asked it casually; only Jane knew what was in his mind.

They weren't happy about leaving Alice. Would it be too

hard for her to pull up her roots from Brackleford, the town where she'd spent all her married life? Even suggesting it would be walking on dangerous ground, for her independent spirit recoiled from pity. Jane stayed on with her as, with their change of plans, they didn't look for a house to rent in the town.

The next weeks were eventful for Matthew, in part because he was negotiating selling his practice in Brackleford and buying in Deremouth and, in part, because of the outcome of his letter to the Café Hélène which had enabled him to trace Yvette. Back in her natural environment she was singing three nights a week and Anton had settled happily at an art school.

In her pleasure at being back where she belonged her English was even more haywire than usual as she ended her letter:

If there is someone who would like to buy the house with its tidy flowerbeds and its so dull and dusty hedge, then that would be the happy thing for you to do for it. Me and my French boy Anton, we are glad to be where we are. But I do speak of you to Anton, I know he has fondness for you and I know you have been for always kind to him. He wishes that one day he will come to have a holiday with you and the so handsome cooper's wife.

'Will you mind having a wife who goes to work?' Jane said, for back in Deremouth surely the brewery would need her.

'With your father? I think it would be an excellent idea. Jane, he's very determined, but do you know how much he needs you there?'

She nodded. 'You met him for the first time; but he used to be so different. With me there he'll get better all the time, I *know* he will. It's almost frightening isn't it, how perfect everything is.'

'Nothing is ever perfect, didn't you once say? There is

Alice. We're all the family she has. Not just for her sake, but for our own, Jane, we must persuade her that families, even make-believe ones, should stay together.'

Alice dreaded Brackleford without them, but she shied away from being a burden on their affection.

'You'll probably wish you'd refused when you know what Matthew hopes you'll agree to,' Jane said cheerfully.

'Agree to?'

'I shall go back to the brewery, Dad needs me and I need to do something I'm good at – not like I did at Watford's. Anyway, you know domesticity and I never have seen eye to eye,' she added with a laugh. 'Apart from someone overseeing how the house is run, Matthew will have to find someone to take his telephone messages, keep his appointment book, help with accounts too if you are any good at figures. Things that a doctor's wife would probably do, but I want to get back to the brewery. Alice, if you refuse, we shall have to advertise for someone and that means having a stranger always in the house. We don't want that. It's *you* we want. If you weren't so pig-headed,' but said with so much affection that Alice felt the prick of tears in her eyes, 'you'd agree to come simply because we want you, because the three of us are like family. Say you'll do as he wants, Alice. Then we can all make plans together, share the excitement.'

Also in those weeks Jane had arrangements of her own to make. By Deed Poll her name was changed from Harriman to Bingley. By unspoken agreement Matthew drove her to Ilkingham and there, under a summer canopy of leafy branches, he put a plain gold ring on her finger. From this day forward their lives would be shared, nothing would come between them 'until death do us part,' they promised.

'Until death and beyond.' She echoed Alice's words.

It was August when the brass plate was fixed to the pillar outside a house in Vicary Place overlooking the shore in Deremouth. In the middle of a crescent of large Georgian houses it had space enough for a surgery on the ground floor, for living space for the new occupants, Dr and 'Mrs' Bingley, for two rooms for Alice and for a cook and a housemaid to occupy the attics.

Their departure from Brackleford gave the local gossips something to talk about for a week or so. After that they appeared to be forgotten until a few months later when the local paper carried details of the Harrimans' divorce. Interest was revived, but not for long. There was little satisfaction in a situation where, bad lot though they all thought her, Madam High and Mighty seemed to have come out of the affair unscathed. So the gap they left closed like the waters over a drowning man. At the Queen Charlotte the regulars were treated to an evening of free ale to celebrate Ian and Elsie's wedding, somehow drawing a line under the sad business of the poor man's unhappy union.

In December of that year, Alayne and her ladies of the sewing party were sitting around a blazing fire, stitching in preparation for the Christmas Bazzar.

'You're looking so bonny these days, Mrs Warburton, my dear. Radiant is the word I would use,' one of the more senior members of the group found a tactful way of putting into words what all of them were wondering.

With her needle poised Alayne looked at these dear, good ladies. The image of Yvette was so clear: Yvette, the only person she had ever talked freely to. Sewing had ceased, all eyes were on her.

'I feel radiant,' she told them. 'Perhaps you will feel it's immodest to speak of such things; if so, forgive me. But I know you are all my friends and I ask that you will give thanks, just as I do, that I am to be blessed with a second child.'

'My dear, that is wonderful for you. But what will the parish do without you? With two wee mites to care for you will have to give up some of your work.'

Alayne shook her head. 'Oh no. The Lord has blessed me, I will always do His work.'

They looked at her in awe and reverence, then set their needles to work with even greater determination.

And while they talked, Marcos gazed out of his study window. He would soon have to find another pianist to accompany him on his weekly visits to the orphanage. He remembered the months when he and Yvette had shared Tuesday mornings, he remembered ... he remembered. She had lifted him outside himself, freed his body and mind, taught him the miracle of loving. Since Stephanie's birth, he had moved back into Alayne's room. They shared their work, they shared their lives; gentle, affectionate Alayne was always there for him. But where was the abandonment of the joy of sex, his and hers too? With Yvette it had been a journey of wonder. One day he'd go to Paris, just once he'd be with her again ... his mind rushed ahead of him. No! No! Why did he let temptation into his heart? He had so much in his life, he had everything. He should go down on his knees and be thankful. Turning from the window he draped his long cloak around his shoulders and took up his beretta.

In the biting wind of the winter afternoon the handsome vicar of St Stephen's strode through the town, bowing his head in acknowledgement of greetings from his flock.

There had been ripples in the stream of life at Brackleford, but they were stilled. All was calm.